"This is a wonderful book with many treasures. Written by a clinical psychologist, who has been deeply engaged with Buddhist practice for many years, his wisdom and experience of both Eastern and Western practices clearly shines through. Huxter not only has an extraordinary depth of knowledge but is a wonderful writer and makes complex things clear. I learnt a lot from this very accessible and wise book and will be returning to it many times; it is an illuminating gift to all those interested in this area and a must read."

– Professor Paul Gilbert, PhD, FBPsS, OBE,
Derbyshire Healthcare NHS Foundation Trust

"It has become very popular nowadays to 'secularize' Buddhism in such a way that it is stripped of the depth and richness of the practices and theories that are based on the Buddha's teachings and the wisdom that has grown from the Buddhist tradition. In a refreshing departure from this reductionist tendency, Malcolm Huxter has brought into dialogue many core themes of Buddhism with the practical concerns and insights of modern psychology. Authentic Buddhist practices and ideas have much to contribute to alleviating psychological distress and to cultivating exceptional states of mental health and balance, and this book has much to offer in this regard."

– B. Alan Wallace, President,
Santa Barbara Institute for Consciousness Studies

"This is a deeply sincere and touching integration of the core of Buddhist wisdom and modern psychology. It's immediately practical, bringing the power of mindfulness and compassion to everyday life, and it also contains many guided meditations. Filled with the author's own depth of practice, this is a life-changing book."

– Rick Hanson, PhD, author of *Buddha's
Brain: The Practical Neuroscience of Happiness, Love, and Wisdom*

"For therapists and others who wish to understand the roots of mindfulness, look no further. This book beautifully encapsulates the traditional literature on mindfulness and is written with the sensibility of a real-world psychotherapist and lifelong meditation practitioner. Importantly, the author unpacks how mindfulness is inextricably related to wisdom, compassion, and ethical behavior. As mindfulness goes mainstream, this book will surely be a valuable resource for curious minds."

– Chris Germer, Clinical Instructor, Harvard
Medical School, author of *The Mindful Path to
Self-Compassion*, Co-editor, *Mindfulness and Psychotherapy*

Healing the Heart and Mind with Mindfulness

Healing the Heart and Mind with Mindfulness is a practical book that provides strategies using mindfulness to manage stress, anxiety and depression, as well as ways to cultivate psychological wellbeing. Uniquely, it combines a traditional Buddhist approach to mindfulness with contemporary psychology and current perspectives. Drawing on the author's many years of clinical experience as a psychologist as well as his personal experience in Buddhist meditation practices, it outlines how the Buddha's four applications of mindfulness can provide a pathway to psychological wellbeing, and how this can be used personally or with clinical populations.

This accessible, user-friendly book provides strategies for healing the heart and mind. Malcolm Huxter introduces mindfulness as it is presented in Buddhist psychology and guides the reader through meditations in a systematic way. The practices are clearly explained and supported by relevant real-life stories. Being aware that mindfulness and meditation are simple but not easy, Huxter guides the reader from the basics of mindfulness and meditation through to the more refined aspects. He provides a variety of different exercises and guided meditations so that individuals are able to access what suits them. The guided meditations can be streamed or accessed as free audio downloads.

Healing the Heart and Mind with Mindfulness is aimed at anyone who wishes to use mindfulness practices for psychological freedom. This book provides insight and clarity into the clinical and general applications of Buddhist mindfulness and will be of interest to mental health practitioners, students of mindfulness, professional mindfulness coaches and trainers, researchers and academics wishing to understand Buddhist mindfulness and the general public.

Malcolm Huxter has extensive personal experience in Buddhist meditation practices and is also a clinical psychologist. He currently works as a clinical psychologist and teaches Buddhist meditation practices such as mindfulness and the cultivation of heart qualities (loving kindness, compassion, appreciative joy and equanimity) between his home in Northern NSW Australia and the UK.

Healing the Heart and Mind with Mindfulness

Ancient path, present moment

Malcolm Huxter

 Routledge
Taylor & Francis Group

LONDON AND NEW YORK

First published 2016
by Routledge
2 Park Square, Milton Park, Abingdon, Oxon, OX14 4RN

and by Routledge
711 Third Avenue, New York, NY 10017

Routledge is an imprint of the Taylor & Francis Group, an informa business

© 2016 Malcolm Huxter

The right of Malcolm Huxter to be identified as author of this work has been asserted by him in accordance with sections 77 and 78 of the Copyright, Designs and Patents Act 1988.

British Library Cataloguing in Publication Data
A catalogue record for this book is available from the British Library

Library of Congress Cataloguing in Publication Data
Names: Huxter, Malcolm, author.
Title: Healing the heart and mind with mindfulness :
ancient path, present moment / authored by Malcolm Huxter.
Description: First Edition. | New York : Routledge, 2016.
Identifiers: LCCN 2015027195 | ISBN 9781138851344 (hbk) |
ISBN 9781138851351 (pbk) | ISBN 9781315715902 (ebk)
Subjects: LCSH: Mind and body. | Mindfulness (Psychology) |
Meditation. | Buddhism–Psychology.
Classification: LCC BF161.H89 2016 | DDC 158.1–dc23
LC record available at http://lccn.loc.gov/2015027195

ISBN: 978-1-138-85134-4 (hbk)
ISBN: 978-1-138-85135-1 (pbk)
ISBN: 978-1-315-71590-2 (ebk)

Typeset in Sabon
by Out of House Publishing

Namo Tassa Bhagavato Arahato Sammabuddhasa
Homage to the Blessed One, the Worthy One, the Fully
Self-Awakened One

Buddham Saranam Gacchami	To the Buddha I go for refuge
Dharmam Saranam Gacchami	To the Dharma I go for refuge
Sangham Saranam Gacchami	To the Sangha I go for refuge

Contents

Illustrations

Figures

Tables

Acknowledgements

Like all journeys this book began with a single step when my dear friend Kyogen O'Neil introduced me to the teachings of the Buddha four decades ago. I have been travelling this ancient path ever since. I have appreciated many teachers along the way who have guided me on this path of awakening and contributed to this book. It is not possible to list everyone deserving of grateful acknowledgement. Nonetheless, the following includes some important ones.

I pay respects and express gratitude to the following formal Dharma and meditation teachers: Lamas Yeshe and Zopa; Ven. Phra Khantipalo, Ven. Somdet Phra Nyanasamvara; Ven. Luang Por Baan; S. N. Goenka; Joseph Goldstein and Sharon Shalzberg; Ven. Sayadaw U Pandita; Steven Smith; John Hale; Ven. Sayadaw U Janaka; Zen master Hogan; Patrick Kearney and Dr B. Alan Wallace.

Respectful acknowledgement and immense gratitude is also given to John Hale and Patrick Kearney as informal Dharma teachers and dear friends. Other mentors, informal Dharma teachers and dear long-term Dharma friends with whom I have often met at the junction points of the Buddha's teaching, therapy and clinical paths include: Dr Peter L. Nelson, Kyogen O'Neil, Michael Dash and Tupten Lekshe as well as the students and fellow teachers from the Australian Association of Buddhist Counsellors and Psychotherapists (AABCAP). To all these people who share the path with me I am truly grateful. Not only have I been nourished by our peer supervision and friendships but each and every one of these Dharma friends has provided an indirect contribution to the key theme of this book, that is, the integration of the contemporary with the ancient.

Other professionals that deserve acknowledgement are my colleagues, clinicians and managers, from the various settings I have worked in including community mental health, private practice and the Christmas Island immigration detention centre. The professionals of Lismore Mental Health Service, NSW Australia and other private

xii   *Acknowledgements*

clinicians in Lismore, in particular have provided over 20 years of support and camaraderie. Two clinical supervisors require special mention. Ken Hudson, clinical psychologist, grounded me as a new graduate in the basics of good clinical assessment and wise treatment. More recently in the last decade Dr Wayne Somerville helped to refine my clinical knowledge and skills, especially in the area of trauma.

Gratitude is given to all those who have courageously shared their stories and placed trust in me to provide care. Special thanks go to all the individuals I have seen in private practice, community mental health, inpatient care and detention centres whose names cannot be mentioned. Similarly, gratitude is given to the countless people who have participated in the programmes, courses and retreats I have provided. Even though these names cannot be provided, every individual deserves thanks and acknowledgement for contributing to this book. Thanks also to my supervisees and all the health and other professionals who have attended workshops, courses and retreats over the years. Their participation and feedback has also contributed to the contents of this book. A special thanks is also due to Robin Hall for sharing his wonderful cartoons, as a simple drawing can convey meaning beyond words. I would also like to express gratitude to Drs Paul Gilbert and Rick Hanson for their support, encouragement and very helpful suggestions in the later stages of the production of this book.

In this world of interdependence it is impossible to journey on a path on your own, and this book would not have been possible without the unconditional love and support of my family. Although my parents and my brother are no longer with us, their love, even in their absence, provided me with the energy and confidence to enter the path. For this I am grateful. My three adult sons, Ben, Punya and Liam have taught me the importance and power of love, and I am grateful to them just for being who they are and for the love and acceptance they have given me, just for being who I am. This gratitude also goes to my sisters and our extended family, Noi and John Morrow, nieces, nephews and in-laws who share our family journey.

Possibly most importantly I would like to acknowledge my loving partner, Mary, for the many roles she has fulfilled in the development and production of this book. She has been a home-based dharma teacher, compassionate companion and editor in the trials and tribulations of life and book writing. My thanks goes to Mary for sorting out the many grammatical errors, rearranging the words so that they made sense, helping me to say what I actually meant and teaching me the meaning of *metta*.

Finally, I would like to thank you, the reader, because it is in the reading of any book that makes it meaningful.

Introduction

Some of us live with great psychological freedom, at ease and with joy. For many, however, it is not easy being human. Most of us find the realities of ageing, sickness and death difficult to bear. We often don't get what we want, get what we don't want and are parted from people or things that are dear to us. Many of us experience intense mental or emotional distress. This may take the form of hopelessness, despair, anguish, anxiety, depression, grief, sadness, dread, worry, panic, frustration, confusion, exasperation, shame, harsh self-criticism, rage, terror, loneliness, boredom, humiliation, embarrassment, guilt, or an overwhelming sense of meaningless. We may also feel uncomfortable with less intense feelings such as alienation, irritation, annoyance, ungratified cravings, uncertainties and insecurities. For those fortunate enough to have a comfortable life there may be a subtle discontent that holidays or weekends must all come to an end and that pleasant experiences do not last.

The difficult experiences described above can all be referred to as *dukkha*. The word *dukkha* comes from an ancient Indian language called Pali. *Dukkha* is often translated as suffering but the word 'suffering' does not fully capture the meaning of *dukkha*. The '*duk*' of *dukkha* refers to not being quite right, not good. The '*kha*' refers to the space of the hub of a wheel. *Dukkha* literally translates as a badly fitting axle in a wheel.

This description of *dukkha* as a 'difficult grind' or a 'wobbly wheel' is probably best understood as unsatisfactoriness. *Dukkha* includes a wide spectrum of experience, from the intense and traumatic to the very subtle, and is a part of life. Being human involves the reality of *dukkha*. We differ only in the degree and intensity of our experience. Those people who are suffering with what our society calls mental disorder are merely at a more intense position of the *dukkha* spectrum. Nobody wants or aspires to *dukkha*. We all want to be happy.

I have worked as a psychologist for well over 20 years and every person I have met in my professional capacity has wanted to be happy. Every individual has been presented with some form of *dukkha* and they have all wanted to be free from it. They have all aspired to psychological freedom. Mindfulness is a practice that can help individuals find relief and freedom from *dukkha*. One way of describing mindfulness is: remembering to be attentive to present moment experience with care and wise discernment.

I became interested in mindfulness and related practices when I was a teenager. In 1974 I was 18 years old and I wanted to be happy. I worried about the Vietnam war, the nuclear threat, the pollution of the planet, my health and the fact that I would, sometime or other die. I was a worrier. I discovered that if I thought things through realistically and I avoided intentionally harming myself or others it seemed to help with my worries and concerns. Attending art school and also travelling throughout Australia and nearby South East Asia I met with people from different cultures and learnt about different philosophies and ideas and was introduced to Buddhism. I started attending Tibetan Buddhist meditation retreats in 1975. Meeting Tibetan meditation masters had a profound effect on my perception of the world and my self. The teachers of these retreats were masters of many skills including logic and reason. Thinking clearly was one way I learnt to deal with the many challenges of life and late adolescence. There were times, however, when reason and logic did not help. Nonetheless, I persisted. One day when I was reasoning my way through a worry, I heard the sound of a bird. The sound was so beautiful that it completely absorbed all my attention. I noticed the subtle nuances and the changing qualities of these notes of life, and peacefulness arose in my heart. The peace did not last, of course, but from this experience I developed confidence that release from worry was possible.

In 1976 I met an English-born Theravada Buddhist monk (Ven. Khantipalo) who reinforced my understanding that through mindfulness and present centred awareness I need not get lost in worry and rumination. From then on I aspired to psychological freedom and this became my most important desire and life direction. Not only could mindfulness lead to personal freedom but it could also provide the presence and clarity of mind to most effectively negotiate and deal with concrete problems in the world. I decided to ordain as a Buddhist monk in 1977. I travelled to Thailand and practised in the Theravada traditions of North East Thailand. The monastic life was intense and involved training in an ethical lifestyle, the cultivation of attention, mindfulness, and the development of wisdom. The experience of being a monk left a lasting impression on me and gave me a perspective on life where ethics, mindfulness and wisdom were essential on the path to psychological freedom.

When I returned to Australia two years later I trained and worked as a Shiatsu therapist. Shiatsu is a body therapy based on working with Chi or energy meridian systems as utilised in traditional Chinese and Japanese medicine. Working as a Shiatsu therapist and trainer provided an opportunity to cultivate compassion and mindfulness, a livelihood aligned with my life goals and aspirations. I worked with many individuals presenting with a wide range of physical, emotional and mental conditions. In my work as a body therapist it became evident that non-cognitive, non-talking body oriented therapy could resolve many mental and emotional problems. Part of this healing seemed related to how body therapies encouraged present centred awareness. I didn't learn about contemporary psychological approaches such as Behaviour Therapy (BT), Cognitive Therapy (CT) or Cognitive Behaviour Therapy (CBT) until I began university in the mid 1980s. Though lacking any overt reference to ethics many of the principles described in these contemporary approaches seemed very similar to some of those I had learnt in both Tibetan (Mahayana) and Theravada Buddhist traditions.

I began working as a psychologist and developing mindfulness programmes in 1991. At this time mindfulness and meditation were not yet understood or accepted within mainstream health settings so the programmes I developed and ran were referred to as 'stress management' programmes. By the late 1990s some mindfulness-based therapies were gaining credibility as supported by scientific evidence. By the end of the first decade of the twenty-first century, many contemporary psychotherapeutic approaches referred to mindfulness as a key therapeutic factor. These approaches were coined the 'third wave' therapies by one prominent psychologist because he thought they had advanced in many different ways from the earlier conventional practices of BT and CBT (Hayes, 2004). Mindfulness has become increasingly popular in contemporary psychology in the last 20 years and now there are many different third wave therapies. The foundational third wave therapies include: Mindfulness Based Stress Reduction or MBSR (Kabat-Zinn, 1990), Mindfulness Based Cognitive Therapy or MBCT (Segal, Williams and Teasdale, 2002), Dialectical Behaviour Therapy or DBT (Linehan, 1993) and Acceptance and Commitment Therapy or ACT (Hayes, Strosahl and Wilson, 1999).

Currently, mindfulness is regarded as a meditation practice, a coping skill, a mode of being and a key factor in therapy. It is both a therapeutic stance used by therapists and a skill that can be taught to individuals seeking treatment, therapy, life-coaching and stress management. Mindfulness can be learnt individually or within group settings and is not limited to any one particular mental, emotional or spiritual approach. In the fields of health, therapy and neuropsychology, overwhelming evidence is accumulating to suggest that learning mindfulness and related practices improves health and wellbeing.

In its adaptations to Western health services mindfulness has had to, understandably, be free from many of the religious and cultural additions these teachings had acquired over the centuries. The ways that third wave therapies frame and teach mindfulness are different from the ways in which I learnt these skills in a traditional Buddhist setting. Nonetheless, I am enormously grateful to the research practitioners and third wave therapists who have served to make mindfulness and related practices a validated approach to mental and emotional health and wellbeing. I also appreciate the ways in which they have creatively explained and taught these skills and related concepts to our Western culture. Without these adaptations mindfulness may not have emerged from the domains of Eastern religions and gained credibility in contemporary psychology. I have used many of the strategies and ideas developed by the third wave therapies to great benefit. In this book I integrate the benefits of contemporary psychology and ancient Buddhist psychology.

If you feel that you experience *dukkha* and you aspire to be free from this anguish, then the perspectives and strategies explained in this book may be helpful to you. Over the years I have written several programmes with corresponding workbooks for different populations and specific manifestations of *dukkha*. I have written and conducted specific programmes for generalised anxiety disorder, panic, bipolar disorder, generalised stress, older adolescents, head injury and the many varied issues that people bring along to community mental health services. This book includes ideas from all of these workbooks and is helpful for people who experience stress, anxiety and depression, which, if we are honest, is most of us. I have written this book so that it may be useful to everyone regardless of his or her psychological status. To make it relevant I have included stories based on the people I have seen professionally over the years. The specifics of the stories have been changed, of course, to maintain confidentiality.

As well as conducting many programmes for people presenting with *dukkha*, I have also taught many seminars and workshops to therapists and written about a Buddhist approach to therapy. Some ideas from these writings are also included in this book.

Whilst trying to make this book as easy to understand as possible, I will be using a few Pali and Sanskrit terms. I feel that the explanation and use of these terms enriches meaning and ultimately how you learn to cultivate mental and emotional health.

As we journey through this book I will outline a discourse given by the Buddha about mindfulness called the *Satipatthana Sutta*. The information and step-by-step instruction will get progressively more sophisticated and possibly more challenging until Chapter 6, reflecting the sequence provided in the discourse. In the last chapter I will suggest ways to continue so that mindfulness is an ongoing practice helping us throughout our individual lives. Please take your time reading this book. If you feel that you are not ready to move on to a more advanced step, spend a while practising where you find it most helpful. Alternatively, you can skip through sections that do not seem relevant for you and focus on what is. There are written instructions in every chapter and you will be invited to try the practices as you progress through the book. If you would like to listen to the instructions, audio tracks are available for free download from www.malhuxter.com (go to 'resources') or from www.routledge.com/9781138851351.

Health warning

Please be aware that everything we do, including meditation, involves a risk to our mental and physical health. Even drinking water, which is essential for life, can be done in a way that is a risk. Too little or too much water can be harmful. Similarly too much meditation practised in an incorrect manner can be harmful whilst too little may be ineffective. Meditation is also like medication in that it often needs to be tailored to the individual and in the right dose. Though this book can be used in a self-help manner, if you are prone to, or suffer with a clinical condition such as severe depression, debilitating anxiety or some form of psychosis, guidance and tailoring the practices may be important for you. Even if you do not suffer with a clinical condition, it is important that you approach the exercises wisely and with moderation, and guidance from someone who has experience is always helpful, if not essential.

Don't be concerned if some of the meditations do not suit you, as this is normal. The Buddha taught different practices dependent on the particular temperament or issues of individuals or groups of individuals. It is best to bring an open mind to the learning process and experiment. If it works for you then use it. If a chosen meditation seems to be developing understanding, is helpful, leads to a sense of integration or is calming and peaceful continue the practice. If, however, after giving it a good try, a particular meditation practice is not helpful, don't be discouraged and try another meditation or way of practising. If a particular meditation exercise causes distress that is unsettling and overwhelming, suspend using that exercise for a period and utilise coping skills that are helpful. Later, as confidence builds and it is timely, the distress-eliciting meditation could be revisited in a gradual, sensitive and wise manner, or you may choose to put it off indefinitely. If you feel you are experiencing negative side effects from meditation, don't hesitate to speak to an experienced meditator or a mental health professional. Just as when we use a magnifying glass things look bigger, when we stop and become aware of our psychological patterns they too can appear to be magnified and may seem to get worse before they get better. Don't be discouraged and seek help or advice if you need it.

Thank you for reading this introduction and the necessary health warning and now I warmly invite you to step onto a healing path that leads to psychological wellbeing and genuine happiness.

References

Hayes, S. C. (2004). Acceptance and commitment therapy and the new behavior therapies. In S. C. Hayes, V. M. Follette and M. M. Linehan (eds.), *Mindfulness and Acceptance: Expanding the Cognitive-Behavioural Tradition*. New York: Guilford Press.

Hayes, S. C., Strosahl, K. D. and Wilson, K. G. (1999). *Acceptance and Commitment Therapy*. New York: Guilford Press.

Kabat-Zinn, J. (1990). *Full Catastrophe Living: Using the Wisdom of your Body and Mind to Face Stress, Pain, and Illness*. New York: Guilford Press.

Linehan, M. M. (1993). *Cognitive-Behavioral Treatment of Borderline Personality Disorder*. New York: Guilford Press.

Segal, Z. V., Williams, J. M. G. and Teasdale, J. D. (2002). *Mindfulness-Based Cognitive Therapy for Depression*. New York: Guilford Press.

1 Four realities

A starting point and a final destination

Chapter overview

This chapter provides an introduction to the Four Noble Truths and concludes with some basic mindfulness meditation practices. The four noble truths, which are the foundation of Buddhist psychology, can also be described as four realities. These realities affect all humans, regardless of their position in society, their age, race, religion, philosophical views or psychological status. You do not need to be a Buddhist to understand these realities of life or to benefit from the strategies the Buddha recommended for psychological wellbeing. However, a brief summary of the Buddha's life and teachings gives a context for understanding Buddhism and this understanding can help with practising mindfulness.

Buddhism

Like all things, Buddhism is viewed in a variety of ways. Many people do not see Buddhism as a religion but as a philosophy, a psychological perspective and/or a spiritual pathway. In my understanding the word 'Buddha' comes from the Pali root verb 'budh', which means 'to awaken' or 'to understand'. The Buddha is more an honorific title than a name and refers to someone who is awake or fully understands. Western scholars created the term 'Buddhism', an English and Pali mix. The term Buddhism has come to represent the teachings of the historical Buddha who before he became known as the Buddha was a man called Siddhartha Gautama.

Around two and a half thousand years ago India consisted of many small kingdoms. Siddhartha Gautama was born as the son of a leader of one of these small kingdoms. According to historical accounts, Siddhartha was skilled in many ways and excelled in studying the arts and sciences of the time. As a member of a privileged family he had a sheltered and protected upbringing. He married and lived in his father's kingdom until he was in his late twenties. At this time, however, the harsh realities of life from which he had been sheltered became obvious. Not only was he confronted with the realities of ageing, sickness and death but he also realised that most people suffered emotionally and mentally in many different ways and were generally unsatisfied with their lives. Seeing a homeless wanderer seeking the truth inspired him to leave his comfortable existence in search of a resolution for the human suffering he witnessed both within himself and around him. It is said that Siddhartha then studied with the prominent meditation teachers of the time and mastered all the techniques they offered, yet he felt that these techniques did not satisfy. For six years Siddhartha led a homeless life practising many different extreme techniques until he almost died from emaciation and exhaustion. Realising that these extremes were not helpful he decided to care for his body and continue seeking understanding in a more balanced manner. According to accounts, on the full moon night before his 35th birthday in May, he sat comfortably under a Bodhi tree and practised mindfulness of breath. This meditation led to a series of insights and by dawn, it is said that he found the understanding he was seeking and became the Buddha. The Buddha taught about what he had realised for another 45 years and then, according to reports, passed away on the full moon day of May in the year 483 BC when he was 80 years old.

Siddhartha Gautama became a Buddha about 2,550 years ago and taught ways to understand or awaken. He broke away from the social and religious systems of the time and taught to all types of people from all walks of life. Regardless of whether someone was a poor farmer, rich merchant, spiritual seeker or royalty, the Buddha taught individuals equally, according to their individual temperament and needs. He taught that the principles of managing emotional and mental suffering could be realised by individuals for themselves and were not dependent upon an external authority. As a teacher with spiritual and psychological genius, the Buddha taught in such a way that his teachings could be adapted to different cultures, regardless of time or place. Over the centuries these teachings have been incorporated into different cultures. The spread was especially evident throughout Asia in places such as Tibet, Burma, Bhutan, Thailand, China, Japan and Korea amongst other countries. Though the essence of the teaching remained the same, the form of the teaching would change dependent upon the culture within which it was hosted. Different accounts of the Buddha's life and teachings have had a liberating impact on millions of people for over two and a half thousand years. Volumes have been written and stories have been passed down over the centuries since the time he lived and taught in northern India.

The teachings of the Buddha are often referred to as Buddha Dharma. The word 'dharma' originated from Sanskrit, another ancient Indian language, where it literally means 'decree or custom'. Dharma has now found its way into the English language where the Oxford Dictionary refers to it as: 'the eternal law of the cosmos inherent in the very nature of things'. Often it is used in reference to the laws of nature or the truth of the ways things are. The dharma, from a Buddhist perspective, refers to the realities of life and conveys a sense of lawfulness about causes and effects, actions and consequences.

Unfortunately as Buddhism is regularly interpreted as a religion there is often reluctance, especially amongst health scientists, to highlight the connections between Buddhism and mindfulness. However, one does not have to be a Buddhist to utilise a technology developed and refined by the Buddha. Muslims developed algebra and many of the pioneers of contemporary physics were Christians. These religious connections have not stopped the advance of these technologies to benefit human kind. In the same way, the personal benefits of mindfulness and related practices do not depend on adherence to a religious belief system or cultural world view. I have witnessed people from different religions, all walks of life, widely varying occupations and different world views flourish psychologically by practising the strategies described in this book. The message is that one does not have to 'believe' what the Buddha taught to benefit from the teachings of the Buddha. Moreover, the teachings emphasise the importance of knowing for oneself. Personal psychological health and wellbeing can only be verified by one's own experience

Western cultures started translating the teachings of the Buddha into English and European languages in the middle of the nineteenth century. Since the 1960s and 1970s enormous interest in Buddhism has arisen in Europe, USA, Australia and New Zealand. Buddha Dharma has been adapted to Western cultures in many different ways, in particular through psychotherapy. Modern psychotherapists are finding that Buddha Dharma can help individuals understand the nature of life, the possible origins of their psychological distress, the possibility that they can be free and ways to be free. These realisations are consistent with the four truths or realities that form the foundation of Buddhist psychology.

Four realities

Regardless of the many different schools and traditions, the primary aim of Buddhism is the realisation of the Four Noble Truths. 'Noble' is used to signify that the realisations and consequent actions based on these truths are refined and profound. The truths are, in essence, two cause and effect relationships: *dukkha* and its causes, freedom from *dukkha*, and the causes of this freedom. They are:

1. There is *dukkha* (unsatisfactoriness or suffering).
2. *Dukkha* has causes.
3. There is freedom from *dukkha*.
4. There are ways or paths to freedom.

The cause–effect relationships evident in the Four Noble Truths can be applied to the basic patterns evident with all *dukkha*, including psychological disorders, and provides a way out of all types of *dukkha*, or at the least can reduce the severity of these experiences.

The first truth: *dukkha*

Sometimes one hears that Buddhists are pessimistic because they talk about how life is suffering. I don't think this claim is very fair, because *dukkha* is only 25 per cent of the four truths. In fact, Buddhists like to focus on the third and fourth truths: freedom and ways to be free. The aim of the practice includes the realisation or acknowledgement of *dukkha* and not a fixation on it.

In the Introduction I wrote that *dukkha* is probably best understood as unsatisfactoriness. It can be mild or extreme and is characterised by unhappiness and discontent.

The first noble truth, according to Buddhist philosophy, is that *dukkha* is a fundamental aspect of existence, since for most human beings life is characterised by a pervasive sense of unsatisfactoriness and uncertainty. To overcome *dukkha* we must first understand it.

From a Buddhist perspective *dukkha* can be understood in three ways: (1) *dukkha* as ordinary suffering, (2) *dukkha* as produced by change, and (3) *dukkha* as a characteristic of clinging to the belief that we do not change and are separate from the world around us.

The first type of *dukkha*, also called *dukkha dukkha* (or the suffering of suffering), is blatant and obvious. It encompasses the difficulties associated with birth, old age, sickness and death. Also included in this first category is the inevitable fact that individuals often get what they don't want, don't get what they want, and are, at some time or other parted from what they like. Emotional pain, worry, fear, anxiety, sadness, grief, sorrow, lamentation, despair, anger, rage, anguish, confusion, loneliness, alienation and other distressing states are experienced by most people at some time or other and are included in this first type of *dukkha*.

The second type of *dukkha*, the suffering of change, involves the paradox of living in happy and pleasant states and yet knowing these beautiful moments are transient and must inevitably change and disappear. At some time or other the things we cling to as sources of happiness and security will eventually change. The stronger the clinging the more intense is the *dukkha* as the objects we cling to change.

The last type of *dukkha* involves the suffering produced from clinging to the belief that our changing body and mind, that which we call 'I', 'mine' and 'myself', with its sensations, thoughts, feelings and emotions, will last forever and is separate and not connected with the world around us.

Contemporary psychologists generally don't use the word *dukkha*, but it is what they address in groups and individual therapy. A word more familiar, and used more consistently by psychologists, is 'stress'. Whilst the meaning of *dukkha* is much deeper and broader than what most people understand as stress, stress is a relevant aspect of *dukkha* that is worth exploring.

Stress

Stress is a word that everyone uses but there is little agreement on what it means. Originally stress was an engineering term referring to the strain placed on physical objects. Then it referred to the biological response that living things had when toxins were released into their systems. The terms stressor, stress, being stressed and stressing out have come to refer to many different psychological things. Sometimes we may be stressed because something very difficult happens to us, like becoming ill, losing our job, having to move from our home, or when someone who is close to us is dying or dies.

There are many different ways stress is described and explained (Figure 1.1). One way to think about stress is when demands outweigh our ability to cope, and as a result we react physically and emotionally, with our thoughts and with our behaviours. Being overwhelmed by things that are happening within us and around us is another way to describe stress. When we are stressed we may act mindlessly, do things without care and attention and make mistakes. Some of the behavioural reactions involved in stress include acting in ways that are harmful to our self or others either in the short term or long term. For example, being hijacked by destructive urges and hurting ourselves or hurting people we care about. Or we may become slaves to addictions such as too much TV, Internet, chocolate, drinking, smoking or taking drugs as a way to cope. Unfortunately these types of behaviours can lead to heedlessness or becoming physically unwell.

Stress may affect us emotionally, physically and mentally. Emotional reactions such as uncontrollable anger, intense sadness and unfounded fear have been related to stress. Physically, stress may lead to muscle tension, increased heart rate, increased blood pressure, sweating, diarrhoea, nausea, aches and pains, headaches and a whole range of illnesses. Mental reactions to stress include not being able to think clearly, lack of focus and forgetfulness. The *dukkha* of stress can manifest as a depressed mood, anxiety, worry, loss of confidence, irritability

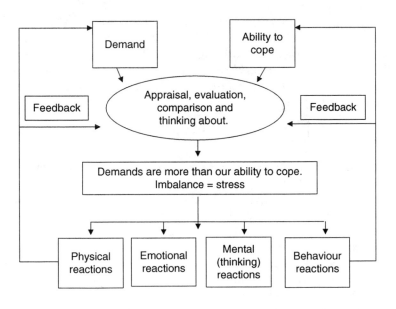

Figure 1.1 A stress interaction
Source: adapted from Cox (1978)

and/or a sense that we have to rush because we never have enough time to do what we need to do.

I mentioned in the Introduction that as people experience varying degrees of *dukkha*, it can be viewed as occurring on a continuum of intensity. Those suffering from anxiety, depression and other 'disorders' are no different than anyone else, except that their *dukkha* may be at one end of the intensity continuum. Few people do not suffer with some kind of *dukkha*.

Like stress, patterns of anxiety and depression can be considered as a sense of being out of balance. Though 'imbalance' may be a more accurate way of describing psychological suffering, the term 'disorder' is used in mental health establishments to refer to particular symptom patterns that are distressing, affect our relationships with other people and/or impact on our ability to cope and function. Sometimes the psychological disorders we experience may form into a personality style, and these are called personality disorders. Often personality disorders are noticed more by other people because of their enduring nature and the way they impact on our relationships.

Psychological disorders

There is a multitude of psychological disorders and in many of these, people experience anxiety and depressive symptoms. Even though there are differences between disorders, symptoms found in one disorder may also be found in others. Further, everyone is different and so, even though many people may have the same disorder, an individual's particular symptom pattern is unique to them. Often people do not clearly fit a particular diagnosis or they feel stigmatised by having what they are experiencing named as a disorder. As long as people do not identify with their disorder, naming them can, however, be very useful. Naming symptom patterns as a disorder can help to share information and ultimately help people understand how best to manage their distress.

Names for disorders have changed over the years and will probably change further as science refines understanding. At the time of writing this book according to the *Diagnostic and Statistical Manual of Mental Disorders* 4th Edition (APA, 1994) some of the anxiety disorders include:[1]

- Generalised Anxiety Disorder or GAD.
- Post Traumatic Stress Disorder or PTSD, where there are anxiety responses related to one or more traumatic situations.

- Agoraphobia, where there is fear of being in places or situations (such as shopping malls, in cinemas, in buses and more) where escape may be difficult or embarrassing.
- Obsessive Compulsive Disorder or OCD, where there may be strange and unwanted thoughts as well as possible compulsions to act in ritualistic ways to neutralise the thoughts.
- Social Phobia, where there is excessive fear of being judged by others in a negative way and as a result the person avoids social circumstances.
- Panic disorder, where panic attacks happen in situations where most people would not be afraid.

Depression as a disorder is very common. There are different types of depression that include:

- Bipolar disorder (manic depression) which is clearly a biological illness that often involves severe mood swings between feeling down and feeling manic.
- Reactive depression, where depressive symptoms emerge after a very difficult circumstance.
- Endogenous depression, in which symptoms emerge without any particular reason except, perhaps, chemical imbalances in the brain.
- Post-natal depression, which affects some mothers within a few months after the birth of a child.

Sometimes depression is categorised as psychotic, melancholic or non-melancholic depending on how symptoms present and how severe they are.

Depression and anxiety

Depression usually involves a sad, discontented and miserable mood, while anxiety usually involves fear and feeling physically excited and on guard. Fear and sadness are defining features of anxiety and depression respectively. Both fear and sadness are, however, natural tendencies that have served an evolutionary and practical role.

Without fear, for example, we may not have survived the many dangers we have had to confront throughout our lives. Sadness on the other hand may be a necessary part of the process of overcoming loss. It is important to honour these emotions and respect that they may have a function and a naturally occurring time frame. In depressive and anxiety disorders, unfortunately, fear and sadness have become excessive and are not functional. As mentioned previously, these conditions may have a range of biological, social and/or psychological causes. One point to consider with these disorders is that in some cases the reactions experienced can be learned or conditioned. For example, we may have experienced justified fear or anxiety in one circumstance but when the fear is generalised to other situations where it is not necessary, it can be problematic. For the most part, fear and the chain of events connected with fear are involuntary and necessary responses for survival. A panic attack in Panic Disorder is a fear response when there is no need for this response. This panic is like a false alarm to a situation that does not warrant the natural flight or fight responses that are needed in a dangerous situation. In these situations individuals may be over-sensitive to triggers and react unnecessarily. They occur very quickly (within ten minutes) and also usually pass very quickly.

Some or all of the following symptoms can occur with a panic attack:

- breathlessness
- a feeling of choking, being smothered or a tight throat
- tingling in the hands and feet, pounding heart
- faintness or dizziness
- pressure, tightness or pain in the chest
- trembling or shaking
- 'jelly' legs
- muscular tension
- blurred vision or spots before the eyes
- nausea or 'butterflies'
- increased heart rate or heart pounding
- sweating
- chills or hot flushes
- de-realisation or a sense that we are in a dream and it is not real
- depersonalisation or a sense that we are outside ourselves
- strong urges to escape or be somewhere else (APA, 1994).

Sometimes panic attacks occur out of the blue without any particular trigger and they take people by surprise. Other times they may be predictable and are cued by reminders of situations, thoughts or physical sensations related to frightening or traumatic events. Panic attacks are common and about one in ten people will have at least one panic attack in their life. Panic attacks can often occur in the context of other emotional problems.

Another very common anxiety disorder is Generalised Anxiety Disorder or GAD. The key feature of GAD is uncontrollable worry for at least six months. Those suffering with GAD may also experience some of the following symptoms to a degree that interrupts their ability to function in life:

- restlessness or feeling keyed up
- being easily fatigued
- difficulty concentrating or mind going blank
- irritability
- muscular tension
- sleep disturbance (APA, 1994).

Many of the experiences of anxiety overlap with depression. The symptoms of depression include:

- depressed mood
- diminished interest and pleasure
- weight loss or gain
- insomnia or hyper-somnia (over-sleeping)
- psycho-motor agitation or retardation
- fatigue
- excessive guilt or feelings of worthlessness
- recurrent thoughts of death
- low self-esteem
- feelings of hopelessness
- poor concentration or difficulty making decisions (APA, 1994).

Worry and rumination are two aspects of *dukkha* that occur in both depression and anxiety. However, worry tends to occur more with anxiety, and rumination more with depression. More details about these two tendencies will be given in a later chapter. Initially, it is enough to understand that these tendencies tend to be very unpleasant, and thus are experienced as *dukkha*. They also tend to be self-reinforcing and so cause more worry and rumination. Worry is driven by fear and avoidance and generally refers to thinking excessively about solutions to problems, somewhere in the future, where the outcomes may be uncertain. Rumination is similar to worry in that thoughts seem to intrude in an uncontrollable manner but it is less future oriented and more passive than worry. That is, one mulls over an issue but does not think of any solutions. With rumination one generally focuses repeatedly on negative aspects of the past or one's current distress and its circumstances. Both worry and rumination often perpetuate stress and are habitual or automatic, in that they seem beyond control and appear to happen without conscious choice.

Anxiety and depression are just two manifestations of the first truth. Unfortunately, these aspects of *dukkha* affect most of us in some way or another. Fortunately there are ways to disengage from the binds of these experiences. The third truth involves the realisation of freedom and the fourth truth represents the path of realisation and how to live it, but first we must discover the second truth.

The second truth: the causes of *dukkha*

In Buddhist psychology the causes of *dukkha* are viewed as cyclic and interdependent. The environment, the places we live, our genetic makeup, our biological predispositions and our social circumstances all impact on the stress we experience. Sometimes terrible things happen in our lives such as the trauma of disaster and great loss. Most people would experience these types of circumstances as suffering. However, the way we cope with traumatic experience varies.

The degree of suffering caused by a difficult experience greatly depends on the way we see and understand the experience. Thus, in Buddhist psychology *dukkha* arises dependent on an interaction between external things and our mind. According to the second noble truth the root causes of *dukkha* are the mental and emotional tendencies of:

- greed – which includes craving, clinging and addictions to pleasant feelings
- ignorance – which involves delusion, ignoring the obvious, being confused about experience, and being unaware of how *dukkha* arises and how to release it
- hatred – which includes aggression, rejection, fear, avoidance, struggle with, resistance and condemnation of unpleasant feelings, or aversion.

In his discourses the Buddha said that as long as individuals' minds were driven by greed, ignorance and hatred then they will experience *dukkha* in some form or another. These three mental tendencies may become complicated cyclical behavioural patterns. Psychological patterns driven by craving and addiction, being unaware or by avoidance and aggression can be the cause of much of our psychological distress. These patterns can also keep us stuck by maintaining the *dukkha*. When stress is understood as a process of being overwhelmed and out of balance with demands, as described earlier, it can lead to anxiety and depression. Worry and rumination, for example, can fuel descending spirals into anxiety and depression. In some cases anxiety and depression may have physical causes including physical illness. In other cases, significant events, such as traumas, occurring throughout our lives, may lead to emotional reactions, anxious or depressed patterns of thought and eventually depression or anxiety. Depression and anxiety may also have strong genetic links and the predisposition to be anxious or depressed can be inherited. For some people, difficult social circumstances or plain hardship may be causal factors. In other cases, depression or anxiety may arise with no particular causes. Sometimes things just happen or don't work out or we lose something and we feel sad.

On the whole, anxiety and depressive disorders can involve numerous genetic, biological, social and psychological factors, which all interact. One point to consider with these disorders is that habitual reactions can be learned. We learn habits, both helpful and unhelpful, in many complex ways. One way we learn is through behavioural reinforcement. Reinforcement refers to strengthening or supporting something. When behaviours are reinforced they are strengthened or increased. When we are rewarded or something pleasant occurs at the same time as, or shortly after, a particular behaviour, that behaviour is likely to increase and get stronger. Or, if an unpleasant experience is stopped or made less after a particular behaviour, then that behaviour is also likely to increase. Reinforcement is one of the main ways in which living creatures, including humans, learn.

Hatred – avoidance and aggression

Many experiences in life are unpleasant. This can include emotions, thoughts, situations and physical sensations. Avoiding what we find unpleasant provides relief, which is reinforcing. Sometimes avoidance is necessary for survival and wellbeing. Often, however, it is not and the more we avoid the stronger the habit of avoidance becomes. Hatred involves rejection, fear, avoidance, and struggle with, resistance to and condemnation of unpleasant feelings, or simply aversion. Aversion can range from subtle discontent and avoidance to being consumed with aggressive hatred, as well as a drive for desperate escape from situations, which may not need to be avoided.

A characteristic of aversion is avoidance of physical and emotional pain. Aversion can be a natural response for survival and protection from harm. When extreme or unnecessary, however, aversion can be an obstacle to living a life free from the anguish of depression and anxiety. Aversion is based on preferences, so that one likes and grasps after some things and dislikes and rejects other things. Aversion can manifest as hatred, anger, fear, frustration, irritation, sorrow and sometimes paranoia. Other varieties of aversion include: irritation, hostility, self-loathing, resentment, repugnance, disgust, wrath, spite, vengeance, envy and cruelty.

Outwardly aversion can become aggression and inwardly aversion can become self-hatred. Those who are depressed are often trapped by aversion and ill will in the form of self-condemnation, harsh self-criticism and unrealistic negative judgement. When aversion isn't necessary for survival or wellbeing it can deceive us by exaggerating, distorting and clouding our perceptions of life, ourselves and other people. Hatred exaggerates the displeasing aspects of something. Hostility can distort the reality of a situation where only the dark, dismal and problematic is perceived. It makes us see only the negative qualities in people, places or things and creates them as intrinsically bad.

Avoidance is a form of aversion, which has gained much attention in contemporary psychology. Avoidance is central to a diagnosis of an anxiety disorder as well as to the development and maintenance of both anxiety and depression. When avoidance maintains anxiety and depression it can involve actively escaping from people, places or things. It can also involve attempts to control or suppress thoughts and uncomfortable or strong emotions.

In depression, avoidance behaviours often reinforce withdrawal and inactivity, which further entrenches depressive patterns and symptoms. Avoidance behaviour also prevents people suffering with anxiety from having the opportunity to learn that the things they are avoiding need not elicit fear. Avoiding some experiences may increase our *dukkha*. If we avoid investigating our stress, for example, it may become entrenched. Avoidance tends to reduce our ability to learn positive coping skills and different ways to think about and respond to difficult experiences.

The flip side of avoidance is aggression. Sometimes we are aggressive, mean and nasty to ourselves, and this is a cause of an enormous amount of misery. Sometimes we get lost in being destructive to things and hostile and aggressive to other people or animals. This also eventually ties us up in contracted knots of unhappiness.

Greed – clinging, craving and addictions to short-term pleasures

Sometimes, rather than avoiding certain experiences we seek them out because they are pleasing and enjoyable. Like avoidance, seeking out experience is often necessary for survival, health and wellbeing. Sometimes, however, the pleasant experience we want may not be conducive to long-term happiness. The experience may provide pleasure in the short term but, in the long run, it may increase our stress and suffering. In such instances clinging, grasping and craving patterns become unhelpful habits. When we are addicted to pleasant experiences at the expense of long-term health, happiness and wellbeing, we are like slaves to habits of pleasure seeking. There are an infinite number of things that we can become emotionally addicted to. Some common ones are tobacco, drugs and alcohol, TV, sex, chocolate, Internet, mobile phone messages and people saying nice things to us.

Craving and clinging can range from subtle attraction to overwhelming fantasy and desperate addiction. When we are craving, our experience is coloured with dissatisfaction about our current reality. Clinging can influence us to believe that lasting happiness is dependent on having a certain person or thing. Clinging is a tendency of mind that is characterised by holding tightly or being stuck. When mud is thrown at a white cloth the colour of the mud sticks to it. When we cling to views and concepts they stick to our mind and influence the way we feel and act.

Holding on to certain views and concepts can be helpful to ensure that our goals are achieved and our values lived. Appropriate desire and wanting can help us to achieve our goals and live in alignment with important life directions. Excessive or habitual wanting, craving or clinging, on the other hand, can involve a struggle or strain to get whatever it is we desire. Craving pulls us out of the present moment so that we become fixated on a desired object. In Buddhist psychology craving is described as fuel for a fire where the fire is our insatiable discontent. Craving is intrinsically unsatisfactory and therefore can be experienced as *dukkha*. Being stuck or clinging to views, concepts and experiences can also be *dukkha*.

An aspect of clinging that causes suffering is the insistence that something should be the way we want it to be, or should not be the way we don't want it to be. The way we use language can be indicative of clinging. For example, as CBT points out, when our language is filled with 'should(s)', have to(s)', 'must(s)', can't(s) or other limiting words, it can indicate inflexibility. Such language may point to the tendency to cling to views, concepts and experience. Merely wanting something to be a certain way is different from insisting that something should be that way. With the latter, when we don't get what we want, we suffer. If we want, without clinging or insistence, we can be more relaxed about outcomes, which can free us from suffering when the outcomes are not what we want them to be. Holding on tightly to beliefs and assumptions of danger and our inability to cope is often a contributing factor to anxiety. Further to this, clinging to dysfunctional and inaccurate concepts, particularly concepts about who and what we are, or self-concepts, often leads to anxiety as well as depression.

Ignorance or delusion

Sometimes experiences are not particularly pleasant or unpleasant yet we fall into habits with them because we are simply unaware of what we are doing. The more we follow unhelpful habits the more they are reinforced. One habit that is hard to break is the belief that true and genuine happiness comes from getting the things that we are addicted to. We may think that when we get the right body shape or a girlfriend with the perfect dimensions, or a plasma TV screen, or whatever it is we crave, that true and lasting happiness will follow. This is a delusion. Delusion can also be driven by aversion or avoidance. For example we may think: 'When I get rid of those age exposing wrinkles and have a perfect make over I will be happy', or 'If I can avoid talking about certain problematic things then they may eventually just disappear'.

In Buddhism ignorance is traditionally defined as mistaking what is impermanent as permanent, what is suffering as pleasure and what isn't me or mine as me or mine. Ignorance involves not seeing, not knowing and being unaware. Delusion is often considered as synonymous with ignorance; however, it is more related to misinterpreting or misperceiving. A deluded person may think they know something; however, they may be unaware of how much they do not know. Delusion can refer to a confused quality of mind that obstructs and obscures clarity of perception and understanding. Delusion includes dullness, laziness and forgetfulness. Misperception and misreading life are aspects of ignorance and delusion and can range from a lack of clarity about something to total confusion, misunderstanding and gross psychiatric delusions.

Habits driven by addictions, avoidance and/or ignorance can become automatic and unconscious. When our lives are ruled by habitually unconscious and automatic patterns our reactions to things may become entrenched. Being trapped in automatic patterns we forget the awe-inspiring mystery of life and instead, life may seem stuck, flat, stale, dull and grey. We are constantly on guard against the possibility that we may meet with something or someone that we are avoiding or lose what we enjoy. When we are slaves to our addictions and our automatic and unconscious habits, we fail to see the possibilities that life has to offer.

Being on autopilot is another way we become stuck in unhelpful reactions. Very often we do things automatically, without noticing what we're doing. We forget to pay attention to our present moment realities and instead get entangled, lost and blinkered by illusive thoughts about the past or future.

Unhelpful tendencies as causes of disorder

In Buddhism, mental, emotional and behavioural tendencies are divided into *kusala* and *akusala* (Pali). *Kusala* translates as wholesome/healthy/helpful/skilful. Wholesome thoughts, emotions and actions are intrinsically good and need no reference to anything outside. They are objectively and universally beneficial. Skilful thoughts, emotions and actions help us to move in a direction towards a desired goal. Together wholesome and skilful thoughts and actions lead us to freedom from *dukkha*. *Akusala* translates as unwholesome/unhealthy/unhelpful/ unskilful. Unwholesome mental, emotional and behavioural tendencies are intrinsically unhelpful and not beneficial. When our goal is genuine happiness for our self and others, the *kusala* lead us in this direction and *akusala* thoughts and actions lead us astray.

The Pali term used for mental affliction is *kilesa*. The *kilesa* are *akusala*. The root of the Pali word *kilesa*, literally means 'to twist', 'to distort' or 'to afflict'. In Buddhism *kilesa* are deemed responsible for mental suffering. They stain the mind causing disturbance and unrest and are also considered as deformations of the mind, giving rise to mental disorder. *Kilesa* are also the driving force behind unskilful action, which leads to further suffering. Thus, *kilesa* can lead to destructive conduct, unhealthy physiological changes and mental unhappiness. Mental affliction can be obvious to see, or it can lie dormant, easily triggered and stimulated under the right conditions.

Different people have different mental afflictions and each individual will be affected by various tendencies in different ways. Everyone is different but common types of affective, cognitive and behavioural patterns that may be afflictive and unhelpful include: misperception, addictive neediness, aggression, jealousy, gloominess, sadness, worry and rumination, impulsive recklessness, guilt, confusion, avoidance, mental dullness, cruelty, hopelessness, self-hatred and so on. Each tendency has its opposite. Table 1.1 outlines some helpful (*kusala*) and the opposite unhelpful (*akusala*).

The Buddha is reported to have said: 'What a person considers and reflects upon for a long time to that his mind will bend and incline.' This statement reflects how both the helpful and unhelpful can be cultivated and developed. The more we engage in patterns and tendencies, the more they are reinforced and strengthened. Patterns become habits that become personal characteristics. The more we are cheerful, kind and generous the more likely that this will develop into our character. The more we tend to fuel greed, ignorance and hatred, however, the more these tendencies develop into the way we are.

This book outlines ways to cultivate the helpful and let go of the unhelpful. It illustrates ways that understanding, skilful action, resolve/determination, mindfulness, focused attention and other skills and qualities can help us to reduce stress and abandon *dukkha*. Mindfulness helps to develop understanding that can free us from enslaving habits. Focused attention gives penetrative power to mindfulness and it can calm and counter negative responses such as

Table 1.1 Examples of helpful and unhelpful tendencies

Helpful	Unhelpful
Insight (wisdom)/rational thinking	Ignorance/misapprehension
Non-attachment/generosity/letting go	Greed/craving and clinging
Love and goodwill/willingness acceptance/tolerance	Aggression/aversion/avoidance/ hostility/self-loathing
Equanimity/acceptance/peacefulness	Worry/rumination and restlessness
Bare attention	Mental proliferation
Balanced: intentions or aspirations, attention, cognition and affect	Imbalanced: intentions, attention, cognition and affect
Composure and calm	Agitation
Mindfulness, awareness	Confusion and mental dullness
Modesty, compunction	Lacking remorse about harmful actions
Empathetic joy	Envy and jealousy
Discretion	Recklessness
Calm acceptance	Anxious fear
Joy	Sadness
Compassion	Cruelty
Faith, confidence or trust	Hopelessness
Equanimity or acceptance	Guilt
Emotional flexibility	Narrow mindedness

unwarranted and excessive fear. When we acknowledge and accept the truth of *dukkha* we are more able to realise its causes and stop feeding them. When we no longer feed the causes of suffering it no longer arises. Nirvana is the Sanskrit term for when there is no more *dukkha*. Nirvana is said to be the highest happiness and is the Third Noble Truth.

The third truth: the highest happiness as freedom from anguish

In Buddhism freedom from *dukkha*, the Third Noble Truth, is Nirvana. According to one translator the word literally means Un (*nir*) + binding (*vana*) (Thanissaro, 1993), meaning to be unbound or free from patterns and habits that lead to *dukkha*. When there are no more mental and emotional patterns associated with craving and clinging, aversion and delusion then there is no more *dukkha*.

The Buddha often used analogies, similes and metaphors to describe the nature of experiences, as verbal descriptions are often inadequate. This was especially the case with Nirvana. He is reported to have said: '[This truth is] profound, hard to see and hard to understand, peaceful and sublime, unattainable by mere reasoning, subtle, to be experienced by the wise'[2] (Nanamoli and Bodhi, 1995, p. 260).

His Holiness the Dalai Lama (2007) believes that the purpose of life is to be happy. He also believes that every being wants happiness and does not want suffering. But, what does it mean not to suffer? What is freedom from disorder? What is mental and emotional balance and health? What is wellbeing and genuine happiness? What does it mean to be free from stress, anxiety and depression?

According to the World Health Organization (www.who.int/topics/mental_health/en/), mental health is 'a state of well-being in which the individual realises his or her own abilities, can cope with normal stresses of life, can work productively and fruitfully and is able to make a contribution to his or her community'. This definition suggests that mental and emotional health is more than just the absence of illness. It suggests that it is a positive state of wellbeing and flourishing.

Like the word stress, the meaning of happiness varies for different people. Positive psychologists see happiness in three ways:

1. The simple feeling of enjoyment and pleasure.
2. The uplifted feelings that are related to getting completely engaged with something, for example, doing a project, reading a great book, surfing, playing music or sport.
3. The sense of wellbeing and peace of mind we get when we do something that is important or meaningful for us. This could include being kind to someone or helping a friend out. For most people loving and being loved are probably the most important and meaningful things in life.

Positive psychologists say that the first type of happiness is healthy and very helpful for a sense of wellbeing. Unfortunately this type of happiness is precarious because, most of the time, it depends on getting what we want. Not only do things that are enjoyable not last, but even if we got what we wanted all the time, the way we feel about our acquisitions could also change. For example, the first time you go to your favourite restaurant it may be very enjoyable. If, however, you had the same meal, over and over again, day after day, the level of pleasure could quickly wane. Advertisers often try to convince us to buy into the first type of happiness. They say that we will be happy when we get what we want. The things that money buys can bring happiness to a certain point, but we all know that in the long run money can't buy happiness. Multimillionaires and lottery winners aren't always happy. There may be short cuts to the first type of happiness such as having endless holidays, going on spending sprees, having affairs, using drugs and alcohol, etc., but unfortunately, the highs of holidays do not last, the money quickly runs out on spending sprees and other short cuts may have hidden costs that eventually lead to misery and despair.

There are no short cuts to the second and third types of happiness because they often depend on us doing something, training in some way or other, or creating positive habits. Being engaged in life and having a purpose are more fulfilling than just getting pleasure and enjoyment. Research shows us that people who have the second and third types of happiness are healthier, live longer, have more success with their work and are more able to cope with life's difficulties.

Matthieu Ricard, a French-born scientist who became a monk in a Tibetan Buddhist tradition, has practised meditation for thousands of hours. Neuroscientists studied Matthieu's brain as he practised a series of different meditations. According to research his brain patterns indicated that he was a very happy man. Matthieu writes that happiness is not just a fleeting pleasurable feeling but 'a deep sense of flourishing that arises from an exceptionally healthy mind' (Ricard, 2006, p. 19). He added that happiness is an optimal state of being and that it is a way of interpreting the world, for while 'it may be difficult to change the world, it is always possible to change the way we look at it' (Ricard, 2006, p. 19). Thus, happiness or mental and emotional health involves a way of seeing and being.

Genuine happiness is not dependent on what we get from the world but rather on what we bring to it. Genuine happiness is internally generated and involves being able to let go of mental and emotional patterns that cause suffering. It also involves acting in ways that are conducive to the long-term wellbeing and happiness of ourselves and others. The cultivation of serenity, insight, compassion and wisdom is also important for genuine happiness. The way to genuine happiness is the fourth truth.

The fourth truth: a path of freedom

People often refer to life as a journey where we follow pathways. Sometimes people lose their way, have no purpose or direction, go down destructive roads, or feel as if they are going around in circles never reaching their goals. Sometimes the pathways we take are blocked or obstructed with difficulties and challenges and we feel stuck, trapped or frozen with fear, helpless and hopeless. Being lost, following destructive ways, going around in circles, feeling stuck, trapped, frightened, etc., are indicators of stress, anxiety and depression.

When we discover a pathway that leads us towards important life goals we feel joy and gain courage. When we choose to cultivate the helpful and let go of the unhelpful then our *dukkha* can fade away. Even if we feel stuck, we can have confidence that a pathway lies beyond the obstructions. This can be enough to bring peace of mind and reduce our stress. The path to psychological freedom involves letting go of unhelpful patterns and cultivating happiness and wellbeing. Easily said, but how do we do this? How do we let go of bad habits and cultivate helpful ones? How do we manage stress? How do we turn off autopilot and switch on to life?

The Buddha described a set of principles that if followed can lead to happiness. These principles are like signposts on a pathway that point in the direction of the desired destination, happiness. They are not strict rules to be followed blindly. Everyone must find their own way on the path. Each individual's pathway to freedom from *dukkha* is unique. Often individual pathways are connected to systems of healing such as those found in therapeutic psychology or spiritual practices. Regardless of the individual and/or the system, there seem to be principles or factors on these pathways that may be considered universal. The principles set out by the Buddha can be summarised as the cultivation of wisdom, consideration of ethics and the practice of meditation, which includes mindfulness. This way was described by the Buddha as the eight-fold path and the factors on this path fit within the principles of wisdom, actions driven by wisdom and the cultivation of the mind. More details will be provided about the Buddha's eight-fold path in the next chapter. For the moment, however, please look at the eight factors of the Buddha's path listed in Figure 1.2.

If we think of stress as having our coping skills and demands out of balance then we can begin to reduce our stress by decreasing the demands placed on us. This may not be easy but we can use wisdom to decide what we commit to, and say no to things that may be overwhelming. If we can't reduce demands, such as when we become ill, we can endeavour to change what needs to be changed and accept the things that can't be changed. We can commit to not harming ourselves or others. We can also increase our ability to cope by learning helpful strategies. We can investigate, change and be creative with the way we see and think about demands. There are many directions we can choose to cope with *dukkha*.

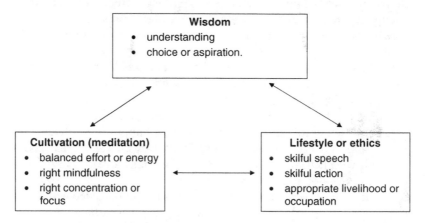

Figure 1.2 The eight-fold path
Source: adapted from Huxter (2007)

Wisdom and ethics

Wisdom is another term that means different things to different people. I often ask participants in my groups what wisdom means to them and I feel honoured to hear what they share. For most people, observing life and being attentive to experience is the way they develop wisdom. Universally, it seems that wisdom is linked to understanding and skilful actions. With wisdom we can choose to act in ways that increase happiness, health and wellbeing and decrease emotional pain, despair and anguish. Wisdom is an understanding that actions have consequences. With wisdom we choose to act in ways that avoid harm and increase wellbeing, not only for ourselves but for others as well.

According to the Buddhist monk Thanissaro Bhikkhu (2006), the Buddha said a good measure of wisdom is: 'the extent that you can get yourself to do things you don't like doing but know will result in happiness, and to refrain from things you like doing but know will result in pain and harm'. This measure of wisdom emphasises the importance of skilful action. What we do impacts on the world and our state of mind. Skilful actions are those actions that avoid harm. Unskilful actions are those actions that, in the long run, disturb mental composure and cause harm, somewhere down the track.

When we act skilfully, we are more able to be present for the experience of life. When we are present we get to know ourselves: our likes, dislikes and our important life directions. We know which actions are helpful and which actions are unhelpful. This knowledge is a form of wisdom and with it we are able to think clearly and accurately, make decisions and act in accordance with our understanding and best intentions. With wisdom we naturally incline to living in line with ethically responsible principles, which are conducive to the long-term health and wellbeing of ourselves and others. This involves caring for our body, heart and mind.

Everyone is different but ways of caring for ourselves include:

- doing regular physical exercise
- engaging in relaxation exercises
- having a healthy diet
- avoiding unwise use of alcohol and illicit drugs
- ensuring we have enough and regular sleep
- being honest with ourselves and others
- remembering our positive attributes and knowing our strengths
- using our strengths in ways that help ourselves and others
- not intending to harm ourselves, others or the environment
- being generous, kind and compassionate and helping other beings
- having enjoyable and satisfying things in our lives
- engaging in enjoyable and satisfying projects
- finding meaning and a sense of achievement in our lives
- doing things that are meaningful
- being assertive with or avoiding people who try to abuse or harm us
- getting to know thoughts and emotions so that we don't get caught up in harmful ones and can create helpful ones
- associating with wise, caring and supportive people
- being able to think clearly about problems and try out solutions
- having gratitude for what we have
- generally respecting life.

Wisdom can develop from hearing or reading wise words, or as is encouraged in CT and CBT, by thinking rationally and clearly. Wisdom can also grow out of meditation and mindfulness.

Introduction to meditation

Without wisdom we remain shrouded in delusion and stuck in *dukkha*. From a Buddhist perspective, meditation cultivates wisdom. In the third wave, mindfulness based therapies, there are different opinions about the value of meditation. MBSR and MBCT programme leaders believe that it is essential to meditate and prescribe formal meditation for 40 minutes a day, six days a week. DBT and ACT practitioners, on the other hand, say that it is not necessary and though it may be helpful, do not prescribe a formal meditation practice. The debate and inconsistency demonstrated between contemporary mindfulness based therapies may be a result of the lack of consensus about what both mindfulness and meditation are. The term 'meditation' has many definitions and is often poorly understood. For some, 'meditation' conjures up mystical unworldly ideas, which are far from the practical realities of many meditation practitioners. Unfortunately the lack of consensus amongst contemporary mindfulness based therapies does not serve to demystify and clarify the practicalities of meditation. So, how do Buddhists meditate and what do they mean when they talk about meditation? I hope that I can answer this question in more detail in Chapter 3 and throughout the rest of the book. For the time being it is relevant to say that one way to understand meditation is as mental training used to develop wisdom and a calm mind. Another way to understand meditation is as 'familiarisation', meaning that we become familiar with ourselves. All meditation involves some form of effort or energy, mindfulness and concentration. From a Buddhist perspective mindfulness cannot be separated from the activity of meditation and meditation cannot be separated from a context of wisdom and a psychologically healthy lifestyle.

Mindfulness

T. W. Rhys Davids, an English/Pali scholar, translated the Pali word *sati* as mindfulness in 1881. *Sati* literally means 'memory', but it refers to memory of the present, rather than of the past. *Sati* is the act of remembering the present, keeping the present in mind. Its opposite is forgetfulness, and the oblivion that characterises forgetfulness (Kearney, 2006). *Sati* can also refer to attention, in the sense that we 'attend to', 'care for' and 'watch over'. Bhikkhu Bodhi, a Buddhist monk, says that to be mindful is: 'to remember to pay attention to what is occurring in one's immediate experience with care and discernment' (according to Shapiro, 2009, p. 556). Immediate experience refers to the experience we are having here now. The discernment of mindfulness means that we make wise judgements about experience. We would not, for example, be in a house sitting on a cushion meditating and notice the smell of our house burning without making a judgement that we should act to put out the fire. Mindfulness includes being discerning about our experience.

Mindfulness can only occur here now, in this moment. However, in Buddhism mindfulness is more than just 'being aware in the moment'. Mindfulness includes recollection and non-forgetfulness. We can mindfully recollect the past, so that we can learn from experience and develop wisdom. Mindfulness can also involve remembering to do something in the future, such as remembering the purpose of what you are doing and not forgetting the suitability, timeliness and appropriateness of what is being done. With mindfulness we can track changes in experience. This helps to develop understanding.

Mindfulness helps us not to be seduced and intoxicated with the highs of life while protecting us from being deceived and lost in the lows. Mindfulness is the opposite of being mindlessly on automatic pilot. With mindfulness it is possible to relax with joyous awe to the mystery and beauty of life. Mindfulness can help liberate us from the suffering associated with anxiety and depression because it helps us remember the lessons from the past, remember our purpose and remember to be here now.

Mindfulness is a powerful healing factor, so powerful that the Buddha is reported to have said that it was an essential factor in being able to realise freedom from *dukkha*. As it is such an important skill it is not surprising that mindfulness or aspects of mindfulness have been used in contemporary psychotherapy for decades. Carl Rogers (1961), the forefather of humanistic psychology, emphasized the importance of being able to 'listen to oneself' over 50 years ago. Gestalt therapists Fritz Perls (1970) and Claudio Naranjo (1970) encouraged 'being in the now' and 'present centredness' as ways to become whole. Behavioural Therapy talks of 'self monitoring' (e.g. Mahoney and Thoresen, 1974),

Cognitive Behavioural Therapy of 'listening to automatic thoughts' (e.g. McKay, Davis and Fanning, 1981) and Cognitive Therapy of 'distancing' (e.g. Beck, 1976). Psychodynamic Therapy involves 'free association' and 'hovering attention' (e.g. Epstein, 1995; Speeth, 1982). All of these therapies contain elements of mindfulness.

For the most part, contemporary approaches to mindfulness explain it as a form of non-judgemental present centred awareness. Mindfulness Based Stress Reduction (MBSR) and Mindfulness Based Cognitive Therapy (MBCT) define mindfulness as: 'the awareness that emerges through paying attention on purpose, in the present moment, and non-judgementally to the unfolding of experience moment to moment' (Kabat-Zinn, 2003, p. 145). Whereas, Linehan (1993), the founder of Dialectical Behavior Therapy (DBT), explains mindfulness as the practice of: *observing, describing and participating with experience, which is done in a non-judgemental, focused (one thing at a time) and skilful manner.* Acceptance and Commitment Therapy (ACT) practitioners say that mindfulness cannot be separated from a context that includes values clarification and committed actions. One ACT trainer in Australia, Dr Russ Harris, defines mindfulness as: *paying attention with flexibility, openness and curiosity* (e.g. Harris, 2008). Another way of describing mindfulness is as presence and being present, here now.

What are we mindful of?

You can be mindful anywhere and with almost everything in life. You can be mindful when you are playing music, eating, talking, walking, running, sitting, lying down and breathing. You can be mindful as you negotiate a business deal, or when you are gardening. Wherever you are able to be aware, you can be mindful.

As mentioned earlier, however, mindfulness is more than just being aware in the moment. Skilful mindfulness has an ethical quality. In order to be successful, bank robbers or snipers need to be in the moment and aware of what they are doing. This type of presence, however, is different than the type of mindfulness that leads to wisdom. Mindfulness applied with discernment and aspiration for long-term psychological health and wellbeing for oneself and others is more likely to lead to wisdom and psychological freedom.

In Buddhism the application of mindfulness can divided into four main domains:

1.   Body and bodily experience, such as posture, actions, physical sensations as well as the breath.

2. Feelings of whether something is comfortable or pleasant, uncomfortable or unpleasant or neither.
3. Moods, emotions, thinking patterns and states of mind such as a happy mind, a sad mind, an angry mind, a peaceful mind and so on.
4. Emotional, mental and behavioural patterns and reactions, both helpful and unhelpful as well as other phenomena.

Related qualities

On the path of freedom, mindfulness is not alone. There are many other skills and qualities that go with it. They all help to develop each other. Some of these skills and qualities are:

Relaxation

Being able to relax is very important, especially in a modern world where everyone seems stressed and tense. Relaxing is letting go of muscular tension. When we can relax we also notice that we can simultaneously let go of worrying thoughts and concerns. Relaxation is the first step in the practice of meditation. Relaxation is a primary ally to being mindful. Relaxation is the bedrock on which you build the stability of mindfulness and has also been the main way that health practitioners have countered the effects of stress since the early 1920s.

Kindness

Kindness is an essential part of mindfulness. Often we are unkind to ourselves, engaging in negative judgement and condemnation. Mindfulness practice requires a quality of tender 'OKness' about ourselves. This does not mean we condone unwise actions or behaviours, but it means that we begin to understand that things arise because of many interrelated causes and conditions. Being kind to ourselves will enable us to have the courage to be open to experience.

Commitment

Commitment is the willingness to put forth effort. Ironically the type of effort needed for mindfulness practice is sometimes described as 'effortless effort'. It involves the motivation and willingness to continue to practise even when it seems boring or unpleasant. It can be compared to digging for water. We need to resolve to keep going even if results do not quickly emerge. The need to practise cannot be over-emphasised. Positive results are more probable with practice.

A beginner's mind

A beginner's mind refers to a quality of interested curiosity about life. As a beginner, one is open to experience and everything is new and fresh. It also refers to a quality of investigation, which means enquiring into the nature of something. This involves an intellectual as well as an intuitive understanding about the changing, interdependent and mysterious nature of our minds and bodies.

Focused attention

Focused attention includes attempting to pay attention to one thing at a time. It involves 'relaxing into' and 'opening up' to an experience rather than forceful concentration. Focused attention requires us to simply bring attention back to the object of attention or action.

Non-judgemental stance

Non-judgement does not imply one should not utilise wise discernment. In the practice of mindfulness a non-judgemental stance generally refers to suspending the filter of evaluating comments so that objects of mindfulness can be perceived as they are. It means suspending unnecessary judgement or condemnation. This involves staying with the facts rather than getting lost in our opinions of the facts, such as 'good', 'bad', 'should', 'should not', etc.

Non-grasping

This attitude has been described as non-striving. It is important to have goals, a direction for action and in some cases apply courageous effort to achieve these goals. The process of how we attain our goals, however, can be more important than the goal. Being too concerned about an outcome can become a hindrance to being here now. A non-striving attitude is important in relaxation and meditation. A non-striving attitude means that when you do a mindfulness exercise it is not done with attachment to a goal in the future. Rather, an exercise is done for its intrinsic value or for its own sake. Non-grasping is the best way to describe this attitude because this highlights the importance of not being attached to outcomes.

Acceptance

Acceptance refers to the willingness to experience whatever happens in our mind, body and life. Acceptance does not refer to apathetically condoning dysfunctional patterns or events. Rather it means seeing things as they are in the present moment. Acceptance may not always be best in situations that are negative or not constructive. In the realm of private internal experiences like thoughts and emotions, however, acceptance allows choice in how we may react. Acceptance refers to being open to experience and being willing to learn from what has been offered by life. This opens us to the mystery of life with a big 'yes' as opposed to rejecting life's experiences with a 'no' or a 'yes but . . .'.

Patience

Patience is like acceptance. One cannot push the natural unfolding of experience and change. Patience involves opening up to experience in every moment as it arises and giving our minds the space to be aware of the experience. Patience also involves the understanding that as we learn to cope, emotional or mental distress will arise from time to time and it may be intense. We can develop patience and tolerance when we understand that our distress will change and we allow it time to do so. Patience involves a deep and warm acceptance of our self and the rate of our 'progress'. Remember that breaking old negative habits takes time and judging ourselves harshly makes matters worse.

It is important to understand that all the above attitudes and skills including relaxation develop naturally, in due time and with practice. Do not be discouraged if, at first, they are not present.

Some beginning mindfulness practices

It is helpful to start being mindful with relaxation and simple everyday activities. In this way you can see how mindfulness is a part of life and a skill that you can cultivate and use in all situations.

As muscle relaxation is an important ally to mindfulness, a progressive muscle relaxation exercise is a good place to start. I will provide the basic instructions for Progressive Muscular Relaxation (PMR). PMR is a practice that has been used by health practitioners including psychologists for the promotion of health and wellbeing and stress management since the 1920s. PMR is also very helpful as an introduction to mindfulness. You need to practise mindfulness as you relax and the more relaxed you become the more able you are to cultivate mindfulness.

An important point about relaxation, however, is that occasionally for some people it can trigger uncomfortable reactions. If this is the case for you another good place to start being mindful is by being aware of sounds or an everyday activity. Eating is an everyday activity that is often used to practise mindfulness. Learning to be attentive to eating is one way to experiment with mindfulness, and experience the benefits for yourself.

These three beginning practices, PMR, mindfulness of sounds and mindful eating are described over the next few pages. There are also free audio tracks available for mindfulness of sounds and progressive relaxation from my website, www.malhuxter.com as well as the website of Routledge, <www.routledge.com/9781138851351>.

Progressive muscle relaxation

During PMR you are asked to tense your muscles. It is important not to tense your muscles if it causes you any pain and not to tense your muscles for longer than 6 or 7 seconds. Please be mindful of how your body feels and remember to also cultivate the qualities of kindness, patience and non-grasping. Whilst this relaxation exercise is usually pleasant for most people, should it cause you discomfort please try one of the other exercises and come back to the relaxation another time when you feel you are able.

- Find a comfortable, quiet place to sit or lie down. A place that you will not be interrupted for about 20 minutes.
- Make the intention that for the next 15–20 minutes you will not be too concerned about anything except being mindful in the moment and practising relaxation.
- Remember that you cannot force relaxation to happen; it is something that happens when you let go of tension.
- First, close your eyes and focus on your breathing, keeping it slow and even. Say the words 'let go' to yourself a few times as you breathe out.
- Tense up your right foot, squeezing your toes together and pointing them downwards. Focus on that tension. Slowly release that tension as you breathe out, whilst saying the words 'let go' or 'relax' to yourself.
- Now tense up the rest of your right leg.
- Slowly release the tension as you breathe out saying 'let go' or 'relax'.
- Go through the other muscles in your body, working through the muscles of your right leg, left leg, buttocks, back, abdomen, chest, shoulders, left arm, left hand and

fingers, right arm, right hand and fingers, neck, jaw, lips, eyes, and forehead.

• Breathe out as you relax each body part saying to yourself 'let go' or 'relax'.

• When you finish, scan through your body and make sure most tension has been released. If some areas are still tense you can spend extra time just relaxing those muscles.

• Slowly open your eyes and remember that throughout the day you can remind yourself to let go of tension by saying to yourself 'let go' or 'relax'.

Mindfulness of sound

• Make yourself comfortable, sitting upright and relaxed.

• Scan your body and release whatever tension you may feel.

• Make the intention that for the period of this exercise, you will not follow concerns about things other than being here and now being mindful of sound.

• Also make the intention to be open and kind to other experiences if and when they come up.

• Now bring your awareness to sound.

• Be aware of sound as sound or vibration.

• There may be sounds of music, birds, cars, traffic, air conditioning, wind, rain or just the hum of silence.

• Notice how you may create pictures and names around the sound such 'my favourite music track', 'dog barking', 'traffic', 'birds' or whatever. Don't struggle with the names or the pictures and simply listen to sound as vibration. Notice how the sounds arise and pass away.

• Notice how some sounds are pleasant, some sounds are unpleasant and some sounds are neither pleasant nor unpleasant. Be aware of all your judgements, but don't worry about them. Simply remember to be aware of sound as sound.

• Now arising . . . now changing . . . now passing away.

• Let your mind be as if it is the sky, open, expansive and clear, and let sounds arise and pass through.

• By listening to sounds, as an orchestra of life, you can become very peaceful.

- By listening to sounds and noticing how they all change you can become very peaceful.
- Be content and at peace to listen to sounds.
- When the time is right you can end this period of mindfulness.
- If mindfulness of sounds was helpful for you, remember that you can be mindful of sounds whenever it feels like the right thing to do.

Invitation to eating mindfully

Eating is often an automatic and unconscious behaviour. Sometimes we have barely finished one mouthful before we shove in the next. We are often doing other things like talking with our mouths full, listening to the radio or watching TV rather than simply being attentive to or enjoying our meals.

To break autopilot mode, it helps to do one thing at a time. With eating this involves just eating when eating. That is, not talking, or walking or reading or watching TV or something else while eating. With mindful eating you bring curious and interested attention to all the different parts of the eating process. Before you eat it is also very helpful to think about and reflect on how the food got on your plate, or in your hand. This reflection helps you slow down and develop an understanding of the interdependence of all things including a simple morsel of food. Such reflection also helps to cultivate gratitude, which is a healing emotion.

Eating mindfully

Before you begin to eat your food, sit down and spend a few moments reflecting on how this food got to be in your hand or on your plate. Did someone give it to you? Or did someone spend time and effort preparing it for you? How did it grow or how was it prepared? Reflect on all the things that were needed for it to grow, such as the sunshine, water, and the nourishment from the soil. Reflect on where this food came from. Perhaps it came from far away, in which case there was effort and energy spent bringing it to you. Think of all the people involved in preparing it and bringing it to you.

Feel the food or the spoon or fork in your hand. Notice the weight, shape, size and texture of the food. Be very curious. Look at the food. Notice all the colours and shapes and other things you can see. Notice the way the light shines on it. Smell it. What does it smell like? If you were to describe this smell to someone else how would you describe it? Bring it to your mouth and take a bite. Listen to the sounds that the biting makes then taste all the tastes. Notice all the bursts of experiences and let them come and go. What does it taste like? Notice all your judgements as well. Do you think it is nice, not nice or some-how in the middle? Slow down your chewing so that you can savour the experience. Feel how the morsels move around in your mouth and how your tongue automatically does its thing. Then when the time is right, notice the urge to swallow and move the food to the back of your tongue and down your throat and into your belly. How does that feel?

Now notice if there is wanting for more. If there is wanting, notice this urge to have more and be present with it. Then, when you decide to follow the urge notice how you bring the food to your mouth for another new moment of experience and be mindful of everything and continue to enjoy your food, mindfully.

Remembering to remember

If you did not experiment with the above or similar exercises before reading this, then I suggest that you make a firm intention that you will in the near future, and follow your intention through with action. As we come to the end of this chapter, I would like to invite you to practise another mindfulness exercise. Right now, without flicking back through the pages, experiment with recollecting what you have read in this chapter. You could, for example, just list the important points in your mind. An extension of this memory exercise is to con-template your responses to the information and what would be useful in your life.

Notes

1 At the time of writing these notes PTSD and OCD were considered as anxiety disorders. In the current *DSM V* (APA, 2013), however, PTSD is

classified under the Trauma- and Stressor-Related Disorders and OCD is listed separately in the Obsessive-Compulsive and Related Disorders category.
2 Majjhima Nikaya 26:19 in Nanamoli and Bodhi (1995, p. 260).

References

American Psychiatric Association (1994). *Diagnostic and Statistic Manual of Mental Disorders, Fourth Edition*. Washington, DC: American Psychiatric Association.

American Psychiatric Association (2013). *Diagnostic and Statistic Manual of Mental Disorders, Fifth Edition*. Washington, DC: American Psychiatric Association.

Beck, A. T. (1976). *Cognitive Therapy and the Emotional Disorders*. New York: New American Library.

Cox, T. (1978). *Stress*. London: Macmillan.

Dalai Lama, H. H. (2007). Happiness in a material world. Happiness and Its Causes Conference Proceedings, 14–15 June, Sydney Convention & Exhibition Centre, Sydney, Australia.

Epstein, M. (1995). *Thoughts without a Thinker*. New York: Basic Books.

Harris, R. (2008). *The Happiness Trap: Stop Struggling and Start Living*. London: Constable and Robinson.

Huxter, M. J. (2007). Mindfulness as therapy from a Buddhist perspective. In D. A. Einstein (ed.), *Innovations and Advances in Cognitive Behaviour Therapy*. Bowen Hills, Qld: Australian Academic Press.

Kabat-Zinn, J. (2003). Mindfulness based interventions in context: past present and future. *Clinical Psychology: Science and Practice* 10: 2 144–56.

Kearney, P. (2006). Mindfulness, meditation and a path as therapy. Advanced workshop conducted with Malcolm Huxter at the Hunter Institute of Mental Health, Newcastle, NSW, Australia.

Linehan, M. M. (1993). *Cognitive-Behavioral Treatment of Borderline Personality Disorder*. New York: Guilford Press.

McKay, M., Davis, M. and Fanning, P. (1981). *Thoughts and Feelings: The Art of Cognitive Stress Intervention*. Oakland, CA: New Harbinger Publications.

Mahoney, M. J. and Thoresen, C. E. (1974). *Self Control: Power to the Person*. Monterey, CA: Brooks Cole.

Nanamoli, B. and Bodhi B. (1995). *The Middle Length Discourses of the Buddha: A New Translation of the Majjhima Nikaya*. Boston, MA: Wisdom Publications.

Naranjo, C. (1970). Present centeredness: techniques, prescription and ideal. In J. Fagen and I. L. Shepherd (eds.), *Gestalt Therapy Now*. New York: HarperColophon.

Perls, F. S. (1970). Four lectures. In J. Fagen and I. L. Shepherd (eds.), *Gestalt Therapy Now*. New York: HarperColophon.

Ricard, M. (2006). *Happiness: A Guide to Developing Life's Most Important Skill.* London: Atlantic Books.

Rogers, C. R. (1961). *On Becoming a Person.* London: Constable.

Shapiro, S. L. (2009). The integration of mindfulness and psychology. *Journal of Clinical Psychology* 65: 6 555–60.

Speeth, K. R. (1982). On psychotherapeutic attention. *Journal of Transpersonal Psychology* 14: 2 141–60.

Thanissaro, B. (1993). *The Mind Like Fire Unbound.* Barre, MA: Dhamma Dana Publications.

Thanissaro, B. (2006). *The Integrity of Emptiness.* www.accesstoinsight.org/lib/authors/thanissaro.

2 Having purpose and choosing direction
Steps on a path of freedom

Chapter overview

This chapter outlines some common stress management strategies such as goal setting, time management and problem solving. It also clarifies the difference between goals and valued directions. Clarifying valued directions helps us to make wise decisions about what we do in life. Wisdom, along with ethics and meditation are three components of the path to freedom, the fourth truth, as outlined in the previous chapter. This path of freedom from *dukkha* can be further broken down into eight primary factors. This chapter describes the eight factors of the path to freedom. To conclude, more ways to practise mindfulness will be provided.

Life direction

It is important to have a clear view of our life direction. When we know where we are going with clear vision it is easier to act mindfully in accordance with our chosen direction. Acting with purpose gives us meaning (the third aspect of happiness according to positive psychologists).

When we become depressed we are often overwhelmed with hopelessness. We may be acutely aware of distress in our lives but not be able to see a way out. Life can seem meaningless and the thought 'why bother' can often arise. When caught in depression we may withdraw from social contact and everyday activities. We may retreat into what seems like an emotional black hole. When we are experiencing anxiety our avoidance of activity is related to fear. When suffering with anxiety we may feel as if we are backed into a corner of avoidance. In this way we are often frozen into inactivity and social withdrawal. As explained in the previous chapter, avoidance is a pattern with anxiety and lack of motivation is often a symptom of depression. Anxiety and depression, as disorders, often occur together.

Sometimes rather than being inactive we frantically engage in nervous activity in an effort to avoid feelings such as boredom or a sense of inadequacy and failure. This type of activity is often done in a chaotic and unconscious manner. We may try to get everything done at once. We rush around from one activity to the next not really being sure of what we are doing or why we are doing it. At the end of the day we may feel exhausted and unsatisfied because nothing was achieved. This type of undirected or confused behaviour is stressful and consequently adds to our suffering.

If we act in a purposeless, meaningless manner it is easy to fall victim to destructive, anxious and depressive patterns. However, when we realise that unhelpful patterns are keeping us in reactive cycles of stress we can slowly and gradually confront our avoidance. Acting with purpose decreases the anxiety we feel and, ironically, if we can be more active our motivation increases and depression decreases. Gradually we develop a clear life direction and gain confidence in the path. Confidence gives rise to commitment or motivation. When motivated, we can endure short-term hardships and difficulty because we can see the possibility of long-term release from our suffering.

Related story: Angelo finds purpose

Angelo had a difficult childhood. There was violence in his family. His mother and father were both aggressive to one another and eventually separated when he was 14 years old. At an early age Angelo decided that he would never follow the path of violence. Although he had a brother and sister he rarely contacted them.

Angelo studied at university as a mature age student and graduated at the age of 37. At 39 he moved to a rural community for work and made many friends. He enjoyed his work and felt he did a good job. He had many girlfriends but had never made a long-term commitment.

When Angelo was 43 he began to withdraw from his friends and stay at home on the weekends. Work, which was once very interesting, seemed to lose its appeal and Angelo started to miss workdays because he had no energy. He was still single and there was no one special in his life. He started to stay in bed and watch TV into the late hours of the night. He had little motivation to work on projects around the house because it was rented and he started to feel fatigued. Angelo would stay up until the late hours of the night, then wake in the early hours of the morning and only get back to sleep when the sun started to rise. On the weekends he wouldn't get out of bed until midday. His concentration started to slip and he couldn't follow the stories in the programs on TV but he continued to watch nonetheless. His work performance began to deteriorate. After missing some important meetings and speaking abruptly and inappropriately with a work colleague his boss suggested he have a few weeks off. Despite the time off, Angelo's health deteriorated. He lost his appetite and he rarely exercised.

Angelo started to ruminate and memories of the past began to haunt him. He started to think of difficult past life events and the circumstances around these events. Many things seemed meaningless. He began to question the value of his work and in particular he began to think that he was worthless and that his life was not worth living. Angelo was experiencing depression.

When a friend visited, Angelo shared his thoughts and the friend asked him what he really wanted from life. Did Angelo really want to end it all or were there other directions and possibilities?

Spurred on by his friend, Angelo began to think about what was really important. In particular he began to think about what life directions he valued. Angelo realised that there were many things that he would really like to achieve during his life. In particular, he wanted to meet someone special and share his life with this person. He did not want to grow into a lonely and isolated old man. Angelo realised that if he wanted to achieve long-terms goals he needed to act now by doing things that were consistent with these goals on a day-to-day basis.

Angelo made some commitments to himself and he managed to keep some of these commitments. He started to watch less TV and he visited good friends. He also took up some hobbies and started going to dance classes. By being more active Angelo's energy started to lift and his mood became lighter. He didn't have time to ruminate and he started to appreciate things. Being present for the simple joys of life gave Angelo a different perspective on his past. Angelo became more content and he felt that he had regained direction and that his life had purpose.

Having purpose and direction

Knowing the direction that is important to us makes it easier to manage our stress. When we act in accordance with our best intentions and valued directions we feel a sense of being in the flow of life and we feel joy. When we are in the flow, life becomes so interesting that there is no time to feel bored or miserable. 'Flow' is similar to the second type of happiness explained by positive psychologists in which we are so absorbed in what we are doing that worries and concerns all fall away (Csikszentmihalyi, 1988). The joy of flow is just one aspect of the happiness that arises when we live according to aspirations for happiness, health and wellbeing.

Mindfulness is a strategy that can help us to get into the flow of life. Mindfulness, focused attention, aspiration and actions based on good intentions cannot be separated from wisdom. With mindfulness we are able to confront automatic habits, quell emotional over-reaction and reduce unhelpful learned responses. One aspect of mindfulness that helps us to do this is clear comprehension. With clear comprehension we are able to act in a way that is in accordance with our desired life direction. We are able to see clearly whether or not our actions are timely and suitable.

Goal setting

Goals are important because they give us direction; however, there are risks with goals when we cling to them. We can never be certain about how things may turn out and if we cling to a specific outcome we may be disappointed if that outcome doesn't occur. We need to be flexible and hold goals lightly. If our expectations are too high or unrealistic we will be discouraged when we don't achieve our goals. Goals are also future oriented and so we may forget to appreciate what is happening in the present. To be meaningful and satisfactory, goals need to be realistic, achievable and clearly defined. A useful acronym commonly used in CBT for goals is SMART:

- Specific
- Measurable
- Achievable
- Realistic
- Time measured

Goals provide us with purpose and direction and enhance our ability to live in line with our best intentions. SMART goals, set wisely, are helpful to reduce *dukkha*. Goal setting is a strategy often used in CBT. Goals can be immediate (i.e. daily or weekly), short term (1–12 months) and long term (10 years to life). If we are clear about a desired outcome we are more likely to be motivated to take the appropriate action to make it happen.

In order to achieve something worthwhile it can help to start with an ideal or a 'dream' of how we would like things to be. This becomes a long-term goal. It helps to be specific by clarifying exactly how life could be different and what needs to be changed to achieve this. Then using constructive and realistic thinking we can consider the steps that are needed and make the immediate or short-term goals accordingly. Goals can target thoughts, feelings and behaviours. Goals provide us with a positive framework to counter cycles of stress or suffering.

Having long-term goals is important but trying to achieve those goals all at once may be unrealistic. Therefore, we need to achieve our goals gradually. Having achievable goals is particularly important when we feel stressed or out of balance. If we have realistic and concrete goals this helps to reduce the tendency for avoidance that is common in both anxiety and depression. It is helpful to start by clarifying exactly what we are avoiding and what we would like to achieve. We can then plan how to get closer to our long-term goals. This step-by-step approach needs to involve graduated approximations that meet realistic challenges.

Someone suffering with agoraphobia, for example, may have an intense fear of large shopping centres. A long-term goal may be to be able to go to a large mall, do a few hours' shopping and manage anxiety. The step-wise approach to meet this goal could start by committing to visiting the local corner store for a few minutes, then at a later date, to going to the local small supermarket for 30 minutes. Slowly and over time this person could increase the time they spend shopping as well as the size of the shops they visit.

Someone overwhelmed with depression may not be motivated to set goals and be stuck in inactivity. Yet, if they become active this can build energy and motivation and lift their mood. Participating in pleasant activities and activities that give a sense of achievement can also influence a lift in mood. Goals can be made on a daily basis and can be very simple. Cleaning one's room, for example, can be an achievable goal which, when completed, can give a sense of satisfaction.

It is particularly important to participate in activities that are enjoyable. Such activity increases the possibility that joyful emotions will arise. Joy is a wholesome emotion that helps focus attention and counters despondency and the flat miserable mood of depression as well as the avoidance of anxiety. What is considered to be enjoyable and satisfying varies from one person to the next but could include such activities as: dancing, participating in interesting projects or hobbies, sports, music, reading, visiting friends, movies, being in nature, surfing and so on. As everyone is unique, the types of goals that help overcome destructive patterns need to be designed and planned on an individual basis.

Time management

Time management is another stress management strategy that is common in CBT. Time management refers to being realistic about how long tasks are likely to take and allocating an appropriate amount of time to achieve one's goals. Prioritising the steps helps in making decisions about what should be done first. Effective time management involves setting out the day's goals and prioritising the steps needed to achieve them. Decisions about what needs to be done, and when, involves priorities being given to each task and determining how long each step may take.

Problem solving

Another common sense stress management strategy is problem solving. Sometimes ignoring, denying or not dealing with problems can make them worse. Becoming overly distressed, worried or relying on unhelpful ways to deal with problems can also make the problem worse. One helpful way to deal with problems is to approach them in a realistic, logical step-by-step manner. Problem solving skills often include the ability to think logically and realistically. They involve looking at an issue from an objective perspective and considering a number of alternatives to deal with the problem. Mindfulness can help with problem solving as it enables us to monitor our emotional reactions and ensure that we don't lose our objectivity. If a particular problem is causing stress it is helpful to be mindful and think in a constructive manner. One must be careful, however, not to let such thinking turn into rumination or worry. If a time limit is placed on problem solving activity then it helps to offset the possibility of destructive automatic thinking patterns taking control.

In summary

All the above common-sense strategies to deal with stress are connected by a thread of wisdom, wise lifestyles and mental and emotional development. When we forget these strategies, when our view becomes clouded, and we act unwisely, confusion and misery often follow. Many of the people I see as a clinical psychologist are suffering because of unwise decisions they made. Though they often wish to learn meditation it is appropriate that they first reflect on their actions and adjust their lifestyles so that their behaviours reflect what is important to them.

Related story: Joanne resolves a problem and dispels confusion

When Joanne sat down with a counsellor she said that she was confused. She said that her life was a mess and no matter what she did she felt uneasy and emotionally stuck. She added that her sleep was disturbed and she was tormented by worry and guilt. She had stopped exercising and had been skipping meals. Her physical health had deteriorated and she had the flu. She said that she had learnt how to meditate and relax when she was younger but when she tried to do this to manage her distress it seemed to get worse. She asked her GP for sleeping medication and to try to cope with her emotional pain she had been using alcohol excessively.

When asked what her aim was for visiting the counsellor she said that she wanted to feel better. Mostly she wanted some clarity and peace of mind.

Joanne was 31 years old and had been married for five years. She said that for as long as she had known her husband, John, he had worked very hard. Often he would work long hours and he was rarely around on the weekends. She said that, financially, she wanted for nothing. Emotionally, however, she felt lonely. She felt her husband was simply not available to provide intimacy, which was something that she yearned for.

Bob, who was in a de facto relationship with someone else, was a long-term friend with whom she could talk. A few months previously their friendship had become sexual and without their respective partners knowing, they had continued to have a sexual relationship. Joanne said that she felt torn emotionally because the relationship with Bob fulfilled her yearning for intimacy but at the same time, sneaking away for intimate moments with him was against her values of respecting her marriage vows and being honest.

She said that the feelings of affection that she had once had for her husband had long died off. She had thought of calling it all off with Bob, but the thoughts of being alone, isolated and rejected were unbearable. The pain of telling John all about the affair was also unbearable because she did not want to hurt him.

She asked the counsellor for advice on what she should do. He offered nothing concrete but suggested she reflect on the causes and conditions of her distress, and fully accept it. Joanne found talking to the counsellor very difficult but as she spoke about her confusion, guilt and distress she gained a different perspective on it. The counsellor suggested that she reflect on what was really important for her and then plan concrete actions that would reflect her deepest values.

Joanne went away and thought about how to deal with the issues in a practical and realistic manner. She made some big decisions and acted on them. She decided that honesty and compassion were high priorities in her life and considered how to act in accordance with these values. She was honest to her husband about the affair, and though it was very painful for both of them, separated from him. Joanne wanted to continue with an intimate relationship with Bob but decided that she would only do so if and when he was also honest with his partner. She decided that if Bob stayed with his partner then, despite it being difficult, it would be best to no longer have a sexual relationship with him. Joanne decided that she simply did not want to complicate her life unnecessarily and possibly harm and hurt other parties further. Joanne disciplined herself to establish a routine with eating and exercise. She began to exercise regularly and to cook and eat healthy food. Soon she was able to sleep without the need of sleeping tablets.

The decisions Joanne made about her relationship were extremely difficult for her because she had to face her fear of being rejected and lonely. It was, however, worth it in the long run because she gained some peace of mind. Joanne's alcohol consumption stopped and she was able to meditate in a manner that was calming and relaxing. Joanne felt that she had dispelled confusion and she had some direction in her life.

Goals and important life directions

The destination or goal is important but so is the journey. Important directions are different from goals. Valued directions are what we think or feel are important, our fundamental purpose, and what is meaningful to us. Goals tend to be specific or definable achievements or outcomes. For example, a university student's goal could be the completion of a degree, a specific measurable and achievable outcome. A valued direction in relation to this goal could be to live life in a way that maximises educational potential. If something happened and the university student could not finish the degree and achieve the goal, then he or she need not be discouraged or depressed because it is still possible to live according to the valued life direction of maximising educational potential. Goals are 'there then' whilst valued directions are 'here now'. Living in accordance with what is valued and important gives us vitality and a sense of fulfilment and satisfaction. When we act contrary to valued directions we may feel inner turmoil and this can lead to depression and anxiety.

It is helpful to clarify our valued directions and prioritise the most important ones. If we know our valued directions we are able to make decisions about our actions and we can act with purpose. Mindfulness helps us to ensure that our actions are congruent with our best intentions. This helps us protect our wellbeing and happiness. We often discover our valued directions when we are faced with a life crisis. We can also discover our values when we question what is really important to us and what we really want. Acceptance and Commitment Therapy (ACT) is a third wave therapy that also connects mindfulness to values clarification and committed action. When values are clarified we are more able to commit to actions that reflect these values.

Developing an aspiration is similar to clarifying valued directions. Wholesome aspirations help us steer along a path that leads to genuine happiness and wellbeing and helps to make our vision for the future a reality. Having an aspiration is not the same as avoiding experience or craving and grasping for something different. Having an aspiration for something better is like being in a small dark room but being able to see out a window to a beautiful view. It reminds us that there are possibilities and it gives us something to aim towards. In the last chapter I explained that the fourth truth is the cause of freedom and I provided information about mindfulness as part of the way to find freedom from *dukkha*. I also mentioned that mindfulness cannot be separated from a context. The context in which mindfulness becomes meaningful is the eight-fold path.

The Buddha's eight-fold path

The eight-fold path is often described as the middle way because it does not incline to extremes. It is considered as a path of moderation. It provides a way to balance the imbalances of desire, attention, thoughts and emotions. The eight-fold path is in essence the practice of Buddhism. Just as an elephant's footprint can contain within it all the footprints of other animals, the eight-fold path contains within it all possible healing, therapeutic and awakening principles.[1]

The eight-fold path is a general framework to slow down and stop the patterns of craving/clinging, aversion/avoidance and confusion/ignorance that cause and maintain *dukkha*. This path also nurtures and supports what is best by cultivating optimal ways of being. In summary, the eight-fold path is a process of letting go of the unhelpful and cultivating the helpful.

Each factor on the path starts with the Pali word *samma* which usually translates as 'right'. *Samma* could also be translated as complete, authentic, fully, skilful, appropriate or correct. The eight factors on the path are not necessarily followed in a sequential manner, one after the other. More accurately they are interdependent components 'comparable to the intertwining strands of a single cable that requires the contributions of all the strands for maximum strength' (Bodhi, 2000, p. 13). Traditionally the eight factors are presented in this order:

1. Complete view, or understanding
2. Skilful intention, choice or aspiration
3. Skilful speech
4. Skilful action
5. Appropriate livelihood or occupation
6. Balanced effort or energy
7. Right mindfulness
8. Right concentration or focus

Right mindfulness is the seventh factor on the path and though it is crucial, the other seven factors are equally as important. As mentioned earlier, the eight factors on this path are divided into three basic components: ethics or lifestyle (appropriate action, speech and livelihood or occupation); the cultivation of the mind (suitable effort, mindfulness and concentration); and wisdom (complete understanding or view and skilful intention or vision). The interconnectedness of the eight factors can be seen in Figure 2.1. This diagram was also in Chapter 1, and is reproduced here for ease of reference.

From a Buddhist perspective the eight-fold path has two levels. At a basic level the path leads to a reduction in stress and helps us to lead a happier and healthier life. At a deeper or more refined level the eight-fold path may lead to the realisation of Nirvana or the complete release from *dukkha*. Contemporary psychology could be considered as fitting within the broad framework of the basic level of the eight-fold path and this book is mostly concerned with this level of

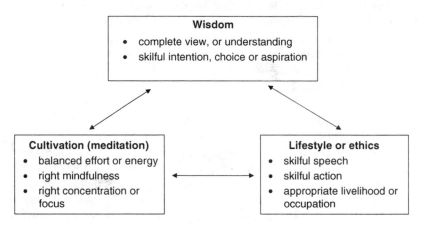

Figure 2.1 The eight-fold path
Source: adapted from Huxter (2007)

the path. However, as we all have the potential to awaken to the realisations of the Buddha, realisations at a deeper and more refined level
are also possible from practising the strategies explained in this book.

Wisdom

Complete view or understanding

Complete view or understanding can be considered the first stage of
the path and also the result of the path. Having a complete and clear
view is like having clean lenses to look through, where our perception
of things is no longer obscured by ideas that are unhelpful. In the traditional Buddhist texts inaccurate views are described as being like a
thicket in which we are entangled.

According to Buddhist psychology inaccurate views include seeing
what is impermanent as permanent, seeing what is not 'me', 'mine' or
'myself' as 'me', 'mine' or 'myself', and seeing things that cannot provide lasting happiness as the source of genuine happiness. Another
mistaken view, according to Buddhist psychology, is the belief that
intentional actions do not have consequences. This means not seeing
that the way we behave in the world has an impact. Such a view may
lead to harmful actions because there is no consideration of the consequences. At a more subtle level this view means not seeing how everything is, in some way or another, connected to everything else, and that
what we do affects others and the environment around us.

Skilful intention or choice

When we are able to see that actions lead to consequences then we are more likely to act in ways that cause less suffering. The decision to act in a manner that will result in less suffering is called a skilful intention or choice. Skilful intentions are intentions that lead to long-term happiness and wellbeing for oneself and others. This type of intention could be referred to as healthy resolve or commitment. Skilful intentions can also be wholesome aspirations as described earlier. Sometimes this factor is called 'right thought'.

Intentions are like choices to act in particular ways. They are impulses to action that steer us through the bigger picture of our life as well as the moment-to-moment actions of everyday activities. Simple actions such as getting up from a chair, scratching our face, going shopping, or saying something to someone, etc., all involve intentions.

At the everyday level we may have thousands of intentions every day. Being mindful of our intentions, both in the bigger picture and in everyday activities can be a very powerful way to give us choice in how we act. As our actions have consequences an intention is a deciding factor that will either lead to happiness or away from it. Intentions based on kindness and compassion are considered to be right intentions.

When complete understanding is the basis of our choices, we endeavour to behave with our speech, actions and livelihood in a manner likely to reduce stress. An ethical lifestyle is the next component of the path. This part of the path emphasises helpful behaviours. However, we should remember that what we refrain from doing is also important.

Healthy lifestyles-ethics

Ethical behaviour, or a wholesome lifestyle, is the foundation of the Buddha's eight-fold path. For the Buddha, practising meditation without the support of an ethical lifestyle is like building a house without foundations – fragile and at risk of collapse. Ethics provide us with direction. An ethical direction is one that leads to long-term wellbeing and happiness for oneself and others.

In contemporary psychotherapy, however, ethics rarely, if ever, get talked about. Contemporary psychology sees itself as a science, and as such many psychologists consider that their practice should be unbiased by value-laden opinions. Also, many therapists refrain from imposing what they feel are society's value judgements on their clients because it is not helpful. However, a therapeutic discussion about ethics is different to lecturing someone about what they should and should not do. A discussion about the ethical nature of behaviour is important because it is fundamental to how someone experiences the world and themselves, something that is of utmost importance to therapy. As a therapist I find that I regularly discuss issues of an ethical nature with my clients.

For some the term ethics is loaded with connotations of social rules imposed by those in authority. For me using the word ethics is the best way I know to describe actions that refrain from intentionally harming self or others. Universal ethical principles are adopted in societies as social laws and mores. Compassion and kindness are often considered universal ethics. The ethical component of the eight-fold path is considered as a personal training that leads to health, happiness and wellbeing. In Pali the word for ethical training is *sila*. *Sila* is often translated as morality or virtue. We undertake this training when we wish to protect the happiness of ourselves and those around us.

Before traditional Buddhist meditation retreats, participants are often asked to strengthen their resolve in this training by voicing their commitment to five principles or precepts. These principles are strong intentions to avoid harm rather than prescriptive rules.

The precepts are often voiced as follows:

1. I undertake the training to refrain from killing living things.
2. I undertake the training to refrain from taking what is not freely offered.
3. I undertake the training to refrain from false speech.
4. I undertake the training to refrain from harmful sexual conduct.
5. I undertake the training to refrain from intoxicants that cloud the mind.

Thich Nhat Hanh, the highly respected Vietnamese born Buddhist monk, skilfully articulates these trainings in a more proactive way as follows:

1. Aware of the suffering caused by the destruction of life, I vow to cultivate compassion and learn ways to protect the lives of people, animals and plants (Hanh, 2008, p. 1).
2. Aware of the suffering caused by exploitation, social injustice, stealing and oppression, I vow to cultivate loving kindness and learn ways to work for the well being of animals and plants. I vow to practise generosity by sharing my time, energy and material resources with those in real need (Hanh, 2008, p. 1).

3. Aware of the suffering caused by sexual misconduct, I vow to cultivate responsibility and learn ways to protect the safety and integrity of individuals (of all ages), couples, families and society (Hanh, 2008, p. 2).
4. Aware of the suffering caused by mindless speech and the inability to listen to others, I vow to cultivate loving speech and deep listening in order to bring joy and happiness to others and relieve their suffering (Hanh, 2008, p. 2).
5. Aware of the suffering caused by unmindful consumption I vow to cultivate good health, both physical and mental, for myself, my family and my society by practicing mindful eating drinking and consuming (Hanh, 2008, p. 3).

When we act skilfully with ethically responsible behaviours, we are able to be present and bring focused attention to our lives. When we intentionally harm ourselves or others it is likely that our minds will be plagued with hatred, guilt or fear.

Skilful speech

There is a common saying that goes: 'Put your mind into gear before you engage your mouth'. This saying exemplifies the commonsense nature of skilful speech.

Skilful speech is closely linked with mindfulness because it involves remembering the purpose of our actions so that we do not cause harm. Spontaneous speech can still be mindful and spoken carefully in a manner that is appropriate to the time and place. Skilful speech inclines towards telling the truth in a benevolent, meaningful and useful manner. The nature of skilful speech, however, is contextual. It may, for example, involve refraining from telling all of the truth to someone if it is not helpful, or telling a mistruth if this reduces suffering. If saying something is not beneficial then keeping silent is also considered to be skilful speech.

Sometimes people speak to each other in harmful ways. Harmful speech can cause suffering to others and regret for ourselves. Harmful speech includes telling lies, backbiting, slander and talk that may lead to hatred and disharmony among individuals or groups of people. Harmful speech can include malicious, callous, cruel and abusive language. Harmful speech can also include mindless speech such as idle, useless and thoughtless gossip. If we lie, deceive and use abusive speech, much of our mental energy may be spent worrying about being exposed or devising ways to defend ourselves against counter attacks.

Speaking and listening are two actions that can either increase our suffering or heal it.

Mindful listening is the reciprocal activity of skilful speaking. It involves putting aside opinionated filters or biases and truly listening to another person. Mindful listening requires hearing the content and meaning of what someone is saying as well as tuning in to their emotions and energetic presence. Truly listening can resolve both inner and outer conflict. Mindful listening involves listening with attention, kindness, compassion and understanding.

I once saw a photo of a poster in a subway. The poster was giving advice to people who use social media such as Facebook and Twitter. It had the acronym THINK which asked the reader to consider the following before they sent anything by social media. I 'think' it is a good way to remember skilful speech.

T = is it True?
H = is it Helpful?
I = is it Inspiring?
N = is it Necessary?
K = is it Kind?

Skilful action

The next factor on the path is skilful action. Skilful actions are consistent with wholesome and wise directions. The five principles of living outlined above are the traditional Buddhist recommendations for skilful actions. We are all different and may have different values but for all of us our actions have consequences. Blatantly unethical acts such as unnecessary killing, stealing or sexual behaviour that hurts someone rarely leaves our heart or minds free of disturbance. The unwise use of alcohol and non-prescription drugs can cloud our awareness and lead to a range of harmful and regretful behaviours. The basic message is that actions have consequences. If we allow harmful intentions to determine our actions it is harder to have the type of mental composure necessary for cultivating mindfulness, focus and wisdom. Acting skilfully, with ethically responsible behaviours, helps us develop the peace of mind necessary for developing focused attention and mindfulness.

Suitable livelihood

Suitable livelihood is closely linked to skilful actions. Making a living, having an occupation and supporting oneself and one's family are a necessary part of life. Much can be written about this topic. In summary, however, suitable livelihood refers to occupations that are ethical and do not involve harming oneself or others.

Cultivating the mind – meditation

The next factors on the path are related to meditation or the cultivation of the mind. As mentioned in the last chapter, meditation can be considered as a form of emotional and mental training that ultimately leads to wisdom. When our mind is relatively free from regret, guilt, fear and other unhelpful mental disturbances, it is more able to settle and be attentive to the present.

Balanced or appropriate effort

Balanced or appropriate effort is the first factor on the section of the path related to cultivating the mind. Balanced effort involves the energy or 'zeal' to let go of what is unhealthy or unhelpful, and cultivate healthy states of mind. Balanced effort is the result of resolve and commitment. Basically, this type of effort has four aims:

1. Preventing unhealthy states from arising.
2. Letting go of harmful states once they have arisen.
3. Developing healthy states of mind.
4. Maintaining healthy states of mind once they have arisen.

Appropriate effort may involve avoiding situations likely to trigger unhealthy states of mind and seeking situations where healthy mind states are more likely to arise. More generally effort requires determination, commitment and willingness to persist with our chosen goals and valued directions.

In the context of meditation practice, appropriate effort may require a non-striving and detached attitude. This type of effort is usually related to relaxed, gentle and open acceptance rather than tense struggle or strain. Effort at a refined level may merely be the energy involved in remembering to be attentive to immediate experience without condemning or grasping. It is beneficial to remember what has worked in the past to enhance mindfulness and concentration, and to apply these strategies. Balanced effort, mindfulness and concentration are inseparable and work together in many different ways.

Mindfulness

Mindfulness helps us remember our true aspirations and prevents us being caught up in reactive habits. Mindfulness is contextual and does not arise independently. That is, mindfulness arises dependent on other conditions such as wise choices and skilful conduct or ethics.

Mindfulness in combination with concentration helps to provide the mental space within which we can see clearly what is happening and navigate our way according to our desired direction or purpose. By bringing attention to our actions and their effects we begin to understand which actions serve our valued directions and which ones don't. The wisdom developed in meditation helps guide our choices and the commitments we make moment-to-moment, day-to-day, month-to-month or year-to-year. Mindfulness will be explained further in following chapters.

Right concentration.

Mindfulness involves balancing effort with a sense of purpose. Concentration provides focus. Just the act of remembering to bring attention to something helps to make attention focused, sustained and penetrating. In Buddhism right concentration refers to highly refined states of concentration. *Jhana* is the Pali term used to refer to these concentrated states. Regardless of whether or not one has achieved a *jhana*, with sustained and applied attention it is possible to see deeply into the nature of our *dukkha*. This focused attention leads to deeper insight, an understanding of what is happening and the development of wisdom. This understanding in turn leads to further skilful intentions, speech, action and so forth.

In summary

The foundation of the Buddha's eight-fold path is ethics, or a wholesome lifestyle. The eight-fold path is characterised by an ethical direction, determined by the cultivation of the wholesome and helpful and letting go of the unwholesome and unhelpful. Here ethics are not rules imposed by society, but guidelines for living. When we enquire for ourselves about what actions of body, mind and speech lead to misery, anguish, stress and despair, and what actions lead to happiness, peace and wellbeing we are able to determine for ourselves whether or not our choices are in accordance with our valued life directions.

Sampajanya – clear comprehension and introspection

Sati is the Pali term for mindfulness and *sampajanya* is the Pali term for clear understanding or clear comprehension. In Thailand these two words are often used together (*sati-sampajunya*) because these two mental factors cannot be separated. They are so linked that it would be remiss of me not to explain this further before I continue in describing mindfulness and meditation.

Mindfulness (*sati*) is the activity of watching over experience and keeping experience in mind over time. Clear understanding (*sampajanya*), on the other hand is the intelligence associated with this activity, monitoring experience through reflective assessment. Together mindfulness and clear understanding create an intelligent presence of mind. When we have clear understanding of an action we know whether that action is appropriate and timely in a given situation. Clear understanding enables us to choose the right actions, track actions as they change over time and remain clear about what is happening without falling into forgetfulness or the delusion of our habits.

When the action we choose to participate in is meditation, *sampajanya* is often referred to as introspection. Introspection will be clarified in the next chapter, which focuses on meditation.

Contemplating body: the first application of mindfulness

The Buddha taught how to practise mindfulness in a detailed and progressive manner. The *Satipatthana Sutta* outlines how to practise the four applications of mindfulness, beginning with the most basic and tangible and progressing to the more subtle and refined. Within each application of mindfulness the Buddha described sub-domains. Applications are also referred to as contemplations. Contemplation is a translation of the word *upassati* (Pali), which means to: '*to repeatedly look at*' or '*to closely observe*' or '*see along with*' or '*track*'.

The first application of mindfulness is contemplating body, which contains six sub-domains.

1. Mindfulness of breathing.
2. Mindfulness of physical postures.
3. Clear comprehension of actions.
4. Contemplating the separate parts of the body.
5. Contemplating the natural qualities or elements of body.
6. Contemplating the impermanent nature of the body.

Most people learn mindfulness in a progressive manner. Mindful contemplation of tangible experience is a good place to start. This can include being aware of our breath as we breathe in and out, or our posture, whether we are standing, sitting, walking, lying down, or moving in some way. Being aware of the sensations we feel on the inside and outside of our bodies is another useful way to apply mindfulness of body.

The capacity to remain grounded in the body can provide a refuge when we are battling with difficult thoughts and emotions. When we pay attention to sensations in the body it is possible to experience a sense of quietude in contrast to being caught up in our noisy mind. Mindful awareness of bodily sensations can bring about psychological insight without rational analysis as body sensations can often be associated with emotional and mental states.

Mindfulness of breathing and body scan are common mindfulness of body practices in contemporary psychology. Body scan is a meditation practice that will be explained later in this chapter. In this practice we pay attention to elemental qualities of sensations, the qualities of temperature (fire), hardness and softness (earth), movement (air) and the quality of fluidity (water).

We need to be sensitive to the context within which mindfulness interventions are used, and the need to tailor interventions to individual needs. All too often there is a 'one size fits all' approach to various mindfulness practices. Unfortunately this may not always be best. For individuals prone to panic, for example, mindfulness of breath can sometimes lead to self-focused attention and precipitate an anxious reaction. Similarly, for those with a history of physical trauma or sexual abuse, body scan can sometimes trigger unwanted reactions. Shifting attention to external phenomena (such as sound), mindfulness of postures (e.g. walking), or mindfulness of ordinary actions can be helpful in these circumstances.

Sometimes we are too restless to sit still, and mindfulness of movement may be more suitable. Mindfulness of daily activities or clear comprehension of daily activities may be helpful for disorders related to impulse control, such as eating disorders or deliberate self-harm. By purposely bringing discerning, kind and honest attention to one's activities, insight about cause/effect relationships is developed and there is an increased likelihood of making choices that are in line with one's values and understanding.

Traditionally the Buddha taught the practice of mindfulness of body to individuals according to their needs. He included practices that encouraged awareness of the body as changing and impermanent.

These practices included contemplation of all the parts of the body (including organs, hair, toenails, etc.) and contemplation of the death of the body. In the time of the Buddha it was not unusual to see dead bodies awaiting burial or cremation. Contemplating body parts or a body without life can impact dramatically on our understanding of what is means to be alive and the preciousness and fragility of our life. These practices help develop an understanding of how we identify with the body and extend our concept of the body beyond the superficial. As far as I am aware these practices are not taught in contemporary psychology and they are certainly not suitable for everyone. Nonetheless, when we contemplate and reflect on the body's impermanence as well its separate parts we can develop wisdom and understanding. This understanding helps us to have more peace with the realities of our body's ageing, sickness and eventual death.

Noting: a tool to develop mindfulness

There are many specific strategies and techniques used in mindfulness training. One strategy used to develop mindfulness is mentally noting, with a name or a label, what we are attentive to. Noting silently to ourselves helps us focus and clarify what is happening.

Noting can be used in our daily activities or busy work life as well as in formal mindfulness meditation practices. We may, for example, use the note 'brushing' when we are brushing our teeth, or 'reaching' when reaching for a door handle. If we are being mindful of the breath we can note 'rising, falling' in synchrony with these movements of the abdomen. Thoughts of the past can be labelled 'remembering', and thoughts of the future, 'planning'. Emotional tendencies can be identified and labelled appropriately such as 'anger', 'worry', 'fear', 'sadness', 'joy', 'peace', 'excitement', etc. Noting can help us cope with painful experiences. Putting a name to a distressing experience can often diminish its destructive power. Noting can therefore help to give us mental and emotional space from destructive habitual patterns. This space provides an opportunity for us to choose alternatives. We must remember, however, that noting is just a tool of mindfulness and we should not become too obsessive about finding names for everything. Noting is useful as we begin our training and it can also be helpful when we are seasoned practitioners and need reminding about what we are doing. As the practice gets deeper, however, noting can become an obstacle and if it is no longer helpful it should be dropped. In addition, if we have a tendency to be obsessive, noting may not be useful to begin with.

When noting, it is important to understand the difference between simple descriptions and negative and unhelpful judgements. The approach used in mindful noting involves simple descriptions as opposed to analytic and opinionated evaluations. For example if you find yourself noting the presence of anger with an angry tone of voice, then noting may not be helpful. Noting is particularly useful for maintaining a continuity of mindfulness during day-to-day activities.

Mindfulness of daily activities

It is possible to be mindful of whatever we do throughout the day. Mindfulness in activities generally means being attentive to what is being done while it is being done and doing it in the best way possible. When we are being mindful, we are likely to do things more skilfully and effectively, and in a manner that is not harmful to anyone. This means we are more aware of the purpose of our actions so that they are in harmony with our goals. In addition, you are more likely to get into flow and fully engage with what you are doing. Actions that may have seemed boring might become really interesting and enjoyable.

Mindfulness in daily life can be naturally relaxed and begin from the first moments of awareness as you wake up in the morning. Greet the new day with a fresh beginner's mind.

When you wake up, wake up to your senses: look, listen and remember to be present, instead of getting caught up in habitual autopilot with regrets about the past and worries about the future. Tune in to what is happening in the present moment and be openly curious about it. As you go about your daily activities you can remember to PAUSE, RELAX and BE AWARE, even it is for just a few moments.

Throughout the day, you can purposefully choose to be present and engaged with life and the world around you in everyday activities such as: washing up, cleaning the house, talking on the phone, etc. When you do these things try to bring all your attention to what you are doing. When you notice that your mind has gone off task, simply bring it back. If you choose to do activities that are enjoyable or interesting, you may notice that it is easy to focus and be mindful because the mind naturally wants to stay anchored on interesting or enjoyable things.

Body scan

Body scan is a practice in which we direct our attention to physical sensations in a progressive and systematic manner. It involves scanning or sweeping attention throughout the body thus becoming more sensitive to how the body is experienced at an elemental level. Body scan is usually relaxing because there seems to be an untangling and a 'letting go' of muscular tension, like that experienced in progressive muscle relaxation. In body scan, however, you do not tense your muscles up first, you are simply attentive to the experience. As a word of caution some people occasionally find body scan disturbing and unsettling at first and not relaxing at all. People who are prone to panic sometimes find focusing on physical sensations triggers panic attacks. Those people who have suffered some form of physical violation, such as sexual abuse, can also be sensitive to body scan. If you find body scan makes you feel uncomfortable rather than relaxed it may be better to put this practice aside for a while and do something else such as mindfulness of sound or mindful movement. Slowly, gradually and in a very sensitive manner, returning to body scan will eventually de-condition these reactions. If difficulty is experienced, discussion with an experienced practitioner or therapist is advised. As with most of the guided meditations described in this book a recording of body scan is provided in the websites provided in the Preface and Chapter 1. Written instructions for body scan are below. The exercise basically involves becoming aware of the physical sensations throughout your body in a systematic way.

Perhaps you could have a go at this practice right now?

Body scan

- Allow yourself to be as comfortable as you can either lying face up or sitting on a chair or cushion.
- Make the intention that, for the next 20 or so minutes, you will try not to fidget or move unnecessarily or be too concerned about anything other than being here now and bringing attention to the sensations in your body.
- When thoughts, emotions, sounds or other things pull your attention away from physical sensations do not struggle. Let these experiences arise and pass away but have them on the edge of your awareness.
- Let physical sensations be the central focus.
- At first bring attention to your body as a whole and with the out breath, let go of tension in your legs, body, arms and head.
- Then bring curious, focused and open-minded awareness to the top of your head.
- Notice sensations as they are, without thinking that they should be other than the way they are.
- Then begin to scan with your awareness so that it progressively and systematically covers the whole of your body from the top of your head to the tips of your toes.
- Feel and be aware of whatever sensations there are without feeling that you need to change them.
- Slowly shift attention to your forehead. Be aware of sensations in your forehead.
- Try to be open to experience without condemnation or unwarranted negative judgement.
- Then bring awareness to your face, your eyes, your nose, your cheeks, your mouth, your jaw and your whole face. Feel the experience.
- As you bring mindfulness to the various parts of your body it is as if, without trying, whatever tightness may have been there melts and falls away.
- Bring awareness to the physical sensations at the back of your head and the top of your neck. Your neck, your throat, the top of your chest and the top of your shoulders.
- Move attention around every corner and aspect of your shoulders letting your awareness touch on every sensation.

- Bring awareness to your arms, the inside of your arms, the outside of your arms, your biceps, moving down your arms to your elbows, your forearms, your wrists and your hands.
- Know and be aware of physical sensations with a curious and open mind.
- Bring awareness to the top of your chest, upper back, your whole chest. Move and scan with your awareness through your body, being open and accepting of experiences as they are.
- If there is any pain or discomfort, try to be gentle, kind and compassionate.
- It is as if when you bring compassionate awareness to distress it is healed.
- Be mindful of your belly, back and hips.
- Slowly and bit by bit scan with awareness to the sensations from the top of your thighs down to your knees.
- Shift awareness down to your shins, your calves, your heels, your ankles, toes, top part of the feet, and base of the feet.
- Then bring attention to the whole of your body.
- Bring attention to the quality of aliveness in your whole body. This aliveness may feel like vibrations.
- If you are feeling relaxed and it feels good sit or lie back and enjoy these feelings, without clinging to them. When your mind wanders off somewhere simply remember to bring it back to the pleasant feelings. Continue to do this for a few minutes.
- As you end the exercise slowly move your fingers and toes, then your hands and feet, become aware of the room that you are in, open your eyes, give yourself a stretch, and go about your daily activities with the understanding that you can be aware of your bodily sensations as you need and it can help you to feel peaceful and relaxed.

Remembering the day's events

As explained in the last chapter, an aspect of mindfulness is remembering or recollecting. When you can remember the day's events wisely without being entangled in negative judgements, you can start to see how one thing affects another. In this way you can begin to understand any negative patterns and reactions you have as well as what has worked to bring focus, happiness and joy. Spending a few minutes at the end of the day to recollect the day's events and actions can help to develop understanding. In particular, it is very helpful to remember the positive things that happened and how they came about. This type of recollection also provides a boost to mindfulness the next day because we begin to pay attention in a way that helps us to remember what happened and how it unfolded. If you feel it would be helpful for you, you could use the daily experiences diary to make a record of some of the things that happened throughout the day. To begin with, see if you can remember pleasant events. Later, as you progress and are less likely to get caught up in thinking negatively about events, you can remember difficult situations and how you coped with them. Bring curiosity to the events, so that you can remember what happened, what thoughts you had, what emotions occurred or what mood you were in, how it felt in your body, how you responded and so on.

I have included another written exercise in the appendices as Appendix A. This exercise involves reflecting on the outcomes of actions and considering ways to increase the helpful and decrease the unhelpful. People who have attended my programmes have found this useful and you may too.

Note

1 This analogy is adapted from one used in the Buddha's discourses which can also be found in Bodhi (2000).

References

Bodhi, B. (2000). *The Noble Eightfold Way: Way to the End of Suffering.* Onalaska, WA: BPS Pariyatti Editions.

Csikszentmihalyi, M. (1988). The flow of experience and human psychology. In M. Csikszentmihalyi and I. S. Csikszentmihalyi (eds.), *Optimal Experience: Psychological Studies of Flow in Consciousness.* Cambridge: Cambridge University Press.

Hanh, T. N. (2008). *For a Future to be Possible.* Berkeley, CA: Parallax Press.

Huxter, M. J. (2007). Mindfulness as therapy from a Buddhist perspective. In D. A. Einstein (ed.), *Innovations and Advances in Cognitive Behaviour Therapy.* Bowen Hills, Qld: Australian Academic Press.

3 Meditation
Cultivating the heart-mind

Chapter overview

The aim of this chapter is to clarify the meditation component of the pathway of happiness and freedom. It introduces meditation as it is understood in the Theravada school of Buddhism (Theravada literally means the way of the elders) and provides an overview of the *Satipatthana Sutta* mentioned in the previous chapter. It explains the basics of the second, third and fourth applications of mindfulness. The distinguishing features of insight and serenity meditations are explained and a related story illustrates this. The chapter concludes with meditation instructions, reference to five psychological obstacles to meditation and some cautions about mindfulness of breath.

To begin with, however, I would like to invite you to practise a few minutes of meditation. So, please read the instructions below then put this book down and practise as instructed. If you are already familiar with this meditation, please practise settling your mind in whatever way works for you.

Grounding in earth element-meditation

Please find a quiet and peaceful space, loosen up any tight clothing and establish a comfortable posture. You may like to sit on a chair or cushion or lie down if you prefer. Ensure that you will not get too hot or too cold.

Make the intention to develop mindfulness and focused attention for the next 5–10 minutes by being grounded in physical sensations. As best you can, try not to fidget or move unnecessarily and incline towards stillness.

Firstly, let your attention sink into your body and put aside thoughts about things in the past or the future. Remember to be here now and find quietude in physical sensation. Put aside craving after things not here, and let yourself become present by anchoring attention in the immediate experience of your body's contact with the ground. Feel the contact of the chair holding you, or if you are lying on the floor, the ground supporting you. Let your attention become centred on the tangible experience of hardness and softness, the tangible experience of solidness. Let your attention be stilled by the simple stability of earth element.

Even though you may notice movement in your mind in the form of thoughts, let both the movement of the mind and movement in your body be on the edge of your awareness and allow the stability of the contact with the floor, chair or cushion, be your central focus.

Sink your attention into solidity and allow whatever tension you may feel, fall away. Simply release tension both in the mind and the body. Find peace in the simplicity of the earth element as it is represented by hardness and softness and tangible solidity . . .

When you notice that your attention is swept away by the movements of the mind, such as thinking, do not struggle. Do not be concerned about the various movements of the mind, but simply remember your intention and remember to return your attention to the quietude of stillness by being aware of and attentive to contact with hardness and softness as your body contacts the chair, cushion or ground beneath you. Continue to practise for a few more minutes remembering to return to the stillness and solidity whenever you have forgotten.

Thank you for your attention.

Buddhist meditation

Buddhist mediation is not limited to the stereotyped image of a yogi seated in the lotus position. There are over 40 different forms of formal meditation practices described in classic Theravada Buddhist texts. The Buddha did not teach a fixed and rigid approach to meditation. Rather, he taught a dynamic and flexible approach to individuals or groups dependent upon their personality, temperament, life circumstances and the situation. Meditation instructions for the different practices were collected from the discourses of the Buddha. The Buddha taught that as long as it was not causing harm it was possible to meditate in all postures and in a variety of different activities. Meditation connects with one's lifestyle, attitudes and day-to-day decisions and is an integral part of the eight-fold path.

Meditation involves a skilful balance and interplay of effort (energy), mindfulness and concentrated attention. As mentioned earlier, effort in meditation is not the same as strain or struggle. Right effort is the balance between having too much or too little energy, such as being either too enthusiastic or too slack. Just as a guitar string can be tuned too tight or too loose, the effort for meditation is a level of energy that is not too much or too little. With right effort we know when there is too much energy or enthusiasm, too much pushing and force, and we can balance this with letting go or just letting be. Sometimes meditation requires courageous effort as we face up to things we would rather avoid.

In Theravada Buddhism Pali terms that are often used for meditation are: *bhavana*, and *citta bhavana. Bhavana* means 'bringing into being', 'causing to be', 'developing' or 'cultivating'. *Citta* (pronounced as chitta) is the Pali term for mind. In Western culture the mind is often thought of as the part of us that thinks and uses reason. *Citta*, however, is more than this. *Citta* more accurately translates as heart-mind, which implies both reason and intuition. *Citta* is also considered as the aware part of a person or the subjective knower of experience. The heart-mind not only thinks, but also feels and experiences. Moreover, according to His Holiness the Dalai Lama, the heart-mind has the qualities of knowing, luminosity and clarity (Dalai Lama, 2009). *Citta bhavana* therefore translates as cultivating the heart-mind. The qualities that are cultivated are wholesome, healthy and beneficial. Meditation or *bhavana* involves the repeated practice, training and development of energy, mindfulness and concentration so that the *citta* develops serenity and insight. *Samadhi* and *vipassana* are two other terms used for meditation in Theravada Buddhism. These terms represent, respectively, the qualities of serenity and insight, which are the two sides of Buddhist meditation. Please note that from here on in this book, the terms heart-mind, mind and *citta* will be used interchangeably.

The cultivation of serenity

The Pali terms *samatha* and *samadhi* are created from the combination of *sam* which means 'with', *a*, which means 'towards' and *dha* which means 'to put or place' (Kearney, 2006). These terms refer to unifying the heart-mind so attention rests in a single place. *Samadhi* is a term that is often used for meditation but its literal meaning is concentration.

Serenity meditation (*samatha* – Pali, *shamatha* – Sanskrit) is based on cultivating *samadhi*. In Tibetan Buddhism the term *shamatha* also refers to a highly refined and transformative state of concentration. *Shamatha* is an entry state to the even more refined states of concentration called *jhanas*. Both the terms *samatha* and *samadhi* refer to a collected, calm, centred, unified, quiet, still and stabilised state of heart-mind. The terms serenity, calm, tranquillity and quiescence are English words all used to describe this aspect of meditation.

You can bring attention to almost anything in order to develop a concentrated, unified heart-mind. It is important, however, that on a path of happiness we don't concentrate in a way that will be harmful. Neutral objects of attention are usually most helpful because there is less craving or aversion and rejection. The breath is an example of a neutral object and bringing attention to the breath is possibly one of the most common serenity meditation practices. Other commonly used serenity meditation objects include: mantras, creative visualisations, muscle relaxation, loving kindness, reflecting on peace and so on. Things that are emotionally uplifting or interesting or peaceful are also helpful to use as meditation objects, because they grab our attention and can soothe.

Serenity meditations calm and quell emotional and physical disturbance. They help us to feel at ease, relaxed, happy, peaceful and serene. Sometimes the focus of serenity meditation is considered to be like a funnel or tunnel that narrows our attention. Other times the attention is broad and wide and just like when a shaken snow dome is stilled and the snowflakes settle, serenity meditation can be experienced as a stilling, stabilising, centring and settling of the heart-mind. In this way serenity meditation serves to collect attention and create a sense of composure and integration. Of course other objects may come to mind. However, as interest in the object of attention grows, concerns, worries, hankerings or desires about other things lose significance and attention becomes absorbed into the object of interest. When attention is focused and absorbed in our chosen meditation object some of the normal activities of the mind fall away, and perhaps even stop. This can be experienced as beautiful silence.

Contemporary psychology has utilised the principles evident in the cultivation of *samadhi* in many different ways. One of the most common uses has been as a way to cultivate the relaxation response (e.g. Benson, 1975). The relaxation response is a natural bodily response that is the opposite to tension and the types of arousal we experience when we are confronted with danger or other demands. The relaxation response involves the parasympathetic nervous system. One of the functions of this response is to restore body–mind balance when a demand, crisis or emergency passes. With a relaxation response, muscular tension decreases, breathing becomes slower and rhythmical, heart rate reduces, and many bodily functions rest and rejuvenate. The healing and therapeutic effect of the relaxation response is well known and has been utilised in contemporary psychology for decades.

Several prominent twentieth-century psychologists have used concentration, and the altered states of consciousness they lead to, in therapeutic ways. Milton Erickson (1979, p. 1) pioneered hypno therapy: 'as a process whereby we help people utilize their own mental associations, memories, and life potentials to achieve their own therapeutic goals'. Erickson had many creative techniques for inducing therapeutic trance and the fixation of attention (concentration) was one. Having the client gaze at a swinging pocket watch, a spot, a bright light, a candle flame, a revolving mirror, or the therapist's eyes have been classic objects of attention fixation with hypnosis. Erickson understood the unconscious as an organised system of psychological processes, which work to maintain emotional wellbeing. He also viewed the unconscious as a process that helped by providing psychological protection. Therapeutic trance allows individuals to access unconscious, intuitive and healing aspects of themselves.

Another prominent contemporary psychologist who described and advocated using focused attention is Csikszentmihalyi (1988). Csikszentmihalyi researched and wrote extensively about the experience of 'flow', which bears many similarities to states of concentration or *samadhi*. When Csikszentmihalyi studied flow, he noticed that artists, musicians, sports people, athletes and surgeons often develop flow. He also noticed that flow would often occur when people were engaged in enjoyable leisure activities. Something as simple as going surfing, watching a sunset, listening to music, or going to an inspiring movie can help to focus and uplift one's mind. People often get into flow when they do something that requires a lot of concentration and or they do something that is so enjoyable that their attention becomes completely absorbed into what they are doing.

When people are in flow they are so engaged in what they are doing that there is simply no mental space left for worries and concerns. They are absorbed in what they are doing and everything else falls away. It feels pleasant to be in flow and whatever is done is done well. In flow, our sense of time can drop away. Being in flow, or 'in the zone' is an optimal way of being. Not only does it feel uplifting, we also do things in the best possible way. These optimal ways of being are very helpful on the path of happiness.

The traditional Buddhist approach to serenity meditation begins with one's intention. When it is our intention to put aside worries and concerns and focus attention, then it is easier for our actions to follow. We make the time to practise and ensure that, as much as possible, we will not be disturbed. We find a quiet space and adopt a comfortable posture.

Relaxation is an important starting point for practising serenity meditation. In contemporary psychology four factors described as important for the relaxation response are:

1. A passive attitude that is not attached to goals.
2. An object to focus on.
3. A quiet space.
4. A comfortable posture (Benson, 1975).

Serenity meditation follows a sequence of relaxation, stability and vividness (Wallace, 2006).

Relaxation involves releasing both muscular tension and distracting thoughts. In serenity meditation we don't investigate thoughts and emotions but just let them go. There is a conscious release of struggling and striving to achieve something. Our intention is to let go, settle, and rest in peacefulness. At this stage we may make a conscious choice to not engage in thinking and rather turn attention towards mental quietude. Although finding a quiet place in our internal babble is easier said than done, with a firm intention and practice, it is possible.

Stabilising attention requires centring and maintaining our focus on the object of meditation. This may be very difficult at first because the mind might be scattered and wild. With patience, persistence and practice, attention becomes more stabilised.

Vividness of perception involves sharpening our perception so that whatever is perceived becomes richer and increasingly more lucid. With enhanced focus details that were not noticed previously, because of a distracted mind, become vividly clear.

In summary, the basic instructions for serenity meditations are:

1. Make a determination to practice.
2. Choose an object of attention.
3. Relax tension.
4. Stabilise attention on the object.

5. Use whatever helps attention stay focused (for example being aware of the pleasantness that may arise in the body and mind as a result of focusing).
6. Let go of whatever blocks the flow to allow absorption into the object.
7. Become sensitive to the subtle details of what is being attended to.
8. Let go of grasping or holding on to ideas, expectations or experience and allow transformation to occur.
9. Let go of ego resistance and simply become completely absorbed.

Please note that as one develops meditative concentration on the chosen object of attention, such as the breath or a constructed visualisation, the object may disappear and be replaced by a vision or other mental event. It is as if rather than choosing an object to pay attention to, it chooses us. These mental events are created from one's own mind and are unique for the individual. They may often be visual in nature but not necessarily limited to this mode of perception. If these events begin to occur for you on a regular basis it is best to discuss this with an experienced meditation practitioner who can explain how to work with them.

Serenity meditation can lead to wellbeing and happiness. The calm and joy that arise from unified attention naturally counter any feelings of anxiety and depression and the development of a concentrated mind is worthwhile in and of itself. However, on top of this, the cultivation of serenity also leads to wisdom. A famous Thai meditation master, Ajahn Chah, once compared a concentrated heart-mind to a still forest pool (Kornfeild and Breiter, 1985). When there is no disturbance and the pool is still and quiet, all sorts of beautiful animals that would normally be too shy come out to drink. When our heart-minds are still and quiet, we notice things about ourselves that we normally would not see. With a quiet, still and tranquil heart-mind, insight and understanding can arise and we can discover many beautiful things.

Introspection with serenity meditation

Sampajanya (clear comprehension) is an important factor in all meditation. As mentioned in the last chapter, *sampajanya* cannot be separated from mindfulness and it ensures that what we do is suitable and timely in accordance with our purpose and goals. When we meditate *sampajanya* is often referred to as introspection. Introspection is a form of meta-awareness and quality control. When meditating, mindfulness remembers to prevent attention straying from the object and *introspection* recognises that attention has strayed. Introspection helps us monitor the process of the continuity of mindfulness and the meditation process in general. Serenity meditation often requires balancing slackness (i.e. spacing out and losing clarity) and excitation. Excitation usually involves getting caught up in an object, either grasping after it or rejecting it with aversion. Introspection helps us to be aware when we have slipped into slackness or excitation so we can then adjust our attention. We can adjust our attention by arousing it when we are slack or spaced out and by stabilising it when we are caught up in excitement.

The cultivation of insight

The aim of insight meditation is, as the name implies, the cultivation of insight. Insight is the realisation of the four truths. When we realise the four truths we understand that certain types of actions lead to unhappiness and misery and other types of actions lead to wellbeing. We understand what leads to what and how things arise and pass away. As a component of wisdom, insight helps us to know how to lead a life free from *dukkha*. In Buddhist psychology insight is the knowing and seeing component of wisdom. It includes understanding three universal characteristics of existence, which according to Buddhism are:

1. *Annica* (Pali): Impermanence or change. All things change. All that arises must also pass away. Nothing lasts. Everything has a transitory or impermanent nature. As all things change they are also uncertain.
2. *Dukkha* (Pali): Unreliability, ambiguity or uncertainty. Here the term *dukkha* is used in a slightly different way than it is when referred to as the first truth. As a mark of existence it means that transient things are not able to bring ultimate satisfaction, that they cannot be the source of complete happiness. Transitory things are also uncertain and ambiguous because we can never be really sure of the outcome.
3. *Anatta* (Pali): Interdependence, no-thing-ness, no self-ness, insubstantiality, contingency or emptiness.

A *note on* anatta

Things change because of causes and conditions. Things do not arise and pass away independent of context or circumstances. This means that all situations, events, people and things are contingent on other things for their existence, and so, according to Buddhism there are no separate independent situations, 'selves' or events. In Buddhist terminology 'emptiness' and 'not self' mean that all things, including what we refer to as self, are empty of separate existence. Emptiness can also mean that things are empty of our assumptions, unhelpful opinions, complicated stories and problems. Being empty of assumptions means that things are just the way they are. In Buddhism, 'such-ness' is another term representing emptiness meaning that things are just as they are (Batchelor, 1997).

In contemporary psychology emptiness refers to a feeling of being like an empty shell, or a nothing, devoid of any positive feelings. In Buddhism, however, emptiness refers to the interdependent nature of existence not a feeling. That is, all things are empty of an independent existence and are interdependent or dependent on other things for their existence. When we realise the nature of emptiness (in the Buddhist sense) rather than being a hopeless nothing we are free to be dynamic, creative and unique because we are not bound by limiting concepts about the world or ourselves. Realising emptiness, realising interdependence and realising such-ness are all the same. This realisation brings with it a sense of being fully alive, vital and present for life as it unfolds.

Satipatthana vipassana

The Pali term that translates as insight is *vipassana*. When we break down the meaning of this term, *vi* denotes separate, intense or distinct, and *passana* means seeing. Therefore *vipassana* literally means seeing separately and seeing distinctly (Kearney, 2006). That is, we see our experience of life as it is rather than seeing through our veils of delusion.

Satipatthana is a compound word derived from *sati* and *patthana* or *sati* and *upatthana*. *Sati*, as mentioned earlier, literally means memory and is the Pali term for mindfulness. *Patthana* means keeping present and it can also mean foundation or source. The *patthanna* of *satipatthana* refers to remembering where attention is directed. *Upatthana* refers to 'establishing near or setting up near' with the idea that an object is kept closely in mind. *Satipatthana* is therefore a compound word that collectively refers to the foundations and applications of mindfulness and refers to remembering to deliberately place close attention or turn the mind to what is happening (Kearney, 2006).

In Pali the term used for mindfulness meditation is *satipatthanna vipassana*. When we closely observe and track changing conditions of body and heart-mind we begin to understand ourselves and the three characteristics of existence. In this way, mindfulness meditation leads to insight.

The four applications of mindfulness are at the heart of Buddhist meditation and they encompass the full spectrum of body-heart-mind experience. They also work in a way to help us break free from patterns of *dukkha*. The first application, mindfulness of body, was explained in the previous chapter. I will briefly outline the three other applications below, and further clarify them in later chapters.

Mindfulness of feelings

Feeling, in this context, does not refer to emotions as we normally understand them. Feeling refers to the quality of our physical or mental experience, whether it is pleasant, unpleasant or neither. Emotions, physical sensations and thoughts can all have a feeling quality of pleasant, unpleasant or neutral. Happiness may have a pleasant feeling, an injury to our body that causes sensations of pain may have an unpleasant feeling and thinking about what to cook for dinner may have a neutral feeling, that is, it may be neither pleasant nor unpleasant.

Another dimension of feelings described in the *Satipatthana Sutta* is noticing what triggers our feelings and what flows from them. For example the unpleasant feeling associated with pain may be exacerbated by thoughts of aversion or the emotion of anger, or the pleasant feeling associated with happiness may change to unpleasant if we react to our happiness with guilt. Being aware of feelings can short circuit unnecessary over-reactions to experiences that come our way. In this way we can have a peaceful mind despite having unpleasant feelings associated with painful physical sensations or emotions.

Feelings are more refined than body, and this domain of mindfulness is a progression from mindfulness of body.

Contemplating citta, *mindfulness of heart-mind*

Mindfulness of heart-mind includes remembering to be attentive to emotions and thought patterns. The heart-mind or consciousness becomes the object of mindfulness. This domain includes awareness of specific mind states both wholesome and unwholesome. It begins by becoming aware of whether the mind is coloured (to varying degrees of intensity) with one of the root causes of *dukkha*, which are: greed, hatred or delusion.

Being aware of intensely distressing emotions is included in this domain of mindfulness. So too is being aware of very subtle and refined states of heart-mind such as those associated with high levels of concentration or insights. This domain includes being aware of various thinking patterns, such as rumination and worry as these patterns can be experienced as states of heart-mind.

For the most part we identify with our heart-mind. Practising this domain helps to provide some space from this identification as well as rein in the tendency for unwholesome states of heart-mind to run rampant. Tracking changes in states of mind promotes understanding and a sense of freedom rather than identification with them. Noticing the changing nature of painful emotions, for example, helps to break reactive patterns often associated with these states.

Mindfulness of heart-mind is a progression from mindfulness of feelings.

Mindfulness of phenomena

This domain is also referred to as mindfulness of mind objects or the contents of the mind. This involves being aware of psychological patterns and emphasises maximising the skilful and minimising the unskilful.

Letting go of the unhelpful and cultivating the helpful are, of course, the essential features of many therapies. In the meditation of mindfulness of phenomena we pay attention to psychological patterns and develop an understanding of how to let go of patterns that block our progress and how to cultivate patterns that are helpful. I will explain more about mindfulness of phenomena in Chapter 6, a chapter about reactive cycles and how to exit them.

Even though formal periods of meditation enhance and refine our skills, the practice of mindfulness is not confined to these times and we can practise the four applications of mindfulness every moment of our waking life. The four applications of mindfulness can be likened to four gears on a motor vehicle. We need all gears to travel and change gears dependent on the nature of the road or the terrain we are travelling through, using the appropriate gear for the job.

Practising *satipatthana*

The instructions in the *Satipatthana Sutta* are directed towards cultivating insight and reducing clinging, aversion and delusion. Even though these instructions were originally taught 2,600 years ago to monks in ancient India they are as relevant today in contemporary culture as they were then. The four applications of mindfulness can be adapted to personal temperament, environmental and situation. They are relevant for a wide range of contemporary issues and disorders.

Practitioners usually begin with mindfulness of body practices and progress to more refined applications of mindfulness such as mindfulness of feeling, mind or phenomena. However, even when we are advancing along with our practices, mindfulness of body practices are often used as a grounding anchor to come back to when needed. Regardless of which application of mindfulness we choose to make central to our meditation practice, they all ultimately lead to freedom from the internal habits and patterns that are the root cause of our emotional suffering.

The Buddha spoke about three stages in the development of mindfulness: focusing, noticing change and maintaining unshaken attention (according to Thanissaro, 1996). To begin with, we apply purposeful and diligent energy to bring an object into focus. The object can be something internal (such as sensations, thoughts or emotions) or external (such as the people, places and things we come into contact with). Regardless of whether the object of our focus is internal or external, the focus of attention is on current experience. We track the experience with our awareness so we can see how it changes. Noticing change and the factors related to change, promotes understanding and wisdom. At the final level we are aware of the object with a sense of peacefulness. This level is also sometimes called bare attention because awareness is present with the object, uncluttered by stories about it. Awareness is simple and direct, moment-to-moment. In reference to this last stage of mindfulness the *sutta* describes awareness as free, independent and unsustained by clinging.

The instructions of the *Satipatthana Sutta* are repeated regularly for every application of mindfulness and its sub-domains. These instructions include directions to identify clearly what is happening, then notice the arising and passing of the experience. In *satipatthana* one is curious about WHAT is happening and HOW it is happening. Discovering the WHAT of our experience involves being aware that a particular experience is happening. Exploring the HOW of experience invites curious investigation about the experience. Though we may want to understand the WHY of experience, this line of enquiry is generally not followed with insight meditation practices because it can give rise to unwarranted assumptions that may be completely untrue. If, however, we explore the WHAT and HOW of experience, answers to the WHYs of experience may naturally emerge.

The essence of *satipatthana* is being aware of an experience then tracking how it changes so that we understand it. What is of most interest is how different experiences connect and condition each other, thereby cultivating within us an understanding of cause–effect relationships. The most important cause–effect relationships we may wish to understand are the four realities: *dukkha* and its causes and freedom and its causes. These cause–effect relationships can be generalised to the whole range of our experience and are relevant to whatever we may be struggling with. When we explore experience with mindfulness we begin to develop an understanding of what leads to what. With this understanding we are more able to make choices in our lives and thus move away from *dukkha*.

Insight meditation

In Buddhist traditions there are a number of different insight meditation practices and there are several styles that are popular in the West. In general, however, the terms *satipatthana vipassana*, mindfulness meditation and insight meditation are synonymous. With insight meditation we investigate the nature of the world around us and of ourselves. We begin by focusing on one object but our focus could change to something else.

In some schools of insight meditation, such as the Mahasi Sayadaw[1] approach, there are primary objects of attention and secondary objects of attention. Primary objects of attention are generally objects that are easy to bring attention to. Physical experiences (body) are often chosen as primary objects because they are tangible and easier to bring into awareness than less tangible experiences such as thoughts and emotions. Since physical and mental phenomena are constantly changing, it is normal that many objects will come into our awareness during insight meditation. If objects, other than the chosen primary one, become so strong that they draw our attention away, we then make those objects 'secondary' objects of our attention. We stay mindful of secondary objects until they no longer stand out, and then return our attention to the primary object. Primary objects become a resting place for our attention. For example, we may choose to be mindful of the experience of the breath as it rises and falls in our abdomen. If the sound of a jackhammer outside our meditation room pulls our attention away from the breath, then we would make 'hearing' the secondary object and pay attention to sound. When the sound seems no longer dominant, when it no longer grabs our attention, we then return to the primary object which is the breath. The rule of thumb in this particular approach is to pay attention to whatever is strongest in awareness. In insight meditation one stays present, being attentive to the flow of changing experience.

Insight meditation also aims to develop an understanding of the three characteristics of existence; change, unreliability and interdependence. At advanced levels of practice we can make the following enquiries:

1. Is this experience permanent or impermanent? Is there anything that does not change and pass away?
2. Is this experience a reliable and enduring source of genuine happiness? Can I be 100 per cent certain about anything?
3. Can I call this experience 'me', 'mine' or 'myself'? Can I find an experience within this body and mind that I can call an independent and a separate self? Does anything arise independent from anything else or are all things interdependent?

Insight into the three characteristics of existence can be developed by deep reflection and analysis. However, it is generally developed simply by noticing change.

Practising insight meditation could be analogous to walking on a path in a mysterious forest. We need to journey along the path with mindfulness and clear comprehension paying attention to present moment realities yet also keeping in mind our direction. We also need to track and remember significant markers on the way so we don't get lost. In this way we become familiar with the environment of our body-heart-minds and we cultivate wisdom.

Insight and serenity working together

The insight and serenity aspects of meditation support and strengthen each other and cannot be separated. Insight meditation requires

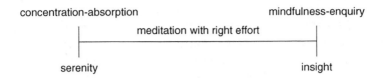

concentration-absorption   mindfulness-enquiry

meditation with right effort

serenity   insight

Figure 3.1 The meditation spectrum

concentration to ensure depth in awareness and serenity meditation requires mindfulness to monitor and sustain concentration.

The serenity and insight aspects of meditation can be considered as the two ends of a stick. When someone picks up one end of the stick the other end follows (Figure 3.1).

Serenity and insight are inseparable as opposite ends of the meditation spectrum. Some meditation practices are at the extreme end of serenity, some practices are at the extreme end of insight and some practices are in between. All meditation practices are either serenity meditation practices, insight meditation practices or a mixture of the two. Serenity and insight meditations often overlap, insight meditation also develops calm and serenity meditations can develop insight.

Serenity meditations are concentration-based and every effort is made to sustain single-minded attention on a chosen object. Objects other than the chosen meditation object are put aside. Suppression is a feature of many serenity meditation practices. Suppression is a conscious choice not to focus on something. It is different from repression which is more likened to an unconscious avoidance. The continuous quality of concentration in serenity meditation results from repeatedly bringing attention back to a chosen object and choosing not to focus on distractions. Attention is sustained and focused on one particular object.

In insight meditation attention can be directed to different objects. There is no such thing as distraction because whatever is happening, and is dominant in awareness, becomes the object of attention. We stay with the immediate body-heart-mind experience of now. Awareness is brought to the specific characteristics of the meditation object, such as a peaceful nature of a mind state or physical sensations of hardness or softness, and also to the general characteristics of change, impermanence, uncertainty and interdependence/emptiness. Insight meditation brings attention and enquiry to actual experience occurring in the present moment. It explores the connections between experience and the three characteristics of existence: impermanence, uncertainty and interdependence.

82   *Healing the Heart and Mind with Mindfulness*

The specific details of the meditation object are seen in serenity meditations only after we cultivate relaxation and stability of attention. With serenity practices there is a sense of collecting, bringing together, fusing with and absorbing into the object of attention. Insight meditation works in an opposite manner where objects of attention are seen separately, clearly and distinctly. With serenity practices, attention generally rests and stays with an object but with insight practices attention often penetrates or 'insights' an object with a sense of enquiry and questioning.

Sometimes meditation practitioners consciously develop serenity meditations first so that their minds are stilled. When they then investigate the nature of an object of attention it is seen clearly and distinctly with insight. Sometimes meditation practitioners find that they can't concentrate well and they cultivate moment-to-moment curious attention and this builds the power of more sustained concentration for serenity meditations. With experience, meditation practitioners may switch back and forth between serenity and insight aspects of meditation, sometimes within the one meditation session.

Insight practices help to uproot negative stressful patterns and serenity practices help to keep the negative patterns at bay providing peace and wellbeing. By directly looking at and investigating patterns of experience, insight influences and often alters the way we see things. Serenity can also give rise to understanding by altering the way we experience things. These altered states of consciousness can range from a subtle feeling of being more relaxed to significant strong feelings of pleasure and wellbeing.

Whether a meditator chooses to practise serenity meditation or insight meditation is very much dependent on their temperament, the availability of teachers, and their particular mental, emotional and behavioural tendencies. Individuals who like to investigate and understand phenomena (such as scientists) may naturally incline towards insight meditation. Individuals who like to 'go with the flow' and become absorbed in what they are doing (such as artists) may naturally incline towards serenity meditation.

Teachers tend to teach whatever they are skilled at. Those who are skilled with insight meditation will teach this pathway and those skilled at serenity mediation will teach the path of serenity. According to one scholar of Buddhism (Kearney, 2006), the Buddha recommended that if a meditator was skilled with insight she should seek out a teacher of serenity and if a meditator was skilled with serenity she should seek out a teacher of insight. Ultimately individuals learn the dynamic relationship between serenity and insight and they learn to skilfully develop both mindfulness and concentration.

Serenity and insight meditation working together can lead to freedom from *dukkha* and complete awakening. Used creatively they can lead to a reduction in severity or the resolution of many common conditions such as anxiety, depression and panic.

Related story: Joe manages panic with mindfulness and concentration

Joe had always been a nervous worrier. He began having panic attacks when he was 45. He could not pinpoint a reason for the panic attacks but knew that they started when he was physically run down and there were a number of stressful events in his life. When he had his first panic attack he thought that he was having a heart attack and death was imminent. After all the medical checks, however, the doctors said that his physical symptoms – increased heart rate, rapid breathing, chest pain, feeling dizzy, sweating, blurred vision and tingling feelings in his fingers – were the results of a panic attack.

Joe's panic attacks were so distressing that he avoided anything that reminded him of them. In the weeks and months that followed he avoided putting himself in any situations where they might occur. He stopped doing physical exercise because he didn't like the physical sensations related to breathing quickly and worried that this may trigger more panic attacks.

When Joe was first diagnosed as having a panic disorder he was told that he should learn slow breathing and progressive relaxation. He bought a progressive relaxation tape and tried it but, rather than relaxing, he became panicky because the voice on the tape asked him to focus on physical sensations. When he tried slow breathing it was sometimes helpful but he also found it difficult. Joe found that bringing attention to his breathing seemed to make him focus on his body again and this was often anxiety provoking. Though trying to slow his breathing down helped sometimes, Joe mostly managed his panic attacks by manipulating his environment so he could avoid panic triggers. This situation placed limits and restrictions around how Joe lived, worked and related in life. It was very difficult.

One day he read how avoidance can reinforce panic reactions and a way to manage panic was not to over-react and 'catastrophise' the symptoms. He also found some information and instruction on 'panic surfing' (Ballie and Rapee, 1998). In essence panic surfing involved using mindfulness to note the physical sensations of a panic attack, without turning attention away. Panic surfing also involved being realistic about the symptoms and reminding oneself with self-talk what was really happening. For example, rather than thinking that chest pain meant that death was imminent, Joe reminded himself that the chest pain was merely a symptom of a panic attack. Joe found that by using panic surfing his panic attacks became more manageable.

Joe also discovered walking meditation. Joe had always wanted to meditate but felt too restless to sit still and quiet for more than a few moments. Rather than sitting still, by doing walking meditation Joe could cultivate mindful focus by moving. To his delight, Joe also found that he could synchronise his breathing with his steps and this was a way that he could slow down his breathing without too much difficulty. Walking meditation became a way for Joe to calm down and sharpen mindfulness. Periods of walking meditation were a respite from nervous worry that used to cause Joe distress. Joe noticed that the calm that was cultivated during walking meditation periods flowed over to other times in the day and he became generally more peaceful. Joe also noticed that the calm concentration cultivated during the walking meditation made panic surfing easier and more effective.

Joe used both calm from concentration and insight from mindfulness to manage panic disorder. The panic attacks slowly reduced in intensity and frequency and eventually did not occur at all. Joe maintained the walking meditation practice and started to practise sitting meditation as well. A regular practice of both sitting and walking meditation as well as mindfulness with daily activities seemed to prevent further panic reactions.

Posture with meditation

Posture is an important part of meditation. Whether we sit, stand, lie or move, the basic recommendation is to ensure that your posture is comfortable and does not block a healthy flow of life energy. If you are sitting, sit with minimal or no muscular tension, an erect back, shoulders relaxed, chest open, head upright and hands placed comfortably on your legs or in your lap. A posture reflecting peace and dignity is helpful when meditating. You need not sit on the floor or a cushion to meditate as chairs are fine. If you feel you need to lie down to be comfortable please follow your needs.

Recollection

Being able to recollect what happened during the meditation period is helpful for meditation practice. After a formal meditation period it is highly recommended to spend a few minutes recollecting and reflecting on what happened during the meditation period. Being able to remember what happened, how difficulties were negotiated and the mindfulness and concentration cultivated, promotes understanding and wisdom.

Mindfulness of breath

The breath is a traditional meditation object and remains popular as a focus for meditation for a number of reasons. The breath is generally neutral and as long as we are alive we breathe, and so it is always there as an object to be attentive to. Being attentive to the breath encourages diaphragmatic breathing, which has numerous benefits on a physical level, and also helps us monitor our mind. In this way it provides a way to integrate and connect the heart-mind and body.

Like digestion, breathing is a function that is automatic, occurring without us trying. However, unlike digestion we can also exert some control over our breathing. We can, for example, hold our breath, breathe rapidly or slow our breath down if we choose to. Slow breathing is very helpful when we are anxious. Slow and regular breathing emphasising a long exhalation is also very helpful to reduce stress reactions and improve general psychological wellbeing.[2] Unfortunately sometimes with people such as those of us who experience panic, trying to control and slow down the breathing can occasionally have the opposite effect and we become more anxious. Later in this chapter I talk about what to do when and if we have anxiety with the breath. For the time being it is important to know that in traditional Buddhist mindfulness of breath practices we endeavour to not control the breath and let it settle into its own natural rhythm as much as possible.

When practising mindfulness of breath we relinquish control. Whatever the nature of the breath, it is accepted and allowed to be as it is. We let the breath breathe us. There are many ways to be mindful of the breath. We can be aware of the breath with an awareness of the whole body. We can simply just know that we are breathing. We can follow the breath as it moves in past our nose tip down into the lungs and back up again. Another way to be mindful of the breath is by noticing the sensation somewhere in our torso, such as the abdomen, as it rises and falls with the breath. In this way we can track changing physical sensations. We follow the experience from the beginning of the rising motion right to the end and note 'rising' as the abdomen is rising. The inward breath movement will stop for a split second and we track that experience. Then as it changes to an outward breath we pay attention from the beginning of the outward breath right to the end and note 'falling'.

Mindfulness of breath can be an insight meditation practice or a serenity meditation practice.

Mindfulness of breath as a serenity meditation practice

Mindfulness of breath as a serenity meditation practice can be used to develop relaxation, stability and vividness. Mindfulness of breath in the whole body or parts of the body is good for developing relaxation. Mindfulness of breath in the abdomen is good for stability and mindfulness of breath at the nose tip is particularly good to develop vividness.

These three places of focus can be used during meditation like changing gears on a car. You can start by relaxing the whole body, then shift to second gear with mindfulness of the belly rising and falling. When you are relaxed and feeling stable with your focus, you can shift to the more refined focus at the tip of the nose. If you feel the need, however, you can change gears back down to the body or the belly. You may feel, for example, you are getting too tense when focusing at the nose tip and decide total body relaxation is needed. Or you may wish to stay in first gear, using the breath to help you relax, for the whole of your meditation. If, however, you are relaxed and stable in your focus, you could set cruise control and stay focused on the sensations at the tip of the nose.

Mindfulness of breath as a serenity meditation practice: instructions

As an act of loving kindness, find a quiet space, secluded from busy circumstances. Establish your posture either lying down face up or sitting on a chair, cushion or mat. Loosen up any tight clothing or other constrictions and make yourself completely comfortable. Make the intention that for the next 20, 30 or 40 minutes you will cultivate a sense of ease, stillness and clarity by remembering to bring caring attention to the breath. Settle your body, speech and mind by bringing attention to the physical sensations of the body as it touches the ground, supporting and holding you. Put aside worries and concerns about the past and the future, and let your attention be present, here now, focused on what you are doing. Quieten your mind by grounding your awareness into physical sensations. Find stillness and quietude by bringing attention to the experience of the body as it touches the earth.

From the stillness and stability of the ground allow awareness to expand upward to movement as you feel it in your body. In particular, feel the movement of the breath as it breathes you. Relinquish control and allow the breath to be completely natural. If it is short, let it be short, if it is long let it be long, if it is shallow let it be shallow, if it is deep let it be deep. Let the breath settle into its natural rhythm without you trying to control it in any way.

1. (Relaxation)

Simply feel the breath in your body and on the out breath let go of tension. Use the out breath to release any thoughts that may be arising. Breathing in be aware, breathing out release and relax. Do not be concerned about any thoughts that may arise. Simply let them come and let them go. Do not struggle with anything. Let it be just as if you are falling asleep, but now, unlike going to sleep you are maintaining a relaxed alertness. Allow the mind to quieten down by remembering to attend to the breath as you experience it in your body. Let your awareness go where it wants to go within the domain of the body, allowing the breath to release tension and soothe both physical and mental unease. Allow mindfulness of breath to bring ease to your body and heart-mind. Simply let go. Simply relax. Relax deeply, finding tension and letting it go, in synchrony with the breath. Allow the breath to soothe and calm you. Let the breath bring a sense of ease and relaxation to your body and your heart-mind. Notice the pleasantness of the experience without grasping or clinging.

2. (Stability/stillness)

You may wish to continue the meditation session by being attentive to the breath in your whole body, relaxing tensions and releasing thoughts. If, however, you feel that your attention is beginning to stabilise on the breath, you may find that it naturally begins to stay with the rising and falling of the breath as you feel it in the chest or preferably the abdomen. If you feel that it is timely you may wish to let your attention become absorbed into the experience of the breath at the abdomen, if so, let your attention go and stay there. If you feel that it does not naturally stabilise on the abdomen or chest as you breathe, then stay with the whole body relaxing with the breath. Otherwise bring close attention to your abdomen or chest as it moves with the breath. Remembering to continue to relax on the out breath, allow your attention to stabilise on the experience of the rising and falling of the abdomen, noticing and sticking close to the stretching and contraction of this part of the body with the breath. Do not force your attention, but stay with the sensations with the aid of relaxation and ease. If you find it useful you can temporarily count the breaths one to ten or note the movement as rising falling, rising falling as a tool to stay focused. Otherwise simply remember to bring continuous attention to the experience, focused at your abdomen or chest as it moves with the breath. Attend carefully, if you can, to the beginning, middle and end of the each rising movement and the beginning, middle and end of each falling movement. When there seems to be no movement, keep your attention focused on the sensations in the abdomen. As best you can, be gently vigilant to keep attention on the target object, and maintain a sense of continuity of attention on the abdomen or chest as the breath breathes you. Be soft and kind with yourself when you find attention strays off. Do not struggle with thoughts or other distractions. Simply notice that your attention has strayed and remember to return attention to the abdomen or the chest. Rising falling, rising falling, remembering to continue to relax on the out breath. Simply enjoy the experience without clinging or attachment.

3. (Vividness/clarity)

You may wish to continue the meditation session by being attentive to the breath in your whole body, relaxing tensions and releasing thoughts. Or it may be timely and appropriate for you to continue to develop stability of attention by bringing it to the movement of the breath in the abdomen as it stretches and contracts with the breath. If however, you find that your attention is becoming more and more reflned or your breathing becoming slower and more subtle, then you are invited to change the object of your attention to the subtle sensations of the breath at the tip of the nose or for some of you, the area above your upper lip. Without tensing up, fine tune your feeling attention so that it becomes sensitive to the delicate sensations at the tip of the nose as air enters and exits your body with the breath. Guard against letting your eyes trying to look at the nose tip. From the base of relaxation and ease in your body-heart-mind, and the stable focus of continuity of attention, allow feeling attention to hone in on this subtle experience. Allow the power of concentration to bring a high resolution to the subtle experience. Stay up close and present. So present and focused that you simply have no time to have your attention pulled away by other experiences, such as thoughts. Allow an interest in the experience to develop. You may notice also that your body and heart-mind feel very pleasant and light with every breath. Simply notice this experience without grasping after it or trying to get more. Appreciate the peace and joy that may arise without attachment. Monitor the process of meditation with introspection. With introspection we guard against excitation where we may become over engaged in thought, and laxity, where we lose clarity about what we are focusing on. Remember to relax. If you seem to be tensing up, trying to force your concentration with a furrowed brow, remember the foundation of relaxation and simply let go of trying. Do not try too hard. Rather, remember that right effort is the energy behind the decision to continue to be absorbed with the experience. Stay with the experience, enhancing vividness and clarity.

When you feel ready you can end the meditation session. Before you go about your daily activities spend a few moments going back over the meditation exercise and remember what worked for you and what happened. Put these recollections in your memory bank for future reference, and then slowly move your body and open your eyes if they were closed. Then go about doing what you do, knowing that you can practise relaxation, stability and vividness when you choose. Thank you for your attention.

Mindfulness of breath at your abdomen as an insight practice: instructions

Practise with mindfulness of breath as a serenity practice for a short period then focus attention on the rising and falling of your abdomen and practise according to the following instructions.

- To help you bring attention to the movement of your abdomen or chest as you breathe, keep your breathing natural, neither speeding it up nor slowing it down. Let yourself be accepting of the breath without judgement that it should be other than it is.
- If you wish you can use noting such as 'rising' or 'falling'.
- Pay attention to the beginning, middle and end of the rising movement and the beginning, middle and end of the falling movement.
- Pay attention to movement and notice how the sensations change.
- Do not struggle with thoughts, feelings or other experiences but let them arise and pass away.
- Notice thoughts, feelings and other experiences and track how they change.
- When they no longer dominate your awareness bring attention back to rest with your breath and noticing sensations in the abdomen.
- You can use noting to help be mindful of the things that draw attention away from the breath, such as 'thinking, thinking' or 'remembering, remembering' or 'hearing, hearing', etc.
- Allow your open, yet focused attention to notice just one breath at a time, connecting mind and body. It is as if the knowing of the breath and the breath are not separate.
- Pay close attention to the specific sensations of movement and notice how they change.
- Remember to remain present with the experience as it changes.
- Continue to remember to be present with experience as it unfolds and use the sensations at your abdomen as it rises and falls with the breath as an anchor, or a stable place of reference.

- When you are ready, make the decision to stop the meditation period but before you start to engage in other activities, spend a few moments recollecting the period of formal meditation. Take note of what worked and what didn't work to cultivate both mindfulness and concentration.

Anxiety with mindfulness of breath

If being mindful of the breath seems to make you more anxious discuss this with an experienced practitioner if you can. Eventually, problems associated with mindfulness of breath can be managed with practice. When practitioners find mindfulness of breath uncomfortable or it triggers unwanted reactions they can substitute something other than the breath as their primary object. It is possible, for example, to pay attention, in a focused manner, to sensations in different parts of your body such as your hands or various 'touch points' such as your feet or the sensations in your buttocks on a chair or cushion. It is also possible to be aware of objects outside your body such as sounds or sights. Noticing and focusing on the quiver of a leaf in the breeze, the changing dance of a flame or the rhythmic movement of the ocean are examples of how objects of sight can become objects of meditation.

Walking meditation

Walking meditation, like mindfulness of breath, can be calming and also serve as an anchor to bring attention back to the present moment. In walking meditation the primary object of meditation is the action, posture and physical sensations of walking. The focus of attention is on changing physical sensations and the relationship between intention and action. The movement of the feet and consequently the way physical sensations change (body) depends on intentions (mentality or mind).

Mindful walking can be done at different speeds. Generally it is best to start each walking session at a fast pace then slow down if this feels comfortable. When you walk very fast the attention is broad and may involve awareness of the whole body moving. At a slower pace attention is brought to the process of walking and is directed to the sensations in the legs or the feet whilst noting 'right', 'left', 'right', 'left'. With slow walking the focus of attention is narrower and usually just at the feet noting 'lifting', 'placing', 'lifting', 'placing' and so on. At a very slow pace the sensations at the base of the feet as they touch, press, shift and lift from the ground can become the focus of attention noting, for example, 'lifting', 'moving', 'dropping', 'touching', 'pressing', etc. If it feels comfortable you can walk really slowly, taking many seconds to make one step. Noting each and every movement helps to ensure that awareness follows the experience of each and every movement from its beginning until its end. Many people find walking mindfully helpful if they are feeling too restless to sit mindfully.

As Jack did in the story earlier, another way to practise mindful walking is to synchronise it with the breath: lifting a foot as you breathe in and placing it when you breathe out. The focus is on the walking and the slowed breathing is secondary. As long as you are walking at a reasonably slow pace, this is one way you can slow your breathing. At the same time you may bypass any problems that sometimes occur when we focus too much on trying to control breathing.

Walking meditation: instructions

- Ensure that there is space enough to walk for at least 6 or 7 paces in front of you and set the intention that for the next 20 minutes or so you will commit to being present here now.
- Begin by standing and bringing attention to your posture. You should be relaxed, upright and dignified, with eyes open looking a few metres in front of you. Let your chest be open, relax your shoulders, make sure your knees are not locked and place your hands where they are comfortable.
- Become aware of sight, sounds and what is happening around you and, without rejection, let these things be on the periphery of your awareness. With curious interest, notice the sensations in your body standing, letting go of unnecessary muscle tension.
- Let 'standing' be the centre of your awareness.

- For a minute or two, enjoy the simple activity of standing.
- Then allow your attention to focus on your feet and the sensations in them, feeling temperature or pressure or movement or whatever the experience is.
- When you are ready, notice the intention to take a step.
- Notice the changing sensations as you shift your weight onto one foot and pick the other one up.
- Notice how your foot feels as it travels through the air and the changing sensation of pressure as you place it on the ground.
- If you wish you can use noting such as 'lifting, moving, placing' or if you wish to walk a bit faster you may use 'left, right'.
- Walk at a pace and find a rhythm that is comfortable for you.
- If you are walking at a slow pace, attention will be more acutely focused on your feet; at a faster pace, the attention can be broader such as your legs or your whole body.
- When thoughts, sounds, sights and emotions pull your attention away from walking, simply note the experience and refocus your attention.
- When you come to the end of your walking pathway, stop, be aware of turning, then walk mindfully back along your pathway.
- If you feel comfortable you can gradually slow the pace and the rhythm down.
- Continue walking for a period that is suitable then let the mindfulness cultivated during mindful walking carry over into your daily life.

Five obstacles to meditation

Meditation is simple but very difficult. As we try to meditate it is natural that hindrances to our practice will arise. Skill negotiating these obstacles develops with experience and it becomes part of our ongoing meditation practice. In essence the hindrances are states of heart-mind, which seem embedded and entangled in our sense of being. Meditation teachers point to five groupings of these states of heart-mind which are considered to be obstructions to meditation and wellbeing.

1. Obsessive sensual desire. An example of this is not being able to get the craving for chocolate out of our minds.
2. Feeling hostile, ill will, hating things or being bored. These feelings can get in the way of getting into the flow of meditation.
3. Lethargy or mental dullness. An example of this is going to sleep during meditation, when you don't need or want to sleep.
4. Restlessness, agitation or worry.
5. Paralysing doubt. This involves being so uncertain about a path to follow that we become stuck and do not do anything. Procrastinating about whether to meditate or not is an example of this. This type of block stops you from gaining mediation experience and learning about the benefits for yourself.

Mindfulness is the main way to deal with the obstacles or hindrances. Being able to identify a hindrance with mindfulness, and note or name it, is one powerful way to overcome and rein in its obstructive power. It also helps not to take the hindrances personally or see them as enemies to be quashed. Rather it is best to see these hindrances as honoured guests that will not stay long. Working through the hindrances is, in fact, the business of meditation and this ultimately leads to psychological freedom.

Being mindful of these five hindrances is included in the fourth application of mindfulness, mindfulness of phenomena. Skilfully working with and through the hindrances are advanced aspects of meditation practice and will be discussed in more detail in Chapter 6. Nonetheless, early reference is made to these hindrances because it is easy for beginners to feel discouraged in the beginning stages of meditation. If you can be aware of the hindrances and realise that they are part of meditation practice, then discouragement may be less likely. As awareness of the hindrances grows, each and every individual learns their own strategies for working with them.

Notes

1 The Venerable Mahasi Sayadaw was a highly respected Buddhist monk teaching in Burma in the mid-twentieth century. His approach has become popular in the West.
2 When we breathe in, the heart rate increases slightly. When we breathe out the heart rate decreases slightly. Slow and regular breathing emphasising an extended out breath will increase heart rate variability (HRV). Research indicates that low heart rate variability is a sign of stress and related mental health issues such as anxiety. High and regular HRV, conversely, is a sign of being able to cope well with stress as well as psychological wellbeing including healthy interpersonal relationships. When we breathe slowly

emphasising the out breath and in a regular manner, the HRV will be optimal and also reflect this regularity. See Porges (2011) for more details.

References

Ballie, A. J. and Rapee, R. M. (1998). *Panic Surfing: A Self-Treatment Workbook for Panic Disorder.* Sydney: Macquarie Lighthouse Press.
Batchelor, S. (1997). *Buddhism without Beliefs: A Contemporary Guide to Awakening.* London: Bloomsbury.
Benson, H. (1975). *The Relaxation Response.* Glasgow: William Morris.
Csikszentmihalyi, M. (1988). The flow of experience and human psychology. In M. Csikszentmihalyi and I. S. Csikszentmihalyi (eds.), *Optimal Experience: Psychological Studies of Flow in Consciousness.* Cambridge: Cambridge University Press.
Dalai Lama, H. H. (2009). What is the mind? The Mind and its Potential Conference Proceedings, December, Sydney (Darling Harbour) Convention & Exhibition Centre, NSW, Australia.
Erickson, M. H. and Rossi, E. L. (1979). *Hypnotherapy: An Exploratory Casebook.* New York: Irvington Publications.
Kearney, P. (2006). Mindfulness, meditation and a path as therapy. Advanced workshop conducted with Malcolm Huxter at Hunter Institute of Mental Health, Newcastle, NSW, Australia.
Kornfield, J. and Breiter, P. (1985). *A Still Forest Pool: The Insight Meditation of Achaan Chah.* Wheaton, IL: Quest Books.
Porges, S. W. (2011). *The Polyvagal Theory: Neurophysiological Foundations of Emotions, Attachment, Communication, and Self-Regulation.* New York: W. W. Norton.
Thanissaro Bhikkhu (1996). *The Wings to Awakening.* Barre, MA: The Dhamma Dana Publication Fund.
Wallace, B. A. (2006). *The Attention Revolution: Unlocking the Power of the Focussed Mind.* Somerville, MA: Wisdom Publications.

4 Mindfulness of thoughts and the freedom to choose to engage or not engage

Chapter overview

This chapter investigates thinking, the content of thoughts and the relationship we have with our thoughts. It discusses what thinking is and some patterns of thinking that often lead to psychological distress or *dukkha*. This chapter also discusses how we can use thinking to lead us to happiness and how understanding our relationship to our thoughts is crucial for this. Mindfulness, serenity meditation and insight meditation provide us with useful tools to work with thinking. Stories to demonstrate this are included and the chapter concludes with some guided meditation practices.

Thinking

Our thinking can lead us to happiness or it can lead us away from happiness. Thinking means different things to different people. For me thinking includes trains of thought that appraise, evaluate, compare, judge and comment. It also refers to impulses, imagery, stories, memories and random and unrelated images or words. What we think, the content of our thoughts, can influence the way we feel. Our relationship to our thoughts also influences the way we feel. If our relationship to thought is driven by attachment, delusion and aversion we will experience *dukkha*. It is possible to change both the content of our thoughts and our relationship to our thoughts.

Cognitive Therapies (CT) and Cognitive Behaviour Therapies (CBT) have excelled at helping individuals to change the content of unhelpful thoughts and they also help to change the unhelpful relationships. The third wave therapies and Buddhist mindfulness practices have excelled at helping individuals change unhelpful relationships to thoughts and they have also helped people to change the content of unhelpful thoughts. It is possible to cultivate healthy thinking patterns and to use thinking creatively to disengage from unhelpful and destructive thoughts. Right intention (which is also called right thought) is one of the factors of the eight-fold path. Having an aspiration for happiness can be a first step in making genuine happiness a reality.[1]

Both the serenity and insight aspects of meditation can be used to work with thoughts to find psychological freedom.

The *dukkha* of thinking

Human language has enabled us to project, conceptualise and communicate like no other species. Conceptual thinking and its connection to language, however, has a cost.

Sometimes our thoughts torment us with what seems like never-ending blah blah blah.

Sometimes, especially when we meditate, thoughts seem to get out of control

and the more we try to stop them or blank the mind the more they grow and grow.

Both the contents of thought or what we are thinking and the way we perceive, interact and understand thoughts and thinking processes, or our relationship to thoughts, can cause and perpetuate suffering. At times thinking can make things that are not real seem real.

How the content of our thoughts can cause *dukkha*

Much of our thinking is automatic. That is, it seems to just 'pop' into our heads and thoughts appear to be involuntary and uncontrollable. Thoughts sometimes convey unhelpful messages that reflect our assumptions and beliefs about the world and ourselves. Some people call the types of thoughts that are unhelpful or prevent the growth of our happiness, 'toxic' thoughts or 'stinking thinking'. Thinking thoughts such as: 'my life is hopeless', 'life sucks', 'everything is horrible', 'my life is a failure and I am a failure', 'everyone one hates me', 'I am not good enough', etc., are all examples of toxic thoughts.

Cognitive therapists say that it is not an event that makes us feel good or bad, but the way it is perceived and interpreted. They say that people often make assumptions about things. Unhelpful thinking often involves assumptions that are unrealistic, not accurate, incorrect, destructive and focused on the worst-case scenario. Just like a dirty lens can distort the way we see the world, unhelpful thinking patterns also distort the way we see things.

Many upsetting emotional consequences are caused by unrealistic, catastrophic, inaccurate, inflexible and self-defeating beliefs about the world, the future and our selves. Unhelpful thoughts tend to have inflexible and absolute words such as: should, have to, must, ought, can't, always, never, etc. The more our assumptions and beliefs are not in line with the way things are, the more likely we will experience emotional distress. Some common thinking patterns often pointed out in CBT as generally unhelpful include the following:

- Over-generalisation
  - The tendency to over-exaggerate. For example, interpreting failure at one task to mean failure at everything.
- Polarised thinking
  - Thinking in extremes of black and white judgements. Things are either totally good or bad and there are no shades of grey.
- Mental filtering
  - Focusing on the negative rather than seeing alternatives or the bigger picture.
- Catastrophising
  - Over-estimating the probability that something 'terrible' will happen and focusing on the worst possible outcome.
- Minimising and magnifying
  - Minimising the positive and magnifying the negative (usually in reference to ourselves and our own qualities or capacities).
- Mind reading
  - Making inferences and assumptions about how other people feel and think without evidence.
- Personalising
  - Taking personal responsibility for events that we are not responsible for, or relating events to oneself when there is no basis to do this.

There are also extreme thinking patterns called gross delusions. Gross delusions are usually associated with psychosis. When an individual is psychotic they generally lose contact with reality in a way that leads to intense *dukkha*. Though gross delusions are less common than the thinking patterns described above, it is still helpful to know about them because this knowledge broadens our understanding of thought and how it can affect us.

Gross delusions usually involve thinking and feeling in an extreme way. They include extreme beliefs and assumptions that are outside the social and cultural norms of the individual experiencing them and not consistent with the shared reality of most people. Gross delusions are not supported by evidence to validate their reality, but for the individual experiencing them, they feel real. Unrealistic paranoia or feeling that everyone is spying on us or out to harm us, or thinking that one is responsible for natural disasters or thinking that we are the next saviour of world, are just some examples of gross delusions. Gross delusions involve both the content of thoughts and the relationship to thoughts. Not only is the content of thought out of line with the way things are, the relationship to the thought is also one of adamant belief.

Although it is hard to question the truthfulness of gross delusions, it is possible to address and change less severe thinking patterns with reason and logic. Like a detective or scientist who investigates the facts, we can investigate the truth of what we are saying to ourselves, or our self-talk. When we question, we look for the evidence about something being true or not true. We also check out the probability of something being true, alternatives for the thought and whether it really matters if the thought is true or not.

Being aware of the content of our thoughts is useful because it allows us to decide whether or not to believe them and so choose to act skilfully. Being mindful of thoughts helps us move them into awareness so that we can skilfully transform them from being unhelpful to being helpful. Mindfulness is extremely helpful in the process of recognition, investigation, skilful action and the transformation of unhelpful thoughts to helpful.

Related story: Pontip disengages from unhelpful thoughts

Pontip was born and raised in a village in northern Thailand. She moved to Australia with her Australian husband when she was 25 years old. She felt inspired by the opportunities living in Australia offered but the cultural shift was difficult. She really missed her family and friends, her community and the children of her village

Pontip's husband's family were very friendly. She enjoyed visiting her sister-in-law and her young nieces and nephews. She loved playing with the children and hugging them. The children also enjoyed her visits. Being with the children reminded Pontip of her home in

Thailand. She wanted to impress her husband's family with her ability to care for young children and took whatever opportunity there was to baby-sit. Pontip was worried, however, that her style of play and affection might be considered strange because of cultural differences between Australia and Thailand.

One day, whilst she was playing with the children she thought she noticed that her sister-in-law frowned. Pontip interpreted this gesture as disapproval, stopped the game she was playing and did something else. As the days and weeks passed Pontip thought more and more about the differences between Australian and Thai culture. She became more and more self-conscious whenever she left her home and mixed with other people. She thought that they thought she was stupid and strange. She began to fear that people would judge the way she spoke and wrote English, the way she looked, the things she bought, how she ate, and generally the way she did things. Pontip started to become anxious in public and felt certain that everyone noticed. So, she avoided going out. Worst of all she avoided visiting her nieces and nephews because she thought her husband's family disapproved of her.

Her fear and avoidance caused a major disruption in her life. She was very embarrassed by her thoughts and she did not want to talk to anyone about them. She tried suppressing the thoughts but they kept surfacing. When she eventually talked to her husband about her thoughts he tried to convince her that his family were not judging in a negative manner. He added that he thought that people in the streets hardly noticed how she did things and it was therefore unlikely they thought she was stupid or strange. Pontip realised, at an intellectual level, that her anxious thoughts might not be realistic. Nonetheless, she continued to have the thoughts and avoided social situations and playing with the children. The situation was distressing for Pontip and she felt trapped by her thoughts. Pontip was not sure how she could cope.

As Pontip was raised a Buddhist she knew that she could seek advice from Buddhist monks and nuns. Fortunately, some Thai nuns lived close by and she visited them. Her trust and confidence in one wise old nun was enough for Pontip to open her heart and tell all that she was embarrassed about. The old nun listened compassionately and reminded Pontip of the basics of insight meditation, a practice she had learnt as a teenager in Thailand. The nun reminded Pontip that her thoughts were impermanent and uncertain and need not be believed as representing the truth. Furthermore, the nun encouraged Pontip to do the things that she was avoiding so that she could realise, at an experiential level, that her fears were not justified. It was a great relief for Pontip to talk to the nun because it reminded her of insights she had had when she was younger. Pontip returned home determined to remember how to be mindful with difficult thoughts and see them as just thoughts and not facts to be believed. Pontip also felt a commitment to slowly reduce the tendency to avoid social situations. She was determined to return to her sister-in-law's and play with the children. She decided that she would not engage in thoughts of being judged and remind herself that they were just thoughts and not necessarily facts.

Pontip practised mindfulness with diligence and rather than suppress the thoughts she noted them and let them come and go. She was able to be mindful of thoughts when she played with the children and noticed that her sister-in-law seemed predisposed to frowning even when she approved of things! When Pontip checked with her sister-in-law about how she felt about her playing with the children, the sister-in-law emphasised how much she appreciated Pontip's contact with them. Pontip realised that the projected fears of judgement were not real. Not only did thoughts of being stupid and strange cause less distress, they hardly arose any more. Pontip also began being more and more social. Best of all, the games with the children became a regular event.

How our relationship with thoughts can cause *dukkha*

When we relate to thoughts in a way in which we think that they rigidly define who and what we are or that they are fixed facts to be believed then they will usually cause us suffering. In the example above Pontip initially believed her thoughts to be true and then identified with them and felt that she was 'stupid and strange'. Trying to push the thoughts away did not help and she felt trapped. When Pontip changed her relationship with her thoughts she was able to be free from their negative influence.

In contemporary psychology, proponents of Acceptance and Commitment Therapy (ACT) use the term 'cognitive fusion' to refer to how we often take our thoughts literally (e.g. Luoma, Hayes and Walser, 2007). It usually involves a process of identification with our thoughts and the belief that thoughts we have about ourselves are facts. Buddhists will often use the term reification in a manner somewhat synonymous with the ACT description of cognitive fusion. Reification is the activity of making something out of nothing, the tendency to identify with something that is not who and what we are.

As we grow up and interact with other people, engage in the environment, notice and observe, think and make logical connections, we develop associations and relationships between words, events, feelings, images and experiences. Through our experiences and related associations we create a sense of who and what we are. This is an essential part of survival. Unfortunately, concepts about the world and ourselves can begin to replace actual experience and we live 'in our heads'. We see ourselves and the world around us through a veil of our concepts and are often ignorant of the way things actually are.

We may have all sorts of thoughts. We may think that we are a failure or that we are wonderful. We may think that something terrible is going to happen even when there is evidence to suggest it won't. Some of the thoughts that arise in our minds may go against our deepest values. We are capable of thinking of things we would never do, such as holding up a bank to pay off bills, blowing up our noisy neighbour's stereo, or worse, killing someone. Fortunately we are able to see such extreme thoughts as just thoughts. Imagine if we took these thoughts literally! Unfortunately when we tend to fuse with unhelpful thoughts that come into our minds and believe them to be the truth of who and what we are we suffer. Worry, rumination, intrusive memories and obsessive thoughts are common unhelpful thought patterns that, when we relate to them unwisely, will cause and maintain psychological distress.

Papanca (Pali)

In Buddhism the process of mental proliferation is called *papanca* (Pali). *Papanca* refers to the way the mind makes more out of an experience than is actually there, complicating situations with proliferating thought. Although creative imagination can be very helpful on the path of psychological freedom, when it is unbalanced it can be destructive. In describing *papanca* some Buddhist scholars say that it is the tendency for 'imagination to break loose and run riot'[2] and it 'includes the whole range of mental processes – thoughts, fantasies, obsessions – that keep us apart from an awareness of present-moment realities' (Chaskalson, 2006, p. 1). Being taken over by unnecessary thinking can disconnect us from life.

In Buddhist psychology the fourth hindrance to meditation is restlessness, agitation or worry. The tendency to think over and over again, be lost, restless and agitated or hijacked by unreliable thoughts, hampers our ability to focus and see clearly with a sense of direction. In Buddhist meditation practices, *papanca* prevents the penetrative power of focused attention and the calm and insight that this stabilised attention can bring. Worry, how we understand it in contemporary psychology, is an example of *papanca*.

Worry

Worry refers to thinking over and over about negative events, usually trying to find solutions to prevent an untoward thing happening. Worry often focuses upon the possibility that something negative will happen in the future. We tend to have 'what if' questions and these 'what if' questions often focus on worst-case scenarios. When we are in the habit of worrying we may develop a 'cognitive bias'. That is, we tend to focus on and select information from the environment that confirms our worry.

Worry is often an attempt to find solutions to imagined problems and cope with uncertainty by thinking through different possibilities. Worry is different to effective problem solving. Problem solving is purposeful, effective and we have the ability to choose when and where we think about our concerns. In addition, with effective problem solving skills, we are calm, focused and able to objectively consider the bigger picture. Worry, on the other hand, is often less effective and more driven by habits of fear and avoidance that are automatic. Worry tends to be intrusive and experienced as uncontrollable or totally unmanageable. It is unpleasant and is often accompanied by distracted nervous agitation. Fear, as a feature of worry, can elicit the flight or fight response in our body. People with uncontrollable worry often experience high arousal, muscle tension, irritability, problems with sleep, and difficulty concentrating.

Worry can be fuelled by our beliefs, often catastrophic, about ourselves or situations and also about the nature of worry itself. Worry can be further perpetuated by the way we react to worry with distressing emotions and avoidant behaviours including trying to control and suppress our thoughts.

Some examples of generally unhelpful beliefs and assumptions about the world that also involve worry include:

- I should always be in control of events and myself.
- I should never have to suffer or feel anything unpleasant.
- If I fail at one thing then I am a total failure.
- Things should always go the way I want them to go and if they don't I just couldn't cope.
- I should be loved by everyone and it is terrible if someone dislikes me.
- If I am uncertain about the future then it is totally intolerable.

When we worry we tend to over-estimate the likelihood of something bad happening and how bad something would be if it actually happened. We may also worry about worry itself! Paradoxically some beliefs about worry are contradictory. For example, we may believe, incorrectly, that we need to worry in order to cope. At the same time, we may also believe that worry is something that we shouldn't engage in because it is making us sick.

Worry can be deceptive and when it takes hold we may believe the content of our worries is true. When we believe our worries they hijack us away from what is actually happening. Unfortunately worry is self-perpetuating because it is reinforcing. We may, for example, feel uncomfortable about the uncertainty of the future, project unwarranted fears into the future and feel we have to find a solution to the possibility that something unwanted may happen. When we worry we may come up with a temporary solution. Though superficial, the imagined solution may be enough to provide some relief from our discomfort, which unfortunately further reinforces the habit of worry. Worry is self-reinforcing because it serves to create an illusion of certainty and predictability and so, in the short term, it reduces anxiety. Unfortunately, the relief is only temporary and when the discomfort of uncertainty arises again we are driven to start to find superficial and unsustainable solutions and worry again. Another way that worry is reinforced is by the relief we feel when the unwanted and often unrealistic things that we spent so much time worrying about don't actually happen.

Related story: Simon manages worry

After many years working in lowly paid, unskilled jobs Simon thought that he would like more satisfying employment so he enrolled at university and upgraded his qualifications. It was difficult being a mature aged student but, with determination, Simon completed his degree and secured a job that had responsibility. Simon, as an expert in his field, was employed as a consultant for the government.

Simon had always been a worrier but since he had started employment in a responsible position, much of his time was spent worrying about it. Simon worried about his competency. There were so many possibilities in relation to the things that Simon had to investigate and report on, it was difficult to be certain about statements he made. Simon felt a sense of commitment to do his best and provide a professional service but he often doubted the value of his work.

It was difficult for Simon to leave work behind at the end of the day. He would often take reports home on the weekends to complete. Worries about work even invaded his sleep. He would lie in bed at night trying to find solutions to problems with work and he would regularly wake up in the early hours of the morning and think things through. He often felt like quitting his work. However, this was not an option because he had a mortgage that needed a reliable income. Worries about finances and the jobs he had to do were not the only topics that occupied his mind. He also worried about his health and his relationships.

Simon had been with his girlfriend for two years and he worried that she might think he was boring and leave him because he was working too hard. He was concerned that she may meet someone more interesting and he would be left alone. Simon found it very difficult to relax and felt it was impossible to control his worries. It seemed that he was always tense and preoccupied with the possibility of making a mistake at work or losing his girlfriend. There seemed a constant gnawing feeling of anxiety driven by the question 'what if'. 'What if something goes wrong? What if there was something I missed in a report? What if someone sues me? What if I can't keep up the mortgage repayments? What if one night my girlfriend is not home? What if she meets someone interesting? What if she leaves me? What if I'm left alone? What if I can't cope?' etc., etc.

Simon seemed to be constantly fretting about some imagined catastrophe in the future. He was irritable, had headaches and digestive problems. His gnawing fear about the future was experienced physically as a tight knot in his belly. Simon could see that worry was affecting his health, his work and his relationship. Ironically, the more he worried about work the less he was able to focus on the tasks he had to do. Simon worried about his health and he became worried about worry, thinking 'What if I worry so much that I have a complete mental and physical breakdown?' Simon was desperate to relieve the suffering that he realised worry was causing. He had tried meditation once before, but, it wasn't helpful. At that time, he had been told that to meditate he should 'empty the mind of thoughts'. However, when Simon tried this it seemed to make things worse.

Someone told Simon about mindfulness meditation and explained that it wasn't necessary to stop thinking. This renewed Simon's interest in using meditation to help him stop worrying. Simon learnt the basics of mindfulness meditation and applied these basics in daily life. It was very difficult to break unhelpful thinking habits but Simon tried nonetheless. When worry arose he tried putting it off for another time and he was able to do this at times. He also experimented with doing nothing when he was reminded of problems that didn't need immediate action. He found doing nothing particularly hard especially when the problems were characterised by uncertainty. With determination Simon learnt the difference between effective and calm problem solving and ineffective fear-driven worry. He was more able to compartmentalise tasks and leave work at work and not take it home and to his bed. Slowly Simon started to have some space from worry and some peace of mind. He felt more secure within himself about the relationship with his girlfriend. To Simon's relief, work became more satisfying and life more satisfying. Simon accepted the fact that worry would arise from time to time yet he felt confident that he could manage it.

Rumination

Rumination is similar to worry. Much that was written above about worry can be repeated for rumination. Rumination is, however, less future oriented and more passive. When we ruminate we mull over an issue without thinking of any solutions. We generally focus repeatedly on our distress and its circumstances, stewing over life's difficulties with a sense of blame and sometimes resentment and bitterness. Like worry, rumination can be intrusive and interfere with successful problem solving. Rumination contributes to a sense of hopelessness about the future, increases negative self-evaluation and often leads to depression.

Rumination is different from wholesome pondering or reflection. Wholesome reflection usually leads to a positive outcome and we have more power to choose when we reflect on the past. Rumination, on the other hand, invades our minds in a way that feels as if we have no power to choose. Rumination leads to repetitive thoughts with negative and distressing themes. When we ruminate we tend to believe that the thoughts we are having, usually about ourselves, represent the truth. With healthy reflection there is an understanding that thoughts may not necessarily represent the truth about the way things actually are.

Intrusive memories

Sometimes if we have intense unpleasant experiences we cannot stop thinking about the experience, even when it is long over. The impact of a particular experience varies greatly from individual to individual. For some, being bullied at work can be shrugged off but for others it can result in the same pattern of symptoms that may emerge with a more intense trauma. Blame, insult, unwarranted criticism, verbal abuse and other types of non-life threatening situations can cause extreme distress because our social relationships are important to us. Associated with the distress is the way the thoughts about the event torment us.

People who have experienced life-threatening traumas will often have intrusive thoughts that come into their mind in an uncontrolled, unwelcome and usually very frightening manner. This type of thought intrusion often occurs with PTSD (APA, 2013). When extreme, these intrusive thoughts may be experienced as flashbacks where strong imagery and other associated memories of a past trauma will recur as if it is happening in present time.

In my clinical practice I have worked with survivors of sexual abuse, war and torture. Some of the experiences that people endure are horrendous and it is often heart-breaking to hear people's stories. Obviously, the suffering related to PTSD involves much more than only struggling with thought. Subsequently, the treatment of this disorder involves more than just changing the content and relationship to thought. Nonetheless, releasing struggle and finding freedom with thought intrusion can be profoundly healing.

Obsessions

Obsessions are thought patterns that involve repeated thoughts, which unlike worry and rumination can sometimes be completely unreasonable and do not make sense. An example of obsessive thinking is when we have a song or some music stuck in our head and we can't seem to get rid of it, no matter how we try.

Obsessive thoughts are a part of OCD (APA, 2013). The thoughts associated with OCD can be offensive, repetitive, bizarre, and intrude in such a way that they cause anxiety, anguish and despair. Those suffering with OCD will often know that the obsession is bizarre and not realistic but are tormented nonetheless. Obsessive thoughts are unpleasant and cause a buildup of anxiety until one feels compelled to do something to have some relief. This may be a personal ritual to neutralize the thoughts, like counting a list of numbers or doing an action which may or may not be related to the thought or it may be an obsessive behavior such as checking doors are locked or washing hands. Unfortunately, acting on the compulsions reinforces them and people with OCD usually feel trapped by behaviours that they know do not make sense.

The suffering related to OCD, like PTSD, also involves more than struggling with thought. Subsequently professional therapy is often necessary. Changing the content of thought and the relationship to thought, however, can help ease the struggle with obsessions.

Understanding thinking

Have you ever had a nightmare? Perhaps you had lost all your money, or your spouse went off with another person, or you were in the middle of a war zone facing death. Then you woke up and realised it was only a dream. What a relief. When we live in a world of concepts, not in contact with actual experience, it is like we are living in a dream. The path that the Buddha taught is a path of awakening. When we understand thinking and see through the illusion of our conceptual world, we wake up to life as we live it and we are free.

What is a nightmare for some is in fact a living reality for others. As a psychologist I often see people who are depressed or anxious because they have lost all their wealth, their spouse has left them, or they live in dangerous conditions. Despite these difficulties, understanding, thinking and waking up to the reality of things can still bring peace. Remember what was said about Nirvana in the first chapter? When there is no cause for *dukkha*, it does not arise. One of the root causes of *dukkha*, according to the teachings of the Buddha, is ignorance.

Ignorance includes not seeing the four truths and the three characteristics of existence (impermanence, uncertainty and interdependence).

Ignorance involves misapprehensions, misperceptions and misunder-standings that are largely driven by our thoughts. When we realise that thoughts, like all things, are impermanent, unreliable and not-self then their potential to cause us suffering is greatly reduced. When we no longer create the cause for *dukkha*, it no longer arises and we realise freedom.

The way of serenity: engaging in the helpful and disengaging from the unhelpful

In relationship to thoughts, a participant of a group that I conducted many years ago said: 'whatever gets your attention gets you'. If we ruminate about our failings or inadequacies, for example, it is easy to become sucked into a descending spiral of depression. If, however, we collect our attention and place it on a neutral or pleasant object, it is possible to become so absorbed in what we are focusing on that unwanted thoughts and unhelpful thinking patterns do not arise. Focusing on something increases the likelihood of becoming absorbed in that 'thing'.

Simon, in our previous example, was suffering with Generalised Anxiety Disorder where worry was the key feature. He purposefully chose to direct his attention to one object and not to another. Though difficult, he was able to consciously put aside worry, compartmentalise responsibilities and focus on the task at hand. In other words, he was able to loosen the grip that worry had on him and be more present for life.

We can uplift our mind in a way that resonates with what we are focusing on. Using creative thought by imagining we are at a beautiful place or with people that love us, for example, can warm our hearts and bring a smile to our faces.[3]

When we are sensitive to the types of thoughts we are having we are more able to choose to focus on the helpful and not the unhelpful. This does not mean that we deny or suppress unhelpful thoughts, but rather, we see them for what they are and choose not to engage with them. There are many ways to use the way of serenity to work with thoughts. The following examples are just a few.

Mindfulness of breath

Mindfulness of breath as a calming meditation practice, as it was described in the last chapter, is often recommended as a way to quieten noisy and sometimes toxic thoughts. Bringing attention to the rhythmic quality of the breath not only soothes the body but it also calms the mind so that there is some internal peace and quiet.

The breath is a neutral object to pay attention to and so is an alternative to being caught up in one's head with thoughts. Sinking attention into the tangible experience of the whole body as it expands and contracts with the breath provides a way to relax tension, as well as calm the mind that is lost in thinking too much. Bringing attention to the abdomen as it rises and falls with the breath, helps to focus and ground attention away from our head. When attention become sufficiently focused it is possible to refine one's focus and enhance the vividness of attention at the nose tip, as subtle sensations change with the breath. As one hones in on the experience of the breath at the tip of the nose, it is as if there is no time to think, because the experience is immediate and absorbing. When thinking is not fuelled, it slows down and blissful silence pervades.

For some people, such as those who are prone to panic, mindfulness of breath may not soothe and calm, but may trigger discomfort and even anxiety. It does this because of the association that bringing attention to the breath may have with panic or other anxious situations. In these circumstances it is better to bring attention to something outside one's body so that there are no reminders. Then, later when one is more able, it is suggested to slowly and gradually bring attention back to the breath. Bare attention to sensory experience outside the body, such as sound, is a good alternative to mindfulness of breath.

Bare attention

Bare attention is the type of attention given to the raw experience of the senses before there is conceptualising about the experience. Joseph Goldstein (1976, p. 20) describes bare attention as: 'observing things as they are without choosing, without comparing, without evaluating, without laying our projections and expectations on to what is happening, initiating instead a choice-less and non-interfering awareness'.

Some contemporary psychologists consider bare attention and mindfulness as the same thing. However, from a traditional Buddhist perspective, mindfulness may include bare attention, but, as we have begun to explore in this book, it is much more. From a Buddhist perspective mindfulness includes discernment and remembering. Bare attention can be activated when we are bringing attention to immediate, here now experience of the senses. Bringing bare attention to experience involves choosing to be attentive to the way one experiences the world through bodily experiences. By bringing attention to the raw experiences of sight, sound, smell, touch and taste or bodily sensations we are able to short-circuit being entangled in worry, rumination and other proliferating thought processes. It is as if we allow our *mind* to become *full* with sensory experience, thereby giving no fuel to the mental proliferation of thinking.

Anchoring oneself in the reality of what one is doing and remembering to remember to be here now is possibly the most powerful way to find some peace from disturbing thoughts.

Settling the mind in its natural state

Another way to disengage from difficult thoughts is to not react to them nor to struggle with, resist, judge or suppress them. Rather, allow them the space to 'be'. In this way we can be attentive to thoughts but from a frame of reference that is distanced from them.

Settling the mind in its natural state (SMINS)[4] is a serenity meditation practice where the focus of attention is directed at the space of the mind and its objects, such as thoughts (Wallace, 2006). Technically SMINS is a serenity practice because attention is brought to a single object and, unlike insight meditation there is no enquiry into the nature of the experience. SMINS is like practising bare attention as described above but instead of focusing on sensory experience the object of bare attention is the mind. We endeavour not to think about thinking, and get as close to the bare experience of thought as possible, without feeding into it or spacing out. With SMINS we try not to place censorship or judgement on depressing, frightening, odd, bizarre, weird, disagreeable or strange thoughts. We also endeavour not to chase after seductive, attractive, pleasing and positive thoughts. With SMINS we do not do anything with the thoughts, rather they are simply allowed to come and go. Just as a ball of string that is tangled up gets worse when we pull and tug at it, distressing thoughts are often best left to unravel by themselves, without us trying to work them all out with logic and reason. The words of a famous Zen master, Shunryu Suzuki, seem to capture this process:

> When you are practicing zazen, do not try to stop your thinking. Let it stop by itself. If something comes into your mind, let it come in, and let it go out. It will not stay long. When you try to stop your thinking, it means you are bothered by it. Do not be bothered by anything. It appears as if something comes from outside your mind, but actually it is only the waves of your mind, and if you are not bothered by the waves, gradually they will become calmer and calmer.
>
> (Suzuki, 1970, p. 34)

SMINS has been compared to plumbing the depths of consciousness.[5] When we plumb the depths, we cannot be certain about what may surface. Sometimes thoughts reflecting our deepest fears may come up. Sometimes thoughts reflecting our deepest passions or highest ideas may arise. The task with SMINS is to greet each thought, regardless of its content, with openness, without pushing the unpleasant away or grasping after the pleasant. In SMINS meditation we try as much as possible to not grasp after pleasant thoughts or struggle with unpleasant thoughts. We are also careful not to space out or lose clarity as thoughts come and go.

The practice of SMINS has also been likened to an old man sitting on a bench in a park[6] watching the clouds in the sky, the trees blowing in the breeze and the children playing. The old man just watches and does not try to change the comings and goings of nature. Nor does he feel he has to control the children or correct them. All he does is watch life in the park live itself.

Thoughts can be like clouds across the sky where the sky is compared to awareness and the changing clouds are like changing thoughts that don't last. Thought can also be like things floating past in a river. Sometimes there are beautiful things and sometimes there is garbage. Either way you don't have to dive into the river of thoughts and swim after them. Sometimes people see thoughts as if they are buses coming down the road. Each bus has its destination clearly displayed and stops to allow you to get on board. If the destination says 'road to misery' you can choose not to board. If on the other hand the sign says 'road to happiness' you can choose to board and figuratively buy a ticket on that thought bus. Another analogy is being a spectator at a circus parade. One just watches the passing parade and does not join the circus. Yet another very useful analogy is that of a doorman at a busy hotel. The doorman greets and opens the door for each guest and politely lets him or her go up into his or her room. The doorman also opens the door as the guests leave the building and wishes them well. The doorman does not follow the guests up to their rooms or out into the streets. Similarly with SMINS we do not chase after thoughts, regardless of whether they are helpful or unhelpful.

At times it may seem as if our mind is overwhelmed with unhelpful and unwanted thoughts. Even though our mind may be flooded, we try, as much as possible, not to follow or get caught up in, or involved with these thoughts. As much as possible we try to step back from the thoughts and develop 'water off a duck's back mind' or a 'teflon mind'.[7] With this type of mind we do not get attached to unhelpful thoughts and they slide away.

As explained in the previous chapter serenity and insight practices often overlap, so that serenity practices also develop insight and insight practices also develop serenity. SMINS is considered a serenity practice because it involves the cultivation of relaxation, mental stability and clarity as the mind focuses on the space of the mind and its contents. However, it also develops insight as the practitioner begins to see and understand the three universal characteristics of existence: impermanence, uncertainty and interdependence.

The way of insight: understanding the nature of thought

In our previous example Pontip misinterpreted her social situations and felt that she was being judged by other people and therefore avoided social contact. Pontip risked spiralling into a deep depression.

Fortunately she was able to change both the content of her thoughts and her relationship to them. She utilised mindfulness and enquiry and she realised that there was no basis to believe the thoughts she was having, and so the credibility of the untrue thoughts simply faded away. For the most part, Pontip utilised an approach that was aligned with insight meditation. She also questioned the truthfulness of what she was thinking as in CT and CBT.

As explained in the previous chapter, practising mindfulness meditation can be a way to develop insight. Though it is possible to choose a specific object of attention to focus on, more generally the object that becomes the focus of attention is what presents itself as life unfolds. We shift into different sub-domains of mindfulness depending on the nature and context of what is arising. To understand thought and thinking processes, the third and the fourth applications of mindfulness are important. As explained in the previous chapter, the third application involves tracking all types of thoughts, feelings, emotions and states of heart-mind. The fourth application, mindfulness of phenomena, involves noticing patterns both helpful and harmful, understanding them and inclining towards increasing the helpful and reducing the unhelpful. There are various strategies we can use to help us with unhelpful thoughts and thinking patterns.

Noting thoughts

When we become aware of something we can make a mental note of it. In some schools of insight meditation, practitioners are encouraged to accompany mental notes with words that describe the experience. This tool for the cultivation of mindfulness was described in Chapter 2 as 'noting'. In the Mahasi Sayadaw approach to insight meditation a common primary object is the rising and falling of the breath at our abdomen. When we practise mindfulness of breath as an insight practice we can note 'thoughts' when they come and then come back to the breath when they no longer grab our attention. However, when thoughts seem to take over our attention, we can make thought the secondary object of attention. In other words we track and are attentive to thought rather than the breath. When we are attentive to thought we can note experience as 'thinking . . . thinking . . .' which helps to clearly identify the WHAT of our experience as well as enable us to step back and not get caught up in the thinking processes. Then we watch what happens. When and if the thoughts seem to fade away we can return to the primary object and track the changing experience of the breath. By being attentive to how attention gets pulled away from the breath we can gain insight about mental events. We can curiously question, for example, 'What are the conditions that keep us focused and what is it that pulls us away?' Sometimes, as we go back and forward between the primary and secondary objects, such as the breath and thoughts, we may notice patterns or themes arising and we can refine our noting process accordingly. We could, for example, note 'worry ... worrying' or 'rumination ... rumination' or another pattern, if this is what is happening. Sometimes practitioners go to the extent of categorising themes such as 'the worrying about my finances tape', 'the [mental] chewing over my relationship breakup track' and so on. As long as it does not become a hindrance to progress, the sub-vocal acknowledgement of what is happening with descriptive words can be very helpful for us to realise freedom and not get caught up in thoughts. Noting and naming are often good ways to catch destructive thoughts before they get out of control.

Curious enquiry with thoughts

The ability to investigate helps to dispel confusion (Pandita, 1992). Investigation can involve realistic and logical enquiry, as encouraged with CT, or it can involve curious and penetrative questioning that is not discursive. This latter type of enquiry does not involve thinking about thinking, in an analytical way, but in a way that quietly observes experience. Helpful enquiry often involves looking at cause–effect, action–consequence relationships. With investigation we can cultivate wisdom because we begin to learn what types of thought lead to happiness and what types of thought lead to being entangled in anguish, anxiety and depression.

For example, when experiencing distressing thoughts and emotions you can ask yourself, 'what is really happening here?', or 'what is the connection between these thoughts and these emotions?', or 'how do I behave when I am entangled in this type of thought?' With mindful investigation we can understand how being lost in unhelpful thoughts may cause despair, whereas engaging in other types of thoughts can lead to happy and peaceful states of mind. When we notice the relationship between a thought such as 'I am a failure at everything' and the consequent feelings of discouragement, we increase our ability to choose not to engage in that type of thinking and let it fade away. We could also mindfully track that thought so that we can understand what feeds it and what flows from it. If the mind is disturbed we can track back, with enquiry, to ask ourselves what the chain of events associated with the disturbance was. Once discovered, we may be able to resolve our disturbance by seeing alternative perspectives. Sometimes it is possible to use concentrated investigation to enquire about what the underlying beliefs that cause distress are. For example, if certain thoughts keep returning, you can ask yourself, or reflect on, what might be driving these thoughts. With investigation, you may discover clinging, attachment or aversion or notice a core belief around an experience is often behind thoughts that keep returning. With concentrated investigation it is also possible to uncover some origins of maladaptive beliefs, such as a significant life event. Such discoveries could answer the WHYs of our thoughts and thinking patterns.

Enquiry can be silent and accompany mindfulness in a way that the tracking of thoughts is completely allowing and uncensored. When thoughts are allowed to unfold we can begin to see into both the content of the thought and the nature of thought as reflecting the three characteristics of existence: impermanence, uncertainty and interdependence.

Curious enquiry can also be retrospective. That is, we can recollect past events and thus gain understanding about our thoughts, emotions and behaviours and their relationships. In some schools of insight meditation, the practitioner is invited to do nothing and simply let the mental events unfold uncensored and unimpeded in an allowing and gentle way. Then, at the end of the meditation session the practitioner recollects the experience, often making a journal of the recollections.[8] The process of remembering a meditation session and journalling it helps to make clear what was previously not clear and thus helps us gain insight.

Insight with thoughts

We need not focus on thoughts in order to develop insight about them. Seeing the impermanence of a falling autumn leaf, can for example, be generalised to knowing the fleeting change and emptiness of an unhelpful thinking pattern, and so not taking this pattern personally and not fuelling it. Though ACT practitioners may not make reference to insight the way Buddhists do, it seems that insight into the characteristics of existence is a therapeutic feature of ACT. Proponents of ACT describe many innovative and creative techniques (such as singing a negative thought in a cartoon character voice) to help individuals 'de-fuse' from toxic thoughts (e.g. Luoma et al., 2007). We 'fuse' with these experiences when we take them literally. From a Buddhist perspective, these techniques can lead to having insight about the nature of thoughts and other experience and seeing clearly that they are not who or what we are.

Other third wave therapies such as MBCT make more direct reference to terms that are shared with a Buddhist approach. One of the aims of MBCT is the development of 'meta-cognitive insight'. Meta-cognitive insight refers to being able to see that the thoughts we experience are not necessarily facts to be believed (Teasdale et al., 2002). When we realise that we need not believe the content of destructive thoughts as facts, we are able to short-circuit descending spirals into depression. Meta-cognitive insight involves shifting the focus to the relationship with thoughts rather than their content, and seeing the general unreliability (the second universal characteristic) of these events. When we can see that thoughts are just thoughts, changing mental events, and not necessarily facts to be believed, we are able to stop believing them and no longer take them personally.

Perhaps the most interesting thoughts to enquire into are those which are self concepts, the thoughts about who and what we are. A central theme of the Buddha's teachings is the study of the self, and understanding the impermanent, interdependent and unreliable nature of our self concepts. There is much that can be said about this topic of curious investigation and it will be discussed more in Chapter 6 of this book under the heading 'Contemplating the self'.

Working with worry

It is important that we acknowledge worry when it arises. There may be a valid reason for our worry and an issue may need attention in the form of calm and effective problem solving. When we acknowledge worry we are in a better position to work productively with it.

Believing in the content of our worry and our beliefs about worry is reduced when we get contrary evidence. If we investigate and experiment, we may realise that what we are worrying about may not be true. This requires us to have the willingness to allow worry to be present and not avoid it by rushing around with often-futile attempts to make it better. Paradoxically, if we can tolerate uncertainty, the habits that reinforce worry can be reduced. This ultimately means that when unwanted worrying thoughts arise, we do nothing. By doing nothing the avoidance is not reinforced. It can be very hard to do nothing, and it requires resolve to let thoughts come and go without reacting to them. It also requires being able to let go of unnecessary and painful emotional reactions. To do this we need to respond wisely to uncomfortable physical sensations rather than engage in denial or catastrophic reactivity.

Mindfulness naturally counters the tendency to be preoccupied with conceptual, future oriented fears. Mindfulness helps us to be particularly aware of the tendency to worry, short-circuit this tendency, confront avoidance, reduce reactivity and gain a helpful perspective.

From a meditative perspective, the fourth hindrance as mentioned in the last chapter is restlessness and worry. Strategies to negotiate peace with this hindrance include developing a calm mind using serenity practices. Doing enjoyable activities and bringing happy themes to mind and focusing on these themes are ways to focus one's mind and cultivate calm. Endeavouring to act blamelessly, ensuring that one's actions are as impeccable as one can achieve, with a commitment to avoid harm are other ways to manage worry about things. When we act wisely, we have less to worry about. Bare attention, as described earlier, is considered as another way to work with restlessness and worry. As will be described in the next chapter about emotions, bringing curious and kindly attention to the experience and getting to know it through un-entangled contemplation is another way to work with this obstacle to peace and contentment.

If we can relax with worry by doing some yoga, getting a massage or practising a full body mindfulness of breath, this can be very helpful. Being able to compartmentalise things that one is worrying about by putting aside a time to problem solve the worrying issue is also very helpful. Choose a specific time to think about the issue and at other times during the day when the tendency to worry arises, simply note it and put it aside.

Working with rumination

Much of what has been written above about worry can also be applied to rumination. As always it is very helpful to firstly acknowledge and clarify WHAT is happening, and we can also use noting to help. Remember, most thinking patterns are fuelled by us engaging with them. Therefore we can choose to put our attention elsewhere. As with the serenity approach, we can consciously put aside, or postpone the issue we are thinking about and place our attention elsewhere. Probably the best place to place attention is with whatever we are experiencing in the five physical senses or with what we are doing. That is, remember the purpose of an activity and bring attention back to the present. We could also choose to do something that is very engaging such as an enjoyable activity. With rumination, doing some strong physical exercise is particularly helpful. Not only may it change the biochemistry associated with depression but it easily draws atten tion away from being caught up in loopy thinking.

Ultimately a way to cope with worry and rumination is to culti- vate tolerance and acceptance of these tendencies, without rejection or condemnation, by developing a sense of acceptance, kindness and compassion with ourselves and our temperaments. Paradoxically, this not only reduces the likelihood that we will be hijacked by worry and rumination but also that these patterns will arise at all.

Working with intrusive traumatic memories

There are many different types of therapies to help reduce the pain and suffering associated with the after-effects of experiencing traumas. Usually they involve a holistic approach that incorporates working with the body and emotions because traumas activate biological survival mechanisms. They also often involve the nourishment of social supports such as friends and family, because this is an important, if not essential, component of post trauma healing. Working with painfully intrusive thoughts is just one important component of recovery. Both the serenity and the insight approach can help us find peace with intrusive traumatic thoughts. The serenity approach helps to give respite from these experi- ences as well as provide the necessary relaxation and calm required to repair the physiological damage that chronic stress creates. The insight approach helps to us review, process and provide new meaning to trau- matic past events so that the pain and anguish associated with them can be released. When we apply the insight approach to the traumatic mem- ories we need to be sensitive to the timeliness of the work. If we are not willing and/or able, the work can backfire and make the situation worse by re-sensitising us to the trauma(s). It is usually best to begin with the serenity approach including compassion, because this approach can give us the calm and supportive resources to cope with what is difficult to bear (e.g. Lee and James, 2012). The final outcome of using the insight approach with painful memories is not that we wipe the memories clean from our minds, but we relate to the experiences in a way that we are free from the *dukkha* associated with them.

Possible serenity-based approaches for intrusive traumatic thoughts

A serenity approach develops a sense that we have more control or choice to engage or not engage with the painful thoughts. A serenity practice, such as mindfulness of the breath, could provide an alternative to thoughts as an object of attention. If one is able, mindfulness of breath also naturally calms and soothes physical and emotional distress. Another serenity approach is to create a special safe place in one's mind, a place that is safe and far away from harm, a place that is restorative, centring, healing and if populated, also has beings who are caring and compassionate. This may involve creative imagination and visualisation, and be linked to an actual place one has been or people who are symbols of care and compassion for us.

Another way to gain a sense of choice with thoughts is to become creative with the imagery, sounds and words of the intrusive memories. Many contemporary psychologies incorporate this approach to help people find some peace with the torment that intrusive memories can bring. One example is pretending that the memories are like a video that we watch on a screen, but we have the power to edit the video, change it from colour to black and white, zoom in and out, turn down the volume or make it mute, play it back to front, fast forward, alter the script, add music, make the script as if it is sung to a cheerful tune or whatever we choose. This playful and creative approach helps to provide a different perspective and a sense of mastery. It also nurtures the ability to choose to engage or disengage.[9]

Possible insight-based approaches to traumatic intrusive thoughts

An insight approach to traumatic memories does not necessarily involve creatively changing our focus or the content of our thoughts, but focuses more on shifting our attention towards the memories. When traumatic memories intrude into consciousness we can note them strongly and with resolve. For example, we could note 'just memories . . . just memories' loud and clear or if there is a visual component to the memory 'just seeing . . . seeing'. When there is an auditory component to the memories we could note: 'just hearing hearing' or 'just the memory of sounds . . . just words'. Sometimes the noting can be accompanied by supportive self-counselling, such as: 'these thoughts are not facts to be believed, they are just illusive memories conjured up by my mind'. Then with kind and courageous resolve turn the mind to the memories and stay with them, track how they change, practise *satipatthana* and see them for what they are and not what they compel you to believe about them. They are just memories and the power they have over us is only the power we give them. Practising *satipatthana* with painful memories is ultimately one very powerful way to be free.

Working with obsessive thinking

As is the case with all potentially problematic thinking patterns, honest acknowledgement is a beginning step in finding liberating space with obsessive thinking. Remember that one way obsessions are reinforced is by acting on the compulsions often associated with this pattern of thought. Therefore, as much is as possible, we try to refrain from neutralising the obsessions by acting on the compulsions. If the discomfort of not acting on the compulsions can be tolerated, then eventually it will become less and less, and the obsessions will lose their grip and possibly fade away. Gaining the insight that thoughts are not necessarily facts to be believed can be particularly helpful with all destructive thinking patterns, obsessions included. Though noting can be helpful with obsessions, we should be careful that the obsessive patterns do not get transferred to the activity of noting. For those inclined towards obsessive thinking, noting could become another unhelpful behavioural ritual, with the distorted belief that the sub-vocal acknowledgement of the pattern will somehow neutralise the obsession. Furthermore, obsession and perfectionism often go together and we could become obsessed with finding the correct words to note the experience with. We could elaborate the experience so much so that accurate and excessive noting becomes the aim of the exercise rather than it merely being a tool for mindfulness. With obsessive patterns the approach should be loose and open, rather than tight and focused. When obsessive thinking arises, and it is not necessary for the situation, it is helpful just to notice in a casual way thereby not giving it the attention that may in fact reinforce it. Somewhat like an uninvited and unwanted guest at a party, you know that the guest is there, but you do not go up and talk to him and thus reinforce his behaviour. Like other patterns, one way to step back and get disentangled with the obsessions is by investing attention in something other than the obsessions. If one feels totally unable to shift attention then the insight approach is the only option. When we feel able, it helps to investigate and look directly at the obsessions, thus developing understanding. This choice, however, will require courageous resolve to tolerate discomfort and so not act in a way that will fuel the obsessions.

Guided meditation: settling the mind in its natural state

Begin by making the intention to practise settling the mind in its natural state and establish your posture so that it is comfortable and at ease. Let your practice be filled with the three qualities of relaxation, stillness and clarity as you settle into your body and allow the breath to find its own natural rhythm.

(Silence)

Bring bare attention to the space of the body, observing sensations arise and pass without distraction and without grasping. Let sensations be as they are without preference and gently open your eyes, gazing vacantly in the space in front of you, and bring bare attention to the visual realm, just as you would observe an abstract painting, notice shapes and colours, tones of dark and light. Put aside concepts about the objects you are seeing and bring bare attention to the raw experience of seeing.

(Silence)

Now without denying the visual field, turn your attention to the domain of hearing. Be attentive to sound as sound or vibration. Bring attention to the sounds of your own body, the close vicinity around you and also sounds that seem off at a distance. Be alert but relaxed and receive sound as it comes to you. There may be sounds of your breath, the ring in your ears, your body as it moves, the sounds of birds, cars, traffic, air conditioning, wind, rain or just the hum of silence. Notice how you may create images and labels around the sound such as: dog barking, traffic, birds or whatever. Don't struggle with the labelling and the pictures but distinguish the sound from the label. Let the labelling or pictures be on the edge of your awareness and direct your attention to sound as vibration.

(Silence)

Now turn your attention to the domain of mental experience – ideas, thoughts and images. With the same open and spacious perspective you may have had with seeing and hearing, observe and listen to the contents of your mind, your thoughts. Notice commenting, evaluating, appraising, judging, planning, calculating, day-dreaming, remembering, catastrophising, overgeneralising, personalising or whatever type of thinking you may experience. Notice thoughts as if they are clouds passing across an expansive sky. Arising, changing, passing and disappearing from view. Or, observe thoughts like birds flying across the sky, sometimes flitting around then moving on. Sometimes just gliding through space. They leave no trace. Sometimes it is as if thoughts babble on like a never-ending stream. Step back from the stream and notice the stream pass by. Notice the thoughts but resist the temptation to dive in and follow the thought. Sometimes, thoughts are like placards in a parade, each having a message, each inviting you in to join the parade. Resist the urge to join the parade and notice messages as thoughts just passing by. There is no need to get caught up in the drama. Let the thoughts come and go. Step back to a place of witnessing and watching the show. Notice how some thoughts are pleasant and some thoughts are unpleasant. Endeavour not to grasp after the pleasant or struggle with the unpleasant. No matter what arises simply observe and listen without distraction, without straying into the other senses. Remember that even frightening thoughts are just thoughts and they only have power over you if you choose to give them this power, they are just thoughts. Don't try to control the thoughts just let them be completely uncensored, with a sense of allowing and gentleness. When you get caught up in thoughts notice the excitation and release any grasping and relax more deeply. At times you might find yourself getting spaced-out and the mind becoming dull or lethargic. When this happens freshly arouse your attention and focus back on the space of the mind and whatever arises within it. Be at peace with thought, regardless of the content. Let disturbing and entangled thoughts disentangle and let the mind settle into its own natural state.

(Silence)

In a few moments we will end this exercise. If you found settling the mind in its natural state helpful in any way, remember what you did and remember you can practise this practice whenever the time is right for you.

So now let's bring this session to a close.

Guided meditation: mindfulness of thoughts to develop insight

Put your body at ease in a posture that is comfortable and set the intention that for the next 15–20 minutes you will settle your body and mind with mindfulness of breath and then you will cultivate insight by bringing curious enquiry to thoughts. Now, let the respiration settle into its own natural rhythm, and relax tension with every out breath. Breathing in and out, relaxing and settling the mind, let go of worries and concerns. Settle your mind in a state of ease, as you release your concerns about the past and the hopes about the future. Set your mind at ease by letting it come to rest in stillness in the present moment.

(Silence)

Now you are invited to let your eyes be at least partly open, gaze blankly into the space in front of you and bring curious attention to the contents of your mind, your thoughts. Settle back and relax like an old man in a park watching clouds pass by. Simply bring curious interest to the flow of nature without trying to change it in any way. Try as best you can to be open to thoughts without preference or condemnation and develop a curious interest about the passing show.

(Silence)

Endeavour not to be pulled into the story that thought can create, and also remain alert, not losing clarity, clearly observing and listening to the flow of thoughts. Observe and listen to thoughts from a place of silent awareness and curious interest. Notice thoughts as if they are clouds passing across an expansive sky. Arising, changing, passing and disappearing from view. Or, observe thoughts like birds flying across the sky, sometimes flitting around then moving on, gliding through space leaving no trace. See thoughts as changing events against the backdrop of spaciousness.

Watch and listen without getting entangled in commenting, evaluating, appraising, judging, planning, calculating, daydreaming, remembering, catastrophising, over-generalising, personalising or whatever type of thinking you may experience. Sometimes there are too many thoughts to note individually. Sometimes it is as if thoughts babble on like a never-ending stream, or like a raging waterfall. Step back from the stream and notice the stream pass by or let the water fall wash over you. Notice the thoughts but resist the temptation to dive in and follow the thought, or be washed away.

Notice how thoughts may tell a story, like a drama, and how we are always in a leading role. Notice how some thoughts lead to emotions and some emotions lead to thoughts. Notice the inter-connections between thoughts and other experiences. Notice and be receptive even to those thoughts that may lead to fear. Try not to struggle with thoughts, no matter how frightening they may be. They are only thoughts. Thoughts only have power over us if we choose to give them this power. Remember that you are not your thoughts. Thoughts are thoughts and they change. Let painful thoughts change without getting caught up in the struggle. Take refuge from tormenting and painful thoughts by stepping back into a place of silent and peaceful awareness.

(Silence)

Bring curious enquiry to thoughts, be attentive to them without getting caught up and taken away or losing clarity. Simply bring curious enquiry to these mental events.

Ask yourself:

- Are thoughts permanent, lasting forever or do they change?
- How do thoughts form and develop and how do they change and pass?
- Where do they come from and where do they go?
- Are thoughts independent or do they change in a way that is dependent on and influenced by other experiences such as what we see, hear, smell, taste, feel and experience?
- Do our emotions influence what and how we think and do our thoughts influence our emotions?
- Are our thoughts about ourselves and the world completely reliable and true or is there room for uncertainty?
- Are thoughts sometimes illusive?
- Are our thoughts a dependable and reliable source of enduring happiness?

Bring curious attentiveness to the experience of thought.

Dwell in a mindful position of quiet and curious interest and allow insight to develop.

(Silence)

Find peace in understanding and being able to watch and listen to thought from a place of awareness and curious, quiet investigation.

In a few moments we will end this exercise. When we finish, before you go about your normal daily activities spend a few moments recollecting the past 15–20 minutes and reflecting on the insights you have gained.

Thank you.

Notes

1 I describe how aspirations for happiness are a part of loving-kindness meditation practices in the companion book in progress with a working title of: 'Harmonious Human Relationships and the Buddha's Path of Warm Friendliness, Compassion, Joy and Peace'.
2 Nanananda (1997, p. 4) in Chaskalson (2006).
3 Creative imagination like this is often used as kindling thoughts in meditation practices based on the four divine abodes: loving kindness, compassion, appreciative joy and equanimity.
4 I am grateful to Dr B. Alan Wallace for providing clarity about this as well as other meditation practices.
5 By Dr B. Alan Wallace on a *shamatha* retreat at Phuket, Thailand in 2010.
6 Ibid.
7 Marsha Linehan the developer of DBT created this analogy.
8 This particular approach is one taught by Jason Siff, who has developed a meditation practice called 'Recollective Awareness'. See Siff (2010).
9 I would like to express gratitude to Dr Wayne Somerville for sharing his clarity and knowledge about an approach to PTSD that he developed called Cognitive Control Therapy (CCT). CCT works on similar principles.

References

American Psychiatric Association (2013). *Diagnostic and Statistic Manual of Mental Disorders, Fifth Edition.* Washington, DC: American Psychiatric Association.
Chaskalson, M. (2006). Aspects of Buddhist psychology and its application to the mindfulness-based approaches. International Conference on Mindfulness and Acceptance. Bangor, UK.
Goldstein, J. (1976). *The Experience of Insight.* Boulder, CO: Shambala.
Lee, D. and James, S. (2012). *The Compassionate Mind Approach to Recovering from Trauma Using Compassion Focused Therapy.* London: Robinson.
Luoma, J. B., Hayes, S. C. and Walser, R. D. (2007). *Learning ACT: An Acceptance & Commitment Therapy Skills Training Manual for Therapists.* Oakland, CA: New Harbinger.
Pandita, S. U. (1992). *In This Very Life: The Liberation Teaching of the Buddha.* Boston, MA: Wisdom Publications.

Siff, J. (2010). *Unlearning Meditation: What to Do When Instructions Get in the Way*. Boston, MA: Shambala.

Suzuki, S. (1970). *Zen Mind, Beginner's Mind*. New York: Weatherhill.

Teasdale, J. D., Moore. R. G., Hayhurst, H., Pope.M., Williams.S. and Segal, Z. (2002). Metacognitive awareness and prevention of relapse in depression: Empirical evidence. *Journal of Consulting and Clinical Psychology* 70: 2 275–87.

Wallace, B. A. (2006). *The Attention Revolution: Unlocking the Power of the Focussed Mind*. Somerville, MA: Wisdom Publications.

5 Emotions

Taming the destructive and cultivating balance

Chapter overview

As the title states, this chapter is about emotions, how to reduce destructive emotions and cultivate helpful emotions. To begin with we will look at what we mean by emotions and explore what we know of emotions from a contemporary scientific perspective and a traditional Buddhist perspective. The chapter will outline how mindfulness can be used to balance our emotions and short-circuit dysfunctional emotions. We will explore anger, fear, sadness and happiness in detail and how mindfulness can be used to understand and balance these emotions. The chapter will conclude by offering some strategies for working with painful emotions.

What are emotions?

The word emotion originates from the Latin *emovere*, which means to disturb. The first part of the word, '*e*' means 'out', and '*movere*' translates as 'to move'. When we need to function effectively in a demanding world, emotions move us to action. There is no direct Pali equivalent for the term 'emotion'. Rather emotions are understood as a combination of physical sensations, feelings (*vedana*), states of heart-mind (*citta*) and mental and physical patterns. Emotions involve complex body–mind interactions.

Emotions are necessary for our personal development, survival and thriving as human beings. They save lives, motivate behaviour and help us form relationships. Balanced emotions are essential for effective communication and the welfare and wellbeing of our families and communities. Unfortunately emotions can be unbalanced, dysfunctional, painful and destructive. At times, emotions can move us to act unskilfully with dire consequences. Emotions can arise and pass relatively quickly. Though it is possible to cultivate and reinforce emotions they often come uninvited. That is, they may come up in a way that seems out of our control because they are either 'hard wired' (part of our neurological–biological–mental systems) or they are conditioned. When we experience an emotion it focuses our attention on the task at hand but it can also bias our perceptions. When we are frightened, for example, there may be a bias to see things that confirm our fear. When we are angry nothing seems to go right and it seems as if the world is against us. When we are sad the world seems negative and when we smile the whole world seems to smile with us. If we are happy everything seems fine.

Emotions: a contemporary perspective

Paul Ekman, one of the world's leading authorities on emotions,[1] describes an emotion as a process influenced by evolution and our personal past that is triggered when we sense something important to our welfare is happening. This results in physiological changes and behaviours to deal with the situation. Ekman describes an emotion episode timeline as the coming together of: the environment, an emotional alert database, automatic appraisal, a trigger, an affect program and a refractory period.[2]

As the name implies a trigger is something that initiates an emotional experience. Some triggers are 'hard wired' or embedded into our emotional systems due to evolution and our genetic inheritance. For example, everyone will express a fear response when they unexpectedly fall backwards. Such a fear reaction is 'hard wired' because we did not need to learn it. Many triggers, however, are learned due to our upbringing and our own unique individual experiences. The emotional alert database is like our own experience library. It contains hardwired or universal triggers, but is mostly filled with triggers that have been learned. Past emotional experiences are embedded in our memory. We automatically appraise the environment by searching for anything that resembles the memories stored in the emotion alert database. Once the automatic appraiser recognises a trigger the affect program begins. The affect program is our emotional response to a situation. There are many affect programs and they vary depending on the emotion that they relate to. Once an emotion has begun there will be a period of time in which it will continue. This period of time is called the refractory period. During the refractory period perception may be narrowed or distorted and our thinking cannot incorporate information that doesn't fit with or justify the emotion. Focused attention on a problem is beneficial in the short term, but if it outlasts its usefulness it can lead to inaccurate perceptions and inappropriate emotional behaviours. Ekman[3] suggests the refractory period may be increased by lack of sleep, alcohol, work stress, a buildup of unresolved resentments and importing 'scripts' from earlier life experience so that they colour the current situation. Therefore ways to reduce the refractory period include living a healthy lifestyle, communicating clearly and being mindful.

In his research Ekman (2003) identified seven basic emotions that have universal facial expressions. These are sadness, anger, fear, surprise, disgust, contempt and happiness. Emotions can be distinguished from moods, traits and disorders. Emotions and moods can influence each other but generally moods are longer lasting than emotions. Similarly traits are more enduring than emotions or moods and tend to colour a person's perception. Disorders occur when emotions become unbalanced. For example, the emotion of fear may have the corresponding mood of apprehension, which may persist to become a trait of shyness and could result in a disorder such as chronic panic attacks.

Emotions: a neurobiological perspective

We know that emotions are often experienced in the body. Sadness, for example, may be felt as heaviness in the chest and the body and fear as churning 'butterflies' in the tummy or shaky legs. Anger is often felt as a tightening of the arm muscles, shoulders and chest and happiness may be described as a sense of light buoyancy throughout the body. From a neurobiological perspective emotions are visceral experiences directed by the brain involving a cascade of biological responses including neural connections and biochemical interactions. At the beginning of the chapter it was stated that emotions save lives, motivate behaviour and help us form relationships. To do this, emotions function within three interrelated systems (Gilbert, 2009; Hanson, 2013).

1. **Avoid, Survival System** (fight, flight and freeze).
2. **Approach, Resource Seeking System** (pursuing and wanting).
3. **Attach, Relationship System** (bonding, safety, soothing).

The first system is related to our basic survival responses. This system includes emotions such as fear, anger and disgust and responses to threat and danger such as the flight, fight or freeze responses. The main biochemicals related to this system are adrenaline, nor-epinephrine and cortisol.[4] These biochemicals are responsible for changes in our bodies such as increased heart rate, alertness, hyper-vigilance and an increased blood flow to the arms and legs in order to hit out, fight or flee danger.

The second system relates to motivation, pleasure and reward. This system includes emotions related to drive, excitement and vitality. The main biochemical in this system is dopamine. Dopamine plays a major role in reward-motivated behaviour. An imbalance in this system may result in depression at one end of the spectrum and addictions at the other end.

The third system relates to feeling safe and developing relationships with others. We feel safe when we are protected, our basic needs are met and we have a sense of belonging. The emotions in this system are related to feelings of contentment, safety and connection and are essential for human health, wellbeing and flourishing. The main biochemical of this system, oxytocin, has a function of soothing distress. The cultivation of loving kindness and compassion are integral components of the Buddha's eight-fold path[5] and represent the development of this emotion system at refined levels.

The three systems are interrelated and when balanced, work together to maintain our safety and wellbeing (Figure 5.1).

Mindfulness of emotions: a traditional perspective

According to traditional Buddhist texts, there are thousands of different states of heart-mind. These range from refined and subtle states of mind, such as sublime peacefulness, to coarse states of mind such as angry rage. Some of these states of mind would be considered as emotions and some would not. As was stated at the beginning of the chapter, in Buddhism emotions are understood as a combination of physical sensations, feelings (*vedana*), states of heart-mind (*citta*) and mental and physical patterns. As mentioned in Chapter 3, feeling (*vedana*) refers to the pleasant, unpleasant or neither pleasant nor unpleasant aspects of all experience. Feelings have the capacity to move us, as when we say, 'that was very moving', or 'I was moved by that'. Feeling, therefore, refers to the aspect of experience that moves us, that stimulates a response.

Feelings in the Buddhist sense and emotions as we understand them in contemporary psychology are not the same. They are, however, related. What they have in common is that they represent the aspect of life that moves us to act. In the context of *satipatthana*, mindfulness of feeling opens us up to the world of stimulus and response, to the

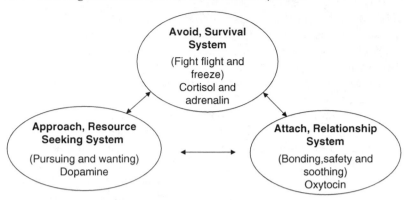

Figure 5.1 The three emotional systems
Source: adapted from Gilbert (2009) and Hanson (2013)

fact *that* we are moved to act and *how* we are moved to act. This in turn can stimulate wisdom, understanding *why* we are moved to act. Mindfulness of feeling is central to working with emotions. It is also central to short-circuit reactive cycles that often involve emotions.[6] The process of taming destructive emotions and cultivating emotional balance requires the skilful application of all four domains of mindfulness. However, the second and third applications of mindfulness are, perhaps, most relevant to emotions.

Contemplating feeling: the second application of mindfulness

Feeling (*vedana*) refers to the pleasant, unpleasant or neutral aspects of experience. We could compare feeling to flavour. When we eat, we experience the physical sensations of the food, its hardness, softness, texture, moisture and so on. We also experience the flavour of the food. Although flavour is distinct from these sensations, it is intimately connected with them. It is the flavour that moves us. We are moved to take more if the flavour is pleasant; we are moved to take less if the flavour is unpleasant; and we are moved to indifference if we can't find any flavour. But what moves us, what stimulates a response, is flavour. Feeling is like the flavour of experience.[7]

According to the *suttas* the Buddha says there are three fundamental aspects of feeling, and these stimulate the three fundamental movements of the heart-mind. These are: pleasant feeling, which moves us to grasp; painful feeling, which moves us to resist or reject; and neither-painful-nor-pleasant feeling, where we don't know what we are feeling, and are moved to dullness, doubt or confusion.

Feelings are not emotions as they are considered in our everyday language, nor are they physical sensations. *Vedana*, the Pali term used for feelings, is often mistakenly translated as sensations. Unfortunately, this translation can be confused with physical experiences of the body such as pressure, heat, movement and so on. Feelings are not solely physical or mental but more like a bridge between body and mind that can be triggered by physical or mental experience.

If we trip and graze a hand and it hurts it may give rise to unpleasant feelings. In this case the unpleasant feelings arise from a physical object. If on the other hand, someone we like smiles kindly at us, and we experience pleasant feelings, it is more related to mental experiences. In some rare cases, what would normally be considered as painful physical sensations, may actually give rise to pleasant feelings. For example, when we get a massage and the masseuse digs into a tight muscle, it may hurt but it also 'feels' good.

Since feelings arise dependent upon conditions that are beyond our control, we cannot control our feelings. We can, however, influence the way we respond to our feelings. Understanding that a feeling is 'just a feeling' can short-circuit the tendency to over-react. For example, pain management may often entail an accepting and peaceful state of mind despite experiencing painful feelings arising from the body. Similarly, as will be clarified in the next chapter, 'urge surfing', which can help substance abusers interrupt the cycles of their addictions, involves mindfulness of feeling.

Contemplating heart-mind: the third application of mindfulness

In the context of mindfulness practice, heart-mind represents our inner state; how we are, at this time. Mindfulness reveals the current situation of our heart-mind, how its naturally transparent awareness is affected by what is arising within it at the time. Is the heart-mind coloured by the wholesome or the unwholesome? What kind of wholesome? What kind of unwholesome? In the contemporary context, this practice entails mindfulness of the thoughts, moods and emotions we find within ourselves.

As explained earlier, contemplation is a translation of the word *upassati* (Pali) which means to: 'to repeatedly look at' or 'to closely observe' or 'see along with' or 'track'.[8] Contemplating the heart-mind or *citta* involves tracking our inner centre of subjectivity. The essence of the heart-mind is awareness or consciousness. An undisturbed heart-mind is compared to a mountain lake, where the water is clear and undisturbed. A person standing on the bank of such a lake could look into it and see clearly to its bottom, seeing fish, plants, rocks and pebbles.[9] On the other hand, the disturbed heart-mind is compared to water mixed with colour or mud, covered with algae, stirred up by the wind or heated until it is boiling.[10] In these situations, the water's natural transparency is lost. According to His Holiness the Dalai Lama the nature of *citta* is luminous and aware. It knows, and it illuminates the objects that it knows. It is also able to illuminate itself. It is easy to confuse the nature of heart-mind with the states that it is coloured by. Mindfulness clarifies this confusion.

In the *Satipathana Sutta*, the Buddha described many sub-domains of the third application of mindfulness. He recommended being mindful of the heart-mind in all its manifestations: wholesome and unwholesome, helpful and unhelpful, gross and subtle.

We have a strong tendency to identify with our heart-mind, to create identity from the movements within it. Contemplating heart-mind helps provide some space from this identification. It reins in the tendency for destructive emotions to run rampant and construct a dysfunctional identity. Mindfully tracking the changing nature of destructive and painful emotions helps us to break reactive patterns often associated with them.

Mindfulness of heart-mind

Ensure that you are at ease with your posture and your body is free from constriction and discomfort. Set the intention that for the next 15–20 minutes you will first ground yourself with mindfulness of body practices then shift your attention to monitoring and contemplating the heart-mind. Know also that being mindful of heart-mind can include being aware of emotions as they arise and pass away, moment to moment.

Let awareness centre on a chosen primary object. The object could be sitting or the rising and falling of your abdomen. It could be strong sensations in your body or sounds. Whatever you choose let that object be like an anchor or a place of reference where you can bring your attention back when you need to. Allow your attention to be open and accepting and be with experience moment to moment. Note whatever is happening in an open-minded, soft, yet clear and distinct manner.

(Silence)

Just as a stage may have many performers and props but a spotlight focuses on only one part of the stage, let the spotlight of your awareness focus on the state of your heart-mind. Do not reject other experiences, but let the state of your heart-mind be the focus of attention. You can shift your attention to rest around the area of your chest if you wish, but let the central focus be on the state of your heart-mind or the general flavour, colour or atmosphere of your mood.

Just as a caring and kind healer may pay attention to the state of your body, bring kind and curious attention to the state of your heart-mind. What are you experiencing right now in the domain of moods, emotions and mental states? Tune in to your heart and ask yourself what is happening here right now. In a manner that is kind, spacious and allowing, ask yourself what am I experiencing in this moment? Try not to identify with the experience. Do not take it personally but see it as it is as a changing event. Try not to be hijacked by thoughts about the experience and as best you can, tune in to the state of your heart-mind.

Is your heart peaceful and calm, or is it disturbed by craving and longing?

Is the state of your mind contracted and frightened or is it open and expansive with qualities of generosity and kindness?

Is the state of your mind, aversive, prickly, frustrated or angry, condemning and judgemental? Or is it loving, open, kind, soft and accepting?

Is the predominant state of mind, sad, depressed and miserable or is it buoyant, light and joyful?

Is it confused and uncertain, restless and distracted or is it clear, confident, calm and focused?

What is the state of your heart-mind right now? Be allowing and open and try to note and name the state of mind objectively and accurately.

(Silence)

Once you have identified the current state of your heart-mind, monitor how it changes.

If there are physical sensations arising in relationship to the state of the heart-mind, tune in to how it feels in your body and notice how this experience changes. Sometimes the state may intensify, and sometimes it may subside. Be content with whatever happens. Try not to grasp after the pleasant or reject and condemn the unpleasant. Simply be allowing and see states of mind as they are without making them more than what they are by thinking unrealistically about them. Notice how the experience arises, changes and passes by.

Rest in awareness of the changing aspects of the heart-mind. Simply be present for the heart of your experience and let it come and go by taking refuge in the quality of awake awareness.

Resting in awareness you can hold and cradle any painful experience with kindness and care. Simply let painful states of mind be. Remember that they are not you and that they change. Let go of struggle and let the experience be. When you give the experience space it is as if you take refuge in awareness. Firmly grounded in mindfulness you can be deeply peaceful with all experience.

By taking refuge in awareness it is possible to tolerate pain. Take refuge in your awareness and allow awareness to be your stable point of reference. It is as if this witnessing is deep and still within the roots of your being. Let awareness be like a solid and stable mountain in the midst of a windy storm. Let awareness be like the still depths of a lake when the surface is turbulent or like a solid island rock in the middle of a rough ocean with strong waves. The states of mind are like waves – coming and going, arising with a distinct energy then rolling on by and changing to something else.

Note the presence of an emotion and name or label it if you can.

Because emotions change they are not you.

Step back, get unstuck from the experience, give it space.

Let it be and let it change. Be at peace with the experience.

(Silence)

Without being caught up, develop curiosity about what is happening when this emotion arises. Also notice how your body feels in response to the emotion. Use noting to help you step back and investigate the experience. Look at and see the experience for what it is, as it is, rather than getting caught up in its story.

If the experience is painful or uncomfortable allow the power of compassion to help you bear and tolerate the distress. Let compassionate awareness be like an open house and see the state of mind like a visitor. Honour it and let it be felt in the body. But then let the door open and let the state pass through.

(Silence)

Resting in a perspective of awareness, nurture wholesome states of mind. Try not to grasp after them. Without you getting in the road, joy and peace can arise naturally and without effort.

Whether the changing states of your heart-mind are wholesome and pleasant or painful and difficult to bear, be kind and spacious with the experience.

Simply stay present and note the experience with openness, compassion and care.

Be like a solid rock island in the ocean.

Be like the still depth of a lake.

Be like a solid mountain.

'Be' with the experience and let it roll by.

Be present completely here and now practising mindfulness of heart-mind.

When you lose mindfulness simply remember to focus your attention, notice how things change, then with equanimity monitor the changing states of the heart.

(Silence 2–3 minutes or as long as you need)

In a few moments this meditation session will come to a close. If you have found it useful in any way remember that you can practise mindfulness as you need in your busy daily activities. Thank you for your attention and may mindfulness of the heart-mind bring peace and joy to all.

Taming the destructive and cultivating balanced emotions

Emotions can be balanced, constructive and functional or they can be out of balance, destructive and dysfunctional. When they are out of balance they can be excessive or deficient. Out of balance, dysfunctional and destructive emotions are evident in a few different ways, such as when we feel and show the right emotion but at the wrong intensity (e.g. over-reacting), or for an unsuitable length of time. When an emotion is out of balance we may have the appropriate response, but express it in a hurtful way such as with passive aggression. Unbalanced emotions are also demonstrated when an emotion is triggered but it is not the right emotion for the job. Emotional imbalance could also occur when the wrong emotions are running rife. Extremes of elation and depression, hope and fear, adulation and contempt, and infatuation and aversion could be examples of emotional excesses. Cold indifference towards self and others when compassion and kindness are needed may be an example of an emotional deficit.

Related story: Bec tames the destructive

Rebecca, or 'Bec', was a 28-year-old employed artist who was generally happy with her life. She did, however, feel her emotions were out of control. In particular she was inclined to frightening outbursts of anger in which she often smashed household objects. Bec was in a relationship and feared that one day she would strike her partner in a fit of rage and thereby destroy a relationship she valued dearly.

Bec was highly motivated to change what she saw as destructive emotions and decided to seek help. She attended individual therapy sessions and a mindfulness programme. In the individual sessions Bec was supported to process painful emotions and memories of childhood sexual abuse. Through mindfulness and compassionate awareness she came to understand triggers for her outbursts such as when she was feeling disempowered. In the group Bec learnt about the four applications of mindfulness and practised both mindfulness and loving kindness meditation. She progressively came to understand her habitual conditioned responses and gained an ability to choose how she would respond to her emotions. Bec learnt how to give emotions space by practising openness, willingness, allowance and acceptance, remembering that acceptance does not mean blindly acting on emotions. She found that she could see emotions as waves coming and going. She neither blocked nor amplified them, but just let them unfold and fade away according to their nature. In this way she practised the second and third applications of mindfulness. Bec progressed to the fourth application of mindfulness in which she explored what fed her emotions and what flowed from them.

In both the group and individual sessions, Bec utilised the practices outlined in the eight-fold path. As she confronted triggers that would normally result in destructive outbursts, Bec was able to remember her intention to avoid harm. Reflecting on her aspiration for peace and happiness helped her to tone down her anger and enhance her wellbeing and interpersonal harmony. Two months after she completed the group programme Bec decided that she was ready to stop therapy. She was very happy with what she had achieved and felt she had gained some freedom of choice in dealing with her angry outbursts.

Balancing emotions

Ekman[11] points out that because emotions are either evolutionarily determined or conditioned to arise under particular circumstances, we cannot control their arising. We can, however, reduce the impact of the triggers, add alternative information to the database, de-automate the appraisers, de-condition the program, and adjust the refractory period. Just as when Bec came to understand what triggered her anger and why, she was able to change her response and bring her emotions into balance.

Balanced constructive emotions get the job of survival, wellbeing and welfare done. They lead to cooperation, collaboration and understanding between oneself and others. Balanced emotions are expressed in a way that is timely and appropriate to the situation.

Marsha Linehan (e.g. 1993), the psychologist who developed DBT, once compared emotions to horses. Horses are powerful animals that can serve us if we train them in a kindly manner. But if we just sit in the saddle and provide no direction, the horse will just go where it wants to go according to its habitual tendencies. In order to direct the horse to where we want to go, we need to connect with it, develop a relationship and understand its needs and particular temperament, yet maintain a sense of authority.

It is easy for emotions to lead us astray down destructive pathways that cause harm and some emotions are simply difficult to bear, even painful. Often, in our attempt to manage our emotions, we may suppress them or try not to feel them. The trouble with this is that they may come out in other ways with secondary emotions such as guilt and shame.

When emotions are painful or leading us in destructive directions we need to develop a kind yet firm relationship with them. Taming and training emotions involves learning new skills and breaking old habits. One way we learn is through behavioural reinforcement. Reinforcement, as explained in Chapter 1, strengthens habits. Sometimes destructive emotions are reinforced by allowing them to run rampant and out of control. This may involve becoming over-engaged, preoccupied, consumed or hijacked by emotions. Avoidance can also be reinforcing. Avoidance of negative experiences can include denial, suppression, substance abuse, dissociation and even self-harm. Avoidance can provide reinforcement because it is a relief to not confront or contact something unpleasant. Sometimes people avoid positive experiences because the experience provokes anxiety or because they are attached to habitual withdrawal and inactivity. At times, in order to train and tame out of control emotions we need to restrain or 'surf' our urges. At other times we need to face up to what we are avoiding.

'Response prevention' is a term used in contemporary psychology that refers to not reinforcing avoidance or other behaviours. In other words, if we choose to not act on our impulse to avoid emotional distress, the discomfort will eventually change and fade away because it is no longer reinforced. In behavioural sciences a term that is used for when a behavioural pattern fades is 'extinction'.

If we face up to what we are avoiding in a very sensitive and graduated manner, our conditioned reactions and old habits can become extinct. If, on the other hand, we face our pain and fears when they are too overwhelming it can make our conditioned reactions worse. Where physical pain is concerned we should respect the need for avoidance and act wisely. It also helps to understand that purposely facing emotional pain is best done when we are somewhat confident that we can cope and it will not make our reactions worse. There is a window of opportunity for the 'extinguishing' process. Too little distress has no effect. Too much distress re-sensitises us to more complicated reactions. The process of tolerating distress and allowing habitual reactions to fade away is best when we proceed in a sensitive, gradual manner and in a way that is timely, suitable and appropriate.

The process of taming destructive emotions and cultivating balanced emotions involves first getting to know and understand them. Once we know what we are working with we are in a better position to make decisions to either reinforce them or allow them to fade away. All emotions are important for our survival, wellbeing and welfare and they can all be in balance or out of balance. On the following pages I will describe four common universal emotions: anger, fear, sadness and happiness.

Anger

Try, for a few moments, looking into a mirror while pulling your eyebrows down and together. Open your eyes wide staring with your upper eyelids against your eyebrows at the same time as pushing your lips tightly together.[12] Do you look unmistakably like someone who is angry? Do you feel angry or are you reminded of a time when you were angry? This expression, according to Ekman (2003), is the universal facial expression of anger. No matter where you go in the world with whatever culture you encounter, the experience of anger is connected with this facial expression. It is a universal sign of anger. It has served a purpose in evolution and, according to biologists, it is essential to the survival of our species that we experience and express anger.

Anger has many grades and variations, from subtle aversion to blind rage. Some words for the various gradations of this emotion include:

Aggravation	Exasperation	Hatred	Rage
Agitation	Fed up	Hostility	Resentment
Annoyance	Ferocity	Irritation	Revulsion
Aversion	Fierce	Loathing	Scorn
Bitterness	Frenzied	Mean-spiritedness	Spite
Blustery	Frustration	Outrage	Torment
Burned up	Fury		Vengefulness
Dislike	Grouchiness		Wrath
	Grumpiness		

The most common trigger for anger is being blocked from pursuing what matters to us, or being stopped in achieving a desired outcome. The desired outcome could be as simple as being able to change lanes in the traffic or as complex as feeling that others do not perceive us in the way we wish to be perceived. Some people seem to get angry at anything and everything. People get angry at injustice, insult, abuse, having freedoms taken away, not getting what they want, being disrespected, criticised or cheated. We can get angry when we are offended by another's beliefs and values or betrayed, abandoned, rejected, falsely accused or when other people break the rules. We can also get angry with ourselves. The list of possibilities is endless but possibly the easiest way to get angry is for others to express anger towards us, as anger seems to breed anger.

Anger gives us the energy to fight against something that is blocking a desired outcome and remove the obstacle. For example, the energy required to protect a young child can be generated by anger and the courage to stand up against oppression and injustice can also be supported by anger. Anger can also be directed inwards and give us the motivation to change something about ourselves that needs to change. Unfortunately anger can be dangerous because it can quickly drive us to act inappropriately in ways that may hurt and harm ourselves and others. Internalised anger can easily degenerate into the fuel of self-hatred and depression and as anger rarely occurs alone it may lead to an array of secondary emotions such as guilt, jealousy and self-loathing. Excessive anger is detrimental to physical health, increasing blood pressure and the risk of coronary heart disease. Unconscious suppression of anger can also increase the likelihood of coronary heart disease and lead to an array of destructive emotional experiences, such as resentment, guilt and depression. 'Anger management' is often a reason for visits to psychologists and participation in self-help courses because anger has a great potential to hurt, harm and destroy property, oneself, other people and our relationships.

There are many strategies for working with anger in contemporary psychology because it is such a desired skill. Assertiveness training, for example, is a popular way of working with anger skilfully so that it minimises harm and demonstrates respect for the rights and wellbeing of all parties. Some other general strategies to work with anger are:

- Being familiar with our personal cues and triggers and knowing what our personal signals for anger are. Ekman says that this type of awareness helps us to 'catch the spark before the flame'.[13]
- Being able to surf the urges to follow aggressive intentions and take 'time out' or do something completely different to acting on anger.

- Applying mindfulness to thoughts so that we know what thoughts may be feeding anger and knowing that these thoughts are not necessarily facts to be believed.
- Being able to note and name anger for what it is, so that we know that anger has arisen in us, but we need not identify with it.
- Choosing not to justify and reinforce violent, harmful and revengeful actions including the way we speak to ourselves and others.
- Practising right speech (including self-talk), which entails not engaging in the types of speech that are toxic to relationships such as shaming, blaming and unwarranted criticism.
- Becoming skilled with exercises that calm the mind and relax the body so that we build up a buffer zone to soften the impact of angry triggers as well as reduce the length of time we are in a refractory period.
- Reflecting on what was helpful and what was not helpful after the episode has passed.
- Cultivating warm friendliness and compassion.

Anger is often the way the hindrance of ill will is expressed. One traditional Buddhist approach to remedy ill will is by cultivating warm friendliness or *metta*. If you refer back to the diagrams about the three emotional systems (Figure 5.1) presented earlier in this chapter, you will notice that there is a relationship between the survival system and the relationship system. The relationship system serves to calm and soothe unnecessary reaction and upset in the survival system, demonstrating how anger can be balanced by *metta*.

Fear

The themes of fear can involve imagined, misperceived, expected, anticipated or actual threats of harm. Most humans fear psychological or physical pain. Fear gives us the energy to escape from danger for the welfare and wellbeing of ourselves or others. Fear is essential for survival and it is important that this experience is communicated quickly to others. Hence, there is a universal facial expression for this emotion. When fear is experienced there is a tendency to move the head back as if pulling away from the experience. The brows are up and pulled together, the lips are stretched horizontally, the eyes are open wide and the upper eyelids are also raised and as wide as possible.[14]

Fear is an emotion of avoidance. The levels of avoidance can range from a mild evasion to an extreme desperate escape from whatever frightens us. At extreme levels, fighting, fleeing or freezing are natural survival avoidance responses to danger.

As with all the emotions there are many grades of fear from subtle avoidance to intense terror and some of the words that are used for the family of fear include:

Afraid	Hysteria	Shock
Cautious	Jumpiness	Tenseness
Dread	Nervousness	Terror
Edginess	Panic	Threatened
Fright	Petrified	Uneasiness
Horror	Scared	Worry

When we are confronted with danger and fear takes hold we will experience a fight, flight or freeze response. The freeze response is a shut down coping mechanism related to danger. A mouse playing dead in the mouth of a cat, as an example, may increase its possibilities for survival. Sometimes we humans shut down emotionally and dissociate in order to cope with extremely difficult experiences. Sometimes these patterns become habitual and they occur when we no longer need them. When this response is no longer helpful mindfulness can help to break the habit. The fight or flight (FoF) response is a more common response to danger.

Adrenaline is the main biochemical that is released immediately when we are confronted with danger so we can avoid or manage injury, act quickly and move away from danger or be able to fight it. In response to demands some of the following physiological changes occur:

- Breathing speeds up so that there is more oxygen for muscles.
- Blood moves towards the muscles to supply energy.
- Muscles tense in preparation for quick responses.

- Heart rate and blood pressure increase so that the oxygen and nutrients the blood carries can be quickly supplied to where they are needed.
- Perspiration increases, in order that the body is cooled should it be involved in strenuous activity.
- Blood vessels may expand and move towards the skin also in order to help cool the body (thus giving a blushed or blotchy appearance).
- Blood clotting ability increases to minimise blood loss should an injury occur.
- We become hyper-vigilant (on the lookout) for danger so that there can be a quick response if needed.
- Digestive processes are stopped or slowed down so that more important and pressing defensive functions are given resources. This may result in such things as nausea and a dry mouth.
- The immune response also slows down as a result of diverting energy to more pressing needs.

The FoF response is an immediate and natural response to threat or danger. After the danger has passed the body should naturally return to a state of balance. However, if something in this complex process goes wrong then the system gets out of balance.

Fear out of balance

As we have discussed throughout this book, fear can be in excess and easily shift from being an important emotion for survival and welfare to an extremely uncomfortable obstacle to living a fulfilling and meaningful life. It some cases, such as with agoraphobia, it can keep us house bound because we fear a panic attack in a situation that we cannot control. With social phobia we may feel desperately lonely because we fear being judged by others. Sometimes fear keeps us caught in meaningless occupations because we fear taking a risk. We may also fear meditation and the insight that it can bring preferring to be entrapped by our own ignorance. At the opposite end of the fear spectrum, a deficiency in this emotion can lead to foolhardy fearlessness.

In many cultural sub-groups fearlessness is often thought of as a desirable state. In the short term, foolhardy courage or self-serving indifference can feel very good, and serve short-term goals such as an adrenaline fix, an ego boost or material acquisitions. Some high risk extreme sports people, for example, could be motivated by an addiction to excitement and a desire to feel fear by participating in dangerous activities. Another example of the problems associated with an imbalance in fear is the harm those who are called psychopaths can cause. As well as lacking compassionate empathy, a feature of a person who fits the psychopath profile is a lack of fear. Like James Bond, they are cool and calm in the face of great risk and danger, thus acting without hesitation in a way that could be harmful to self or others. The psychological profile of a psychopath can also involve no fear of consequences. Fear of negative consequences is, according to Buddhist psychology, considered a helpful emotion. The right fear, in an appropriate amount, in a timely manner consistent with the context and need is a wholesome mental state because it is a disincentive to act in a harmful way.

Anxiety disorders develop when natural functional fear responses become exaggerated, distorted and dysfunctional. When the body's responses to immediate threat are not resolved our systems often do not have an opportunity to bounce back to a state of equilibrium and we become more vulnerable not only to anxiety disorders but also depression and a variety of health conditions. In heavy traffic, for example, when the FoF responses may be at full throttle but we cannot do the things that the body is geared up to do, it may not easily return to a balanced state. If we have repeated FoF responses it can, understandably, affect our emotional and physical wellbeing. When demands become overwhelming, stress responses can become chronic. Cortisol is a stress hormone that is regularly released at different times throughout our day in response to demands. When the stress response becomes chronic the levels of cortisol can also become

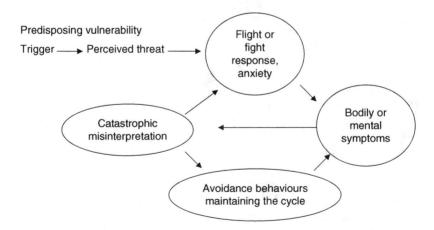

Figure 5.2 The panic cycle
Source: adapted from Wells (1997)

elevated, increasing our vulnerability to long-term illnesses, such as type II diabetes, high blood pressure and heart disease, and immune deficiencies that may increase our risk of cancer. It can also lead to worsening anxiety and depression, and disrupt memory processes.

As we explored in Chapter 1, panic is a fear response when there is no need for this response. Panic is like a false alarm to a situation that does not warrant a FoF response. A panic cycle is illustrated in Figure 5.2 to show how panic can be self-reinforcing.

Panic attacks, in panic disorder are examples of when the natural and healthy emotion of fear develops into a disorder.

For the most part, fear and the chain of events connected with fear are involuntary and necessary responses for survival. We cannot stop fear being triggered. We can, however, change the way we react to fear so that it does not hijack us in an out of control manner. We can reduce our fear of fear and we can also reduce the likelihood that unnecessary fear will arise at all.

Balancing fear

With reference again to the emotional system diagram (Figure 5.1), the relationship system serves to calm sympathetic nervous system responses of the survival system. When we feel safe and a fight, flight or freeze response is no longer necessary, oxytocins released as part of the soothing system stimulate the parasympathetic nervous system, helping the body recover from an incident. Oxytocins slow down our breathing and heart rate and increase the blood flow to digestion. In general they allow our bodies to rest, recuperate and repair. Oxytocins also counter the ill effects of stress and chronically elevated cortisol, improving our health and emotional wellbeing (Kukchinskas, 2009).

As far as psychological treatment for anxiety is concerned, there is an abundance of successful strategies and therapies. Some of these approaches have already been explained in this book. The way the third wave and Buddhist therapies address the excesses of fear are sometimes counter-intuitive. Rather than attempting to get rid of it or eliminate fear and anxiety, the general approach is to embrace and accept it. These approaches provide the opportunity to find freedom from anxiety by understanding it. As far as treating the deficiencies of fear, such as fool-hardy fearlessness, there may not be many conventional therapies available or appropriate. Nonetheless, with the cultivation of the heart-mind and the maturation of wisdom, individuals become more aware of imbalances in their lives and begin to realise ways to address them. Mindfulness is a key if not essential activity to find balance with fear.

Surfing panic with understanding: guided instructions

The following suggestions are strategies to work with a panic attack when it is occurring. These suggestions involve being objective and not reacting to or feeding into a panic cycle and so allowing a panic attack to naturally subside or burn out. The following guidelines follow principles of insight meditation.[15]

- Acknowledge or note the most noticeable experience. You could say to yourself, for example, 'panic . . . panic' or 'panic has arisen'. Remember to be calm with the tone of noting and step back or into a perspective of awareness that is not cut off from the experience but also not lost in it. Be careful not to be hijacked by thoughts about the experience and be as honest as you can about what you notice. Let thoughts about the experience be on the periphery of your awareness and turn your attention to your body and describe, to yourself, what is happening. If your heart is racing note, for example, 'racing heart'. If your body is shaking note: 'shaking . . . shaking'. If you are breathing quickly note 'fast breathing', etc.
- Investigate the experience, and tell yourself something accurate about it. For example, you could ask yourself: 'What is actually happening here?', 'Where do I experience my panic most of all?', 'On a scale of one to ten, how would I rate this particular panic attack?'
- Try to be objective and honest about the experience. Do not note panic if in fact you are not panicking.
- Access your understanding of panic and remind yourself of your insights. Say to yourself statements reflecting your insights such as:
  - This is a natural fear response, which is misfiring.
  - The brain sometimes makes mistakes; this panic is one of those mistakes.
  - This panic is just a false alarm.
  - This false alarm is being fuelled by catastrophic misinterpretations that I need not believe.
  - Any catastrophic thoughts that I may be having are not facts to be believed.

- o   Just because I am experiencing an intense emotion it does not mean I have to act on it.
- o   This panic has a beginning, middle and end and it will tend to dissolve more readily if I let it roll out rather than struggling with it.
- o   Turning attention towards panic rather than reacting and running away from it is one way that I can overcome and heal this problem.
- o   Making friends with panic is therapeutic. Struggling and fighting panic only makes thing worse.
- o   Just because this experience of panic may seem overwhelming, I am not panic. I don't need to be trapped by taking this panic personally.
- o   When I can connect with the part of me that knows and is watching panic, it is spacious and peaceful.
- o   I can be at peace with panic.
- Cultivate patience with panic. Know that in time it will pass and that the less you struggle with it the easier it will pass.
- Try to be completely open and receptive with your current experience. If this is unpleasant note 'unpleasant feelings' and relax into the discomfort without resistance. The more you accept and allow the closer you come to healing and letting go.
- Be completely receptive to whatever unpleasant physical experiences arise. Melt and soften with these experiences, knowing that the more you can soften and open to them the closer you come to healing and being at peace with them.
- Be open and receptive to catastrophic thoughts but remember that you don't need to believe them. They are only thoughts with inaccurate messages. Let such thoughts come and go. They need not take hold and hijack you.
- Notice the urge to avoid the experience and remember that the more you avoid the more the cycle is reinforced. Resist the impulse and urge to move away and rather stay with the experience in this present moment. If you want you can note 'aversion . . . aversion' or 'urge . . . urge'.

- Take refuge in awareness with the knowledge that awareness is like the still depths of a lake buffeted by strong winds. The depths are peaceful while the surface is rough and turbulent.
- Hold firm to the confidence that the turbulence will settle.
- Rest in the peace of awareness and let the panic roll out and finish.
- Maintain a stance of presence and let mindfulness be your refuge.
- Be open, compassionate and kind with whatever presents in your sphere of awareness. Find peace and freedom from panic by being courageously present.

Sadness/grief

If you feel confident that you can cope, think of a time when you lost something that was important to you. It could be the loss of a job, your health or your clear vision or hearing. It could be the loss of self-esteem or the admiration of colleagues or friends or the loss of a dream. The loss could be related to a rejection from a friend or the death of a child, spouse, sibling, parent, friend or pet.[16] How did you feel when those important things were lost? How do you feel now when you reflect on your losses? What do you notice happens to your body? What is the facial expression you feel forming and how is your posture and breathing? What types of thoughts arise and what is the strongest emotion you experience? Can you name it? Do the words that come to mind include grief and sadness, or one of the following?

Abandoned	Disappointment	Hurt	Rejection
Anguish	Discontentment	Insecurity	Sombre
Bereft	Disheartened	Isolation	Sorrow
Crushed	Discouraged	Lament	Suffering
Defeated	Dismay	Loneliness	Unhappiness
Dejection	Futility	Melancholy	Wistful
Depressed	Gloom	Miserable	Woe
	Glumness	Neglected	
	Hopelessness		

The facial expression of sadness is unmistakable. Unless we are blind or impaired in some other way we all know the universal expressions of sadness. Again, if you feel confident that you will cope, find a mirror and pay attention to how you look when you reflect on your losses. If you are not looking sad try the following:

Let your body sag and slump. Then, if you can, raise the inner corners of your eyebrows up in the centre of your forehead. Move attention to your lower lip and push it up slightly, as if you were pouting. Let your eyes drop and look down. Also let the rest of your face relax and sag with the exception of your cheeks, which if you can, try to raise.[17]

When you make a sad expression does it also seem to invoke the corresponding feelings? Or if this emotion was already present, does an exaggeration of the expression make the sadness stronger? The relationship of the body to the mind is highlighted in the way an emotion will bring changes in our posture and expressions and vice versa. If we manipulate our posture and expressions (both verbal and facial) it can illicit the emotion that it reflects. When we are overwhelmed with sadness we may feel a sinking heaviness, particularly in our chest. We may also feel as if our body is collapsing in on itself. Our chest may feel tight and aching, as if our heart is broken. Our lips may begin to quiver and, of course, tears may start to flow. The trigger for sadness is the loss of something important to us. Sadness is possibly the longest lasting emotion and the boundaries between it as an emotion, mood, temperament and disorder can easily become blurred.

Depression is the disorder of sadness and we have discussed some of the features of this disorder in previous chapters. The types of losses involved with depression are many and include the loss of hope and meaning, faith and confidence. Possibly one of the most powerful triggers for depression is the loss of a loved one. When the effects of this type of loss emerge it is commonly called grief. As well as sadness, the normal grief response can involve the following emotions, physical responses, thoughts and behaviours: anger, guilt, anxiety, loneliness, shock, yearning, numbness, helplessness, the heaviness of fatigue, tightness in the chest, a dry mouth, a hollow feeling in the stomach, tightness in the throat, ruminations, obsessions, confusion or even hallucinations, disturbed sleep, social withdrawal, crying, neurotic responses to old possessions and memories, absent-mindedness, searching and calling out, restless overactivity and more.

When you see someone expressing grief, what do you feel like doing? Do you feel like giving them a hug? Interestingly, kind and well-meaning touch stimulates oxytocins, the hormone of human bonding, which is also soothing (Kukchinskas, 2009). One of the functions of the expression of sadness is to get reassurance and comfort from another. From an evolutionary perspective, consoling and helping those who are grieving strengthens bonds and promotes the welfare and wellbeing of our families and communities. When we can practise self-compassion it can help with our own distress (Neff, 2011). In my opinion another function of sadness is to provide an opportunity to process the losses we experience by internalising and withdrawing from our normal way of relating to the world. We come to terms with what it means to be who and what we are in the absence of that person, animal or object that was so important to our sense of identity and wellbeing. When we lose a loved one, the grieving period also provides the time to respect and honour that person's life, the meaning of their life and the impact they had on us.

The effect of grief can be painful and debilitating. If the grief is excessive and not dealt with effectively it can become pathological and the bereaved person is unable to function adequately for months or years. As we have learned throughout the course of this book one cause of psychological suffering is clinging and attachment. To the extent that we are attached to things that change, to that extent we will suffer grief. Paradoxically, it is now scientifically accepted that secure attachments to significant others are essential for healthy human development (e.g. Bowlby, 1988). If a child does not develop an attachment to a carer then that child will be impaired in their social, physical, emotional and or mental development. In addition, if a child perceives and feels that they are not loved and cared for then they also fail to thrive physically and psychologically. Attachment is developed in humans and other creatures that need nurturing because it has a survival value. As attachment is natural, then it is also natural to grieve. In many respects the pain of grief is the price we pay for the joy of love and the commitment we have to those we love and are attached to. Parents, for example, are attached to their children because we know, intuitively, that it is natural and necessary. Most parents wish for their children to grow and develop into healthy and well-balanced individuals.

Grief is the natural and healthy response to the loss of someone who is dear to us. If we notice someone who does not express sadness when a close relative or friend died, then we may think that they are disordered in some way. Sadness, the natural human response to loss, like fear and anger can be excessive or deficient, and therefore dysfunctional. How do we work through the normal grief responses so that the disruption and dysfunction to our lives is minimised? How do we prevent sadness from deteriorating to pathological grief? How do we ensure that sadness is constructive and not destructive and that we process our losses in a healthy and beneficial way?

The treatment of depression is one of the key targets of contemporary psychology and some of the approaches to this common cold of psychological disorders have already been discussed in previous chapters. Contemporary psychology also offers an array of strategies to work with both pathological and normal grief responses. Moving through the normal grief response successfully is often described as working through stages. Different approaches describe different stages. One approach that I have found helpful for people suffering with grief is a task-based approach described by a psychologist called William Worden (1982). The sequence he described is as follows:

- Task 1: Accept the reality of the loss.
- Task 2: Experience the pain of the grief.

- Task 3: Adjust to an environment in which the deceased is missing.
- Task 4: Withdraw emotional energy from the deceased and reinvest it in other social activity, without uncertainty or guilt.

These principles of acceptance, willingness to experience, and releasing one's clinging and moving on, as described above, relate to the loss of a loved one but can also be applied to other losses and provide a way to work with sadness in general. In the beginning paragraphs of the *Satipatthana Sutta*, the Buddha says mindfulness is very helpful, if not essential, to overcome grief.

Happiness

In Chapter 1, three types of happiness were mentioned: (1) simple feelings of pleasure, (2) the joy of engagement and (3) the wellbeing that comes from engaging in meaningful activities. Happiness can be found in all three of the emotional systems outlined earlier (Figure 5.1). Happiness usually happens when we are free from danger and threat, when we have the pleasure of acquiring something that is important to us and or we have a sense of belonging and connection. Happiness is a broad topic and the cultivation of genuine happiness is one of the main themes of this book.

There are possibly hundreds of words that describe happy experiences some of which may include:

Aglow	Delight	Gladness	Pride
Alive	Ecstatic	Glee	Rapture
Amusement	Elation	Happiness	Relief
Bliss	Enjoyment	Jolliness	Satisfaction
Bubbly	Enthralment	Joy	Thrill
Buoyant	Enthusiasm	Jubilation	Triumph
Cheerfulness	Euphoria	Light-hearted	Uplifted
Contentment	Excitement	Merriment	Wonderful
	Exhilaration	Pleasant	Zeal

One cannot mistake the facial expression of happiness as a smile. It is not just the movement of the mouth, however, as a genuine smile also involves the muscles around the eyes. One can tell if someone is feigning a smile by looking at his or her eyes. With a genuine smile the eyes seem to sparkle with warmth as the muscles at the outer corner of the eyes are engaged. The genuine smile is not a forced smile, or a smug smile, or one-sided (which can be a sign of contempt) or the grin that arises when we endure pain. A real smile, which is also called the Duchenne smile,[18] seems to clearly demonstrate the pleasure we experience. There are many types of happiness and many reasons (triggers) for people to smile. According to Ekman (2003) the many different types of enjoyment and reasons to smile can include:

• Contact with pleasing sights, sounds, smells, touch and tastes.
• The types of relief we have when a difficult experience is over.
• The types of elation we feel when we see unexpected acts of human goodness.
• The feelings we have when we succeed at something.
• Amusement, even when it may involve ridicule.
• Schadenfreude, which is a German term referring to relishing in another's misfortune.
• Naches, a type of pride and joy in one's offspring.
• The joy of wonder.
• Gratitude.
• Excitement.
• The bliss and rapture of absorption in something.

Happiness is self-reinforcing. We like to do things that make us happy. Happiness, like the other emotions, has survival value and works towards the wellbeing and welfare of ourselves and others. The emotion of happiness provides reinforcement for actions, it can deepen connections to others and it can also enhance cooperation within our families, associates and communities. A mother's smile and her other expressions of approval and joy serve to stimulate oxytocins both within the mother and the child. They also serve to reinforce social and emotional interaction and are essential for the child's healthy development.[19]

Like all the emotions, happiness can be excessive, deficient or dysfunctional. Mania, with all the problems that it can create, is an extreme example of when happiness is excessive. Over-excitement is a less extreme example but it can also be the cause of problems such as exhausting and turning friends away, thereby disrupting social harmony and cooperation. An example of dysfunctional happiness would be giggling at a friend's or relative's funeral. A lack of joy is the key feature of depression and a very clear example of when there is a deficiency of happiness.

A genuine smile can heal emotional distress at all ages. The experience of happiness can transform our state of being and be curative for depression. Psychologists will often ask people who are depressed to create a pleasant events schedule. This requires the client to schedule activities into their day that may be enjoyable as well as activities that may bring some sense of achievement. These activities can lift a depressed person's mood. It seems that the experience of happy emotions serves multiple functions in our lives. However, as discussed in earlier chapters, the happiness we get from gratifying the senses is limited. The happy emotions that arise from hedonic pleasures only last as long as the pleasure lasts and unfortunately can become addictive. Sometimes our efforts to realise short-term happiness can bring us long-term misery and unhappiness. Sometimes we become entangled and entrapped by our addictions to fleeting happiness and the pleasure-seeking behaviours that are driven by our addictions. As with the other emotions it is important to find balance with happiness so that we can enjoy a fulfilling and meaningful life without falling into a happiness trap.[20]

Nirvana, the ultimate goal of the eight-fold path, is said to be the highest happiness. But the Buddha also taught how to realise simple types of happiness such as the joy we experience when we work in services that help, when we act kindly to another, or give generously or appreciate and enjoy the fruits of our efforts. The Buddha taught how to live a good life by cultivating wisdom, virtuous actions and the heart-mind. The Buddha was not alone in teaching how to live a wholesome and happy life. Aristotle, one of the great Western philosophers, spoke about the importance of hedonic happiness based on health, wealth and beauty and 'eudaimonia', a more sustainable genuine happiness. The primary component of Aristotle's eudaimonia was a virtuous (ethical) life.

The theme of this book and the teachings of most if not all wise sages is the realisation of happiness, not just as a transitory emotion but also as a genuine and sustainable way of being. Every chapter of this book addresses this topic in some way or another and mindfulness is a key strategy to find balance and genuine happiness.

Reflections on mindfulness of emotions

With mindfulness we can get to know and become familiar with our emotional lives. We can become very familiar with the cascade of mental and biological responses that are collectively called an emotion. We can become aware of all the components of an emotional episode and have more choice in how we reinforce or allow our emotional responses to fade away. Mindfulness of emotions includes developing insight about emotions. This involves understanding what triggers them, what fuels them, what quells them, how they can fade away and how we can cultivate the ones that best serve the needs and values of ourselves and others. When we are able to track and understand emotions we are in a better position to choose to abandon the destructive and cultivate the constructive. With awareness, resolve and skilful action we can alter the trajectory of a destructive emotional episode so that it is transformed into something helpful and constructive. When we have an understanding of what an emotion is then we are in a powerful position to be able to tame the destructive and cultivate balance.

Remember Bec?

Bec was one of hundreds of people I have had the honour to teach mindfulness to within a group setting. Everyone comes with different stories and reasons for participation in mindfulness groups. For the most part, the motivation for attendance at a group is to work with painful and often destructive emotions. During the session on emotions I usually provide a double page handout which gives participants some strategies to try when they are experiencing painful and potentially destructive emotions. This information can be found on the following pages as a way to conclude this chapter.

Coping with painful emotions

During formal meditation practices or during daily activities some ways to cope with painful and possibly destructive emotions include:

- Honour emotions. They arise for a reason and they may indicate that we need to act in a particular way. Act on emotions if this is needed and don't force yourself to investigate emotions when they are too overwhelming. Remember always be kind to yourself.
- Note and name the emotions. Say to yourself something like: '_____ (the name of the emotion) has arisen'. Name the emotion with a tone of voice that is not the same as the emotion you are noting. For example, if anger is there, name it with a tone of voice that is not angry. Naming an emotion helps to create space with it. There are lists of words referring to some basic emotions [in

this chapter]. These lists can help find words to describe the emotions you experience.

- Give emotions space. As much as possible let them be without rejecting or suppressing them. If it is painful do not suppress the experience. Let it be. Giving space to emotions is like accepting them and embracing them with kindness.

- Step back from falling into and becoming entangled with the emotion. Step back from them into a space of awareness. Step back and get unstuck by being aware.

- See emotions like waves coming and going. In this way try not to block them or amplify them. Rather let them roll on by. Surfing powerful emotions is like staying balanced and not being dumped by them. Sometimes, it also means being able to dive through them before they pound you into the seabed.

- Practise emotional aikido. Aikido is a defensive martial art. Aikido experts are very good at getting out of the road of destructive energy, neutralising destructive energy and even transforming it to something beneficial.

- Remember that we are not our emotions but rather they are changing events passing through like visitors. Remember you don't need to take emotions personally.

- Practise openness, willingness, allowance and acceptance. Remember that acceptance does not mean that you don't take action when you need to.

- See difficult and painful emotions as an opportunity to develop understanding or insight.

- Remember that all experiences change and painful emotions have a natural time frame, and will also change to something different.

- Be aware of the thoughts related to the emotion but try not to get caught up in them. Relax into how the emotion feels in the body rather than trying to work it out by thinking too much about them. [Practicing softening, soothing and allowing how emotions feel in your body.]²¹

- Enquire into painful emotions. Look directly at emotions and see them for what they are rather than what we construct them to be. Being afraid to look at and investigate destructive emotions can sometimes make them stronger. When we look at them, we might notice that they are nothing to be afraid of, and all the scary parts of them fade away.

- Cultivate the opposites of the painful and destructive emotions, such as, for example peacefulness, kindness, compassion, wisdom, acceptance, etc.
- Unlearn unhelpful responses by not reinforcing old reactive habits. This means that we don't let destructive emotions become the boss of our lives and we make choices to stand up to, and say no to what they are trying to make us do.
- Use helpful self-talk such as: 'it's OK, this will change', 'I am not my emotions', 'this will pass' or 'it is understandable that this emotion has arisen, and I don't need to take it personally'.
- If the emotion is too overwhelming to deal with, use a healthy distraction such as watching a movie, or listening to music. These types of distractions can help the destructive and painful emotions pass by without causing any damage.
- Find a good friend and talk it out.
- Remember to remember to be here now.

Notes

1 Dr Paul Ekman developed a programme with Dr B. Alan Wallace called Cultivating Emotional Balance (CEB). CEB is an evidence-based educational programme that uses the contemporary scientific understanding of emotions and training in Buddhist meditation to help participants enhance emotional wellbeing and reduce the impact of destructive emotions (see www.cultivatingemotionalbalance.org/). With appreciation, I received training in teaching CEB under the guidance of both Dr Paul Ekman and Dr Alan Wallace in 2011. Much of the information related to the scientific perspective of emotions in this chapter is credited to Dr Paul Ekman.
2 Dr Paul Ekman during CEB teacher training, Phuket, Thailand, 2011.
3 Ibid.
4 Please note that the freeze response does not necessarily involve these hormones and is related to the ventral vagal nerve as it shuts down the human system, as one way to cope with threat and danger. See Porges (2011) for more details.
5 The cultivation of loving-kindness as mentioned in the final chapter of this book will be detailed along with compassion, appreciative joy and equanimity in the book currently in progress with the current working title: 'Harmonious Human Relationships and the Buddha's Path of Warm Friendliness, Compassion, Joy and Peace'.

6 Reactive cycles will be the topic of the next chapter.
7 Credit is given to Patrick Kearney for making this comparison on the many workshops we have run together and also in the Dharma teachings on retreats he has led.
8 Credit is given to Patrick Kearney for making this and the many other clarifications about Pali and Buddha Dharma in the many workshops we have run together and also in the Dharma teachings in the talks he has given and retreats he has led.
9 Thanks to Patrick Kearney for pointing out this reference in: The greater discourse at Assapura MN 39. See Nanamoli and Bodhi (1995, p. 370).
10 Thanks to Patrick Kearney for pointing out this reference from the Sangarava Sutta, SN 46:55. See Bodhi (2000, pp. 1612–13).
11 During CEB teacher training, Phuket, Thailand, 2011.
12 Adapted from CEB teacher training in Phuket, Thailand, 2011, credit to Dr Paul Ekman.
13 Ibid.
14 Ibid.
15 These instructions have been inspired and adapted from instructions found in a manual written about panic surfing by Ballie and Rapee (1998).
16 Adapted from CEB teacher training in Phuket, Thailand, 2011, credit to Dr Paul Ekman.
17 Ibid.
18 The Duchenne smile is named after Guillaume-Benjamin-Amand Duchenne (de Boulogne) a nineteenth-century French neurologist who researched which muscles were involved in facial expressions.
19 In an experiment called 'The still face experiment', young mothers are first asked to interact with their 12-month-old babies as they would normally. Then the mothers are asked to maintain a blank and still face. In only a few minutes the babies become very distressed. See www.youtube.com/watch?v=apzXGEbZht0.
20 With acknowledgement, 'The happiness trap' is the title of a book written by a third wave ACT therapist in Australia called Dr Russ Harris. See Harris (2008).
21 "Soften soothe allow" is a practical and effective strategy used in Mindful Self Compassion (MSC), a programme developed by Christopher Germer and Kristin Neff. Also see Germer 2009. I trained in this approach after creating this handout for coping with emotions.

References

Ballie, A. J. and Rapee, R. M. (1998). *Panic Surfing: A Self-Treatment Workbook for Panic Disorder*. Sydney: Macquarie Lighthouse Press.
Bodhi, B. (2000). *The Connected Discourses of the Buddha: A Translation of the Samyutta Nikaya*. Somerville, MA: Wisdom Publications.
Bowlby, E. J. M. (1988). *A Secure Base: Clinical Applications of Attachment Theory*. London: Routledge.
Ekman, P. (2003). *Emotions Revealed: Recognizing Faces and Feelings to Improve Communication and Emotional Life*. New York: Times Books.

Germer, C. K. (2009). *The mindful path to self-compassion. Freeing yourself from destructive thoughts and emotions*. New York: The Guilford Press.

Gilbert, P. (2009). *The Compassionate Mind: A New Approach to Life's Challenges*. Oakland, CA: New Harbinger Publications.

Hanson, R. (2013). *Hardwiring Happiness. The Practical Science of Reshaping your Brain and your Life*. Croydon: Ebury Publishing.

Harris, R. (2008). *The Happiness Trap: Stop Struggling and Start Living*. London: Constable and Robinson.

Kukchinskas, S. (2009). *The Chemistry of Connection: How the Oxytocin Response Can Help You Find Trust, Intimacy and Love*. Oakland, CA: New Harbinger Publications.

Linehan, M. M. (1993). *Skills Training Manual for Treating Borderline Personality Disorder*. New York: Guilford Press.

Nanamoli, B. and Bodhi, B. (1995). *The Middle Length Discourses of the Buddha: A New Translation of the Majjhima Nikaya*. Boston, MA: Wisdom Publications.

Neff, K. (2011). *Self-Compassion: Stop Beating Yourself Up and Leave Insecurity Behind*. New York: HarperCollins.

Porges, S. W. (2011). *The Polyvagal Theory: Neurophysiological Foundations of Emotions, Attachment, Communication, and Self-Regulation*. New York: W. W. Norton.

Wells, A. (1997). *Cognitive Therapy of Anxiety Disorders: A Practical Manual and Conceptual Guide*. Chichester: John Wiley.

Worden, W. J. (1982). *Grief Counselling and Grief Therapy: A Handbook for the Mental Health Practitioner*. New York: Springer.

6 Reactive cyclic patterns and freedom from the bind

Chapter overview

This chapter builds on previous chapters and explains more about reactive cyclic patterns and how to exit them by exploring their connection with dependent arising. The chapter will begin by explaining two terms often used in Buddhism, *karma* and *samsara*, to create an understanding of the principles of dependent arising. Dependent arising explains how things come to be and also how they change. An understanding of the complex principles of dependent arising helps us to understand our reactive cycles, and how to exit them. Finally the chapter will provide strategies to work with reactive cycles by providing a description of the fourth application of mindfulness and its sub-domains, and some guided practices.

Karma

Contrary to popular belief, karma is not fate or predestination. Karma (Sanskrit) or *kamma* (Pali) literally means 'action'. It refers to voluntary acts of our body, speech and mind. Through our actions we are sowing the seeds of our future experiences and we are constantly reaping, in the present, the harvest of our past behaviour. Karma is a basic factor in the unfolding of our lives that determines our wellbeing or misery. What we do impacts on how events will unfold. When we act with helpful or wholesome intentions then it is more likely that useful and wholesome consequences will follow. When we act with unhelpful or unwholesome intentions, it is more likely that *dukkha* will follow. Just as the wheels of a cart follow the hoof prints of the oxen pulling it,[1] the relationship between actions and consequences is considered a law of nature.

The contemporary Buddhist view of karma does not discount the role that other factors such as evolution, the environment, our genetic makeup, social influences and our brain chemistry may play in our life. It does, however, emphasise the role our intentional actions play in constantly creating different outcomes that impact on our experiences in the present and the future. When we begin to understand karma we begin to see the dynamic relationship between ignorance, mental afflictions (*kilesa*) and actions. When we understand the relationships between causes and results, actions and consequences, we are more able to make decisions to act skilfully, short-circuit reactive cyclic patterns and reap the benefits.

Samsara: reactive cycles

When we experience depression or other psychological distress it can feel as if we are caught in a cycle.

These cycles often result in anguish and despair, yet we repeat them nonetheless. Sometimes the cyclic patterns seem to occur internally within our own minds. Other times, like a complicated web, the cycles may include the external world of people, places and things. People, events or situations around us may be triggers for reactions within us, or our own reactions may affect the people and the world around us, and the entangling effects become more and more complicated.

Samsara, which is both a Pali and Sanskrit term, literally means 'a turning' or 'a going around'. It usually refers to cycles of existence. In cultures that believe in rebirth it is called the wheel of life and death and can refer to the cycles of rebirth, ageing, death and rebirth. It is not necessary to believe in rebirth to see *samsara* evident in our everyday existence because it also refers to repetitive patterns of behaviour involving thoughts, emotions, speech and actions.

Reactive cycles or *samsara* can occur over a wide range of time frames. Cyclic and reactive patterns may occur over split seconds and moments or they may take minutes, days, months, years, or be evident the whole of one's lifetime. In classic Buddhist descriptions, the wheel of birth and death is often depicted as occurring over three lifetimes (past, present and future). The issue of reincarnation will not be discussed here, other than to say that many people who call themselves Buddhists do not have a belief in reincarnation either way. That is, in accordance with the themes of agnosticism, they feel that they do not have reliable evidence to know that it either exists or doesn't exist (Batchelor, 1997). The rebirth of conscious experience, on the other hand, is something that is clearly evident moment-to-moment, day-to-day and month-to-month, as a continuum of body–mind experiences.

Even though *samsara* can include very refined moments of joy and fulfilment, when the cycles of existence are driven by greed, ignorance and hatred, Buddhists say that *samsara* is *dukkha*. Nirvana, on the other hand, is the result of exiting the cycles. When we no longer feed our destructive cyclic habits then they fade away. As first highlighted in Chapter 1, when we are no longer creating the cause for suffering then suffering does not arise. *Samsara* is usually considered the basis of *dukkha* and Nirvana is the absence of *dukkha*.

Related story: Jack short-circuits cycles of angry reactivity

Jack was 32 years old and a father of two young children, Samantha 2 and Bobby 4. Jack valued a happy family life and he wanted to have a meaningful and positive relationship with his children but he was uncertain what to do when they were naughty. He would get angry and yell at them or even hit them before he realised what he was doing. Jack felt at the mercy of his reactive outbursts and little Bobby seemed to cop most of the flack.

Bobby started to become angry and defiant with both his parents and started to yell at his little sister Sam, in the same way that Jack yelled at him. Bobby also began to cower whenever Jack approached him. It became obvious to Jack that his angry reactions were having a negative impact on his son.

Jack had not had a good relationship with his own father. Jack's father had used harsh physical punishment with him and when Jack turned 15, he had hit his father back. Jack did not want the same pattern to continue with his own son. The very idea of Bobby cowering from him made Jack feel heavy hearted. In an effort to avoid this unpleasant feeling, Jack started to avoid approaching his son and soon Bobby got no attention from his dad. Jack started to ruminate about the whole situation and felt guilty and thought that he was a failure as a father. This self-concept, in turn, led to a cycle of other reactions and Jack eventually became quite depressed.

Fortunately Jack's relationship with his mum, Dianne, was one characterised by love and support. Dianne was a wise and observant mother and grandmother who noticed Jack's emerging depression and the dynamics between her son and grandson. When Dianne asked Jack about what was happening he burst into tears and spoke about his frustrations and fears. After the emotions settled, Jack and his mum reflected objectively about the cyclic patterns. Together they thought of some ways to exit what seemed to be descending negative emotional and behavioural spirals.

Jack realised that there were a number of opportunities to short-circuit his cycles of reactivity. Perhaps the greatest opportunity was to refrain from acting on his angry urge to hit his son. Jack noticed that the urge to hit was like a wave of energy that built up, had a peak, and eventually subsided if he didn't follow the urge. Instead of lashing out when he thought Bobby was naughty Jack ensured there was a reasonable and natural consequence for a 'naughty' behaviour.

Jack also learnt helpful and effective ways to deal with his children's behaviour. He made an effort to find things that Bobby and Sam did well and made positive comments about those things. Jack also devoted special time just to be with his son by involving him in projects around the house. Jack began to challenge his old interpretations of naughty behaviour and started to see his son in a different light.

Jack made a commitment to himself that he would manage his anger. Rather than being lost in thoughts, Jack began to be mindful of triggers, bodily sensations and urges. He also began to see himself and the thoughts he had about himself differently. The frequency of falling victim to negative and inaccurate self-concepts reduced substantially.

With commitment and effort Jack was able to exit his old reactive cycles and gained control of his aggressive behaviour. As a result the children became more manageable and their challenging behaviours decreased. Bobby in particular appeared much happier and reduced his attention-seeking behaviours. Jack felt better about himself, and a spiral into deep depression was prevented. As a result everyone in the family benefited and the development of more negative reactive cycles was averted.

Interdependence

Things do not occur in isolation and Jack's story is an example of interdependence. Jack's habitual reactions were influenced by the way his father had treated him. Possibly Jack's father was also treated in a harsh and cruel way as a child. Jack was treating his own son in the same way that his father had treated him. In this complicated web, Bobby's behaviour triggered Jack to express his anger in aggressive outbursts, which in a flow-on effect then influenced Bobby to be aggressive towards his sister. Jack also had internal reactions of rumination and guilt leading to a deepening sense of failure and depression. Reactive cyclic patterns can cause us to sink down into the mires and swamps of depression or trigger us to fly off in unwarranted angry outbursts.

In Buddhist cultures the cycle of birth and death is often depicted as a wheel with a central core, six sectors and an outer rim. The central core has a drawing of a pig chasing the tail of a chicken, which is chasing the tail of a snake, which in turn is chasing the tail of the pig. The pig, chicken and snake respectively, represent greed, ignorance and hatred. The six sectors of the middle circle refer to realms of existence and can also represent the different states of mind we find ourselves in, ranging from bliss or heaven, to torment or hell. Around the outer ring there are 12 drawings each representing psychological factors that lead to the continuation of *samsara* and *dukkha*. The 12 factors are linked like a chain reaction where one factor will trigger the next, which will trigger the next and so on. The principle behind the chain reaction is called dependent arising.

Dependent arising

While dependent arising is complex, it is explained succinctly throughout the Buddhist discourses as follows:

> When this exists, that comes to be:
> With the arising of this, that arises.
> When this does not exist that does not come to be,
> with the cessation of this, that ceases.
> (Bodhi, 2000, p. 552)[2]

Dependent arising is the fundamental principle through which the Buddha understood the nature of things. Dependent arising describes the natural laws of cause and effect. The principle of dependent arising is evident in the natural physical world, the non-physical realm of consciousness or mind and in the relationship between physical and non-physical phenomena. Dependent arising has also been called dependent origination, dependent co-arising, interdependence and even life.[3]

Although Buddhism is often viewed as a religion, the teachings of the Buddha tend to be more scientific than religious. The Buddha did not teach that life was created by an almighty, omnipresent and all-knowing God or that our lives unfold in ways determined by forces completely external to our selves. Rather he taught that life comes about because of complex interdependent relationships.

Many of us have learnt to understand that things happen in life in a linear way. That is, one thing leads to another in straight lines or linear sequences, for example when it doesn't rain our plants wither, when we get something we want, we feel happy, if we lose something, we feel sad, etc. Linear causality is a practical and useful way of understanding the mechanics of life and finding solutions for problems. In fact, linear causality was the original basis for understanding how to successfully work with thoughts when applying CBT to a range of psychological problems.

In CBT the principle used to understand thought and how it affects us is often explained as the ABC of thinking (Figure 6.1). In the ABC of thinking, (A) refers to activating events, (B) refers to beliefs or assumptions and (C) refers to emotional consequences. The ABC of thinking explains that it is not always the events of our lives that cause emotional upset but the way we think about them. When we have inaccurate beliefs or assumptions about ourselves or an event it often leads to emotional distress.

Therefore if we want to change the emotional upset (C) we can change the activating event (A) or as is done in CBT, the beliefs or assumptions (B) leading to the problem.

The third wave therapies lean towards interdependence as a way of understanding the causes of disorders and how to resolve them. As indicated in Figure 6.2, with interdependent notions of causality (A), (B) and (C) are mutually dependent.

With interdependent causality (B) is dependent on (A) for its coming into being and (C) is dependent on (B) and if there is no (A) or (B) then (C) does not arise. However, with interdependent causality (A) and (B) are also dependent on (C) for their coming into being. In other

Figure 6.1 Linear causality

words, as symbolised in Figure 6.2, the interdependent co-arisings of things are reciprocally affected by their interaction.

The principles of interdependence or dependent arising are complex and, according to the Buddha, are not fully comprehended until one realises Nirvana. Nonetheless, if you can get some notion of what it is about, it is extremely helpful on the path of psychological health, well-being and freedom. The more one understands aspects of dependent arising, the easier it is to make healthy choices.

An example of a rainforest may be a helpful way to illustrate dependent arising. A rainforest has developed over hundreds of years and is maintained by a sensitive ecosystem. Every part of a rainforest's ecosystem is constantly changing and affecting each and every other part. The system is not centred on one or two organisms but is a subtle web of interactions. As small changes occur a rainforest adapts and transforms. If something dramatic happens such as significant logging then it impacts on the whole system. For example; the rainforest depends on rain for the healthy growth of trees. In Figure 6.2 (A) could refer to the formation of clouds, (B) could refer to rain and (C) to trees. The whole system is interdependent. Rain is dependent on the formation of clouds, which is dependent on transpiration of trees pumping water into the sky, and trees are dependent on rain for their growth. If there were no trees, then there would not be any formation of clouds. When there are no clouds there is no rain. When there is no rain there are no trees. As all elements of the rainforest are interdependent the resultant flourishing of the rainforest, or its transformation to a barren desert, is dependent on these interdependent elements.

The complex unfolding of life is not dependent on one thing, but rather a coming together of causes and conditions within a context. One thing going wrong within a system has the potential to destroy

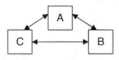

Figure 6.2 Interdependent causality
Source: adapted from Huxter (2007)

the whole system. Conversely if the system is not working then changing something within the system has the potential to resolve the problem. There is a saying in ACT: 'If I continue to do what I've always done, then I'm going to get what I've always got' (Forsyth and Eifert, 2007, p. 11). This phrase exemplifies the mechanics of dependent arising and suggests that if we continue to be stuck in patterns of unhelpful actions then unhelpful results will follow. In the story earlier, the *dukkha* that Jack was experiencing came into being due to a number of factors coming together, and doing what he had habitually done. The reduction of the *dukkha* was due to Jack beginning to change his habitual patterns.

In other words, in the absence of a cause, *dukkha* does not arise. This formula can be applied to the whole range of possible psychological disorders and issues. For example, the panic cycle illustrated in Chapter 5, and re-presented here for your convenience (Figure 6.3) involves a trigger, fight or flight responses, mental and physical experience and catastrophic misinterpretations of the experience.

When something is taken away from the reactive cycle it short-circuits. For example, when the person who panics no longer believes catastrophic thoughts about the experience then the cycle is no longer fueled and a panic cycle either slows down or panic disappears.

Depression is another example. The developers of MBCT (Segal et al., 2002) have found that when ruminative thoughts are not taken as facts to be believed, it slows down or stops rumination. When

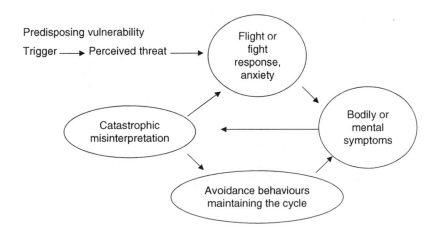

Figure 6.3 The panic cycle
Source: adapted from Wells (1997)

there is less or no rumination there is less likelihood of a relapse into depression.

Every psychological disorder has a pattern of cause and effect relationships involving triggers, physical sensations, thoughts, emotions and behaviours and every pattern can be broken. Regardless of whether *dukkha* receives a diagnosis as a disorder or it is simply the dissatisfaction of something not being perfect, everything is workable. We begin by being aware of the cycles. Then we can act in ways that will exit the cycles.

Classically, as depicted in the rim of the wheel of birth and death described earlier, dependent arising has 12 factors, each depending on another for its coming into being. For example: dependent on contact, feelings arise, dependent on feelings, craving arises, dependent on craving, grasping and clinging arise, dependent on clinging and grasping, action occurs, dependent on action, rebirth occurs, and so on. Another way to understand these interdependent links is illustrated in a flow diagram (Figure 6.4).

A cycle of stressful reactions can begin anywhere in the cycle. As a reference point for example, it might begin with a *situation* or *trigger*. This situation may be an *external event* such as something happening

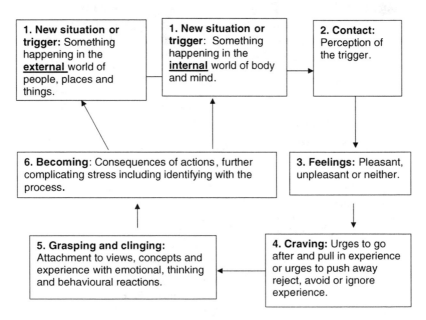

Figure 6.4 Cycle of stressful reactions
Source: adapted from Fryba (1989)

in our world or it could be an *internal event* such as an emotion, or bodily sensations, thoughts, beliefs, etc. In relationship to Jack's story one trigger was Bobby's behaviour. *Contact* is when an event impinges on our awareness and it is perceived. Contact in Jack's case involved the perception of Bobby's behaviour. After perceptions *feelings* will arise. In Jack's case, the feeling was unpleasant when Bobby's behaviour was perceived as being naughty.

Feelings give rise to *urges* (craving) to reject or avoid the experience by pushing it away, or to cling to the experience by pulling it in and holding on to it. If the experience is neither pleasant nor unpleasant we may ignore the experience, have no urges at all and do nothing. In Jack's case the habitual urge was to push away and try to get rid of the unpleasant experience, resulting in an aggressive reaction. Urges involve choice. We can decide to act on the urge and follow through with it, or we can decide to refrain from acting on the urge or do something different, just as Jack decided to resist the urge to hit his children. The choices we make are crucial to how a cycle unfolds. Whether we grasp and cling to pleasant experience, react with aggressive rejection or choose to ignore the experience and do nothing, there will be different consequences. Whatever we do leads to consequences and a new situation emerges. In the cycle of stressful reactions the emergence of a new situation is called *becoming*. This new situation becomes another trigger, which leads to new perceptions and feelings and the cycle goes around and around. It is *samsara*.

Dependent arising is not just a random pattern of events. Nor is it completely determined by forces beyond our control. Dependent arising follows patterns according to the formula referred to earlier: 'When this exists, that comes to be; with the arising of this, that arises. When this does not exist, that does not come to be; with the cessation of this, that ceases' (Bodhi, 2000, p. 552). Dependent arising demonstrates regular patterns and causal sequences. With close observation we can begin to see what leads to what and how we can change the outcomes, if we need to. We see that: *When I act in this way, this results, but if I do something different, something else will result*. When we see that we can work with our situation we are more able to choose to exit reactive cycles.

Exit possibilities

Classically, dependent arising is described in two directions. One direction spirals into *dukkha* and the other leads to freedom. The classic sequence described earlier can be reversed. When there is no craving,

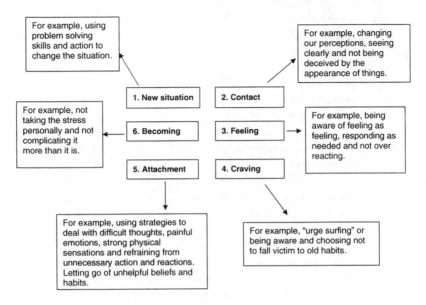

Figure 6.5   Reactive cycles with exit possibilities

grasping does not arise, when there is no grasping, there are no unhelpful actions, when there are no unhelpful actions, then there are no negative consequences of actions, and a reactive cycle of stress does not happen. When we stop doing what drives *dukkha* then *dukkha* also stops. Reactive cycles always have exit and entry possibilities. Figure 6.5 is an example of a cycle of stressful reactions, highlighting exit possibilities.

Remember Jack?

If we go back to Jack's story, we can see that Jack was able to exit a vicious cycle. After speaking with his mum, Jack began to perceive his son's behaviour in a different way and he made a decision to restrain from reacting with aggression. When he was no longer fuelling his angry reactions, they started to fade away. When Jack was less angry, he could see more clearly that he need not treat his son harshly to discipline him. This clarity resulted in Jack being able to parent Bobby more effectively. In direct relationship to Jack changing his behaviour, Bobby's behaviour also improved. Thus, Jack's story includes an example of the broader interpersonal aspects of dependent arising, where Bobby responded well to Jack's treatment of him. One skill that Jack applied to exit this particular cycle was urge surfing.

Urge surfing

Do you remember that right intention is one of the factors of the eight-fold path? Right intentions provide the motivation to act skilfully. Intentions can, however, also be impulses for unskilful action. Sometimes intentions are experienced as quick pictures, or words in the form of thoughts. Intentions can be extremely subtle and we may have thousands of intentions daily, many of which are not acted on. An urge is another way of describing an intention that has more intensity than subtle intentions. An urge may involve strong craving to avoid unpleasant feelings or to have pleasant feelings. If an urge leads us to being entangled in reactive and destructive cycles then we can choose to surf the urge.

'Urge surfing' is an expression coined by Alan Marlatt (e.g. 2002), an esteemed psychology professor who used mindfulness to help people with drug addictions. Mindfulness helps people with substance addiction to be aware of their cyclic patterns and resist reinforcing their habit. Urge surfing refers to not acting on urges or impulses that fuel reactive cycles. In most cases it refers to maintaining awareness and balance while experiencing the wave of craving to pull something towards oneself, or the wave of rejection, experienced as an impulse to push something away or even to be aggressive.

We can experience urges like waves that build up, reach a crescendo then pass on by. The term surfing is used because it is like staying balanced on a surfboard and either riding a wave in the ocean, or moving through it gracefully in some way or other. Staying balanced or moving skilfully through a wave is usually better than struggling with it and being dumped by its force. Urge surfing becomes a way for us to resist getting caught up in and reinforcing unhelpful habits. Following are some instructions for practising urge surfing.

Urge surfing

- Try to be mindful during all your waking hours.
- When an urge appears, note it accordingly.
- It could be noted as 'wanting . . . wanting', 'craving . . . craving' or 'rejection . . . rejection', 'urge . . . urge' or 'pushing away . . . aversion', etc.
- When you notice an urge arising make a decision about whether or not the urge needs to be acted on.

- If acting on the urge is not necessary or not in line with your valued directions, try 'surfing the urge'.
- Just like passing waves in the ocean build up, have a crescendo and then fall away, let urge waves arise and pass on by.
- Just like holding on to something solid and stable in the water, something unmovable when buffeted by the waves, let your awareness and your resolve be unshaken by the waves of wanting and not wanting. Maintain firm mindfulness as an urge wave comes towards you, builds in energy, tries to pull you along and then passes you by.
- Do not follow the urge . . . let it pass by.
- Sometimes you dive through the wave. With minimal surface area to catch you, the urge wave just flows around you smoothly.
- Sometimes it is as if you surf along the side and ride the wave using mindfulness to maintain equilibrium. Using the energy of the wave you can move gracefully down the edge and avoid being swept away, losing control or being dumped.
- Let go of struggle and maintain balance with mindfulness and clear intention.

Exiting reactive cycles requires us to pay close attention to patterns both within ourselves and in the world around us. The function of the fourth application of mindfulness is to develop an understanding of these patterns so that we can choose to reinforce them if they are helpful or to not reinforce them if they are not helpful.

Contemplating phenomena (*dharmas*): the fourth application of mindfulness

In Chapter 1 a variety of meanings for the term '*dharma*' were explained. A *dharma* has two essential aspects: experiencing and what is experienced. When a *dharma* is understood as a phenomenon, it is not a thing out there but an experience-of-a-thing. The focus of the fourth application of mindfulness, contemplating *dharmas*, involves bringing attention to a broad range of phenomena, or experiences. This application of mindfulness focuses on dependent arising and psychological patterns and includes all the experiences of life that are not addressed in the other three applications. The fourth application of mindfulness stands separate from the other three in that there is less passive observation and more active engagement and intelligent discernment. In particular, the fourth application involves paying attention to psychological patterns in order to maximise the skilful and minimise the unskilful. The objects of the fourth application of mindfulness can be as wide and broad as the whole of life and all of our inner and outer worlds. Using the fourth application of mindfulness we can focus on particular areas of life that may be relevant for progress along a path of psychological health and wellbeing. In the *Satipathana Sutta* the Buddha highlighted five sub-domains of the fourth application.

1. Contemplation of the five hindrances or obstacles to the cultivation of heart-mind: obsessive sense desire, ill will, lethargy, restlessness and paralysing doubt.
2. Contemplation of what we normally call our self: body-heart-mind. Body refers to solid tangible experiences and heart-mind includes feelings, perceptions, mental creations and consciousness.
3. Contemplation of the six sense bases: sight, sound, smell, touch, taste and thought (in Buddhist psychology mind is considered as a sense base).
4. Contemplation of seven factors of awakening: mindfulness, investigation, energy, joy, tranquillity, concentration and equanimity.
5. Contemplation of the four noble truths: *dukkha*, the cause of *dukkha*, freedom from *dukkha* and the way to freedom from *dukkha*.

1. Contemplation of the five hindrances

As mentioned in Chapter 3, there are five hindrances to meditation that also block the path of psychological health, wellbeing and freedom:

1. Obsessive and unnecessary sense desire.
2. Hostility, ill will or unhelpful aversion.
3. Lethargy and mental dullness.
4. Restlessness, agitation and worry.
5. Debilitating uncertainty or paralysing doubt.

The nature of the hindrances is illustrated in one of the Buddhist *suttas* by a simile in which meditation is compared to looking at a reflection in water. Analayo (2003, p.189), a Buddhist scholar and monk practitioner, describes this as follows:

According to these similes the effect of sensual desire is similar
to water mixed with dye; aversion resembles water heated to the
boil; sloth and torpor [lethargy] is compared to water overgrown
with algae; restless-and-worry affect the mind like water being
stirred by wind; and doubt is like dark and muddy water. In all five
cases, one is unable to see one's reflection properly in the water
... sensual desire colours one's perceptions; because of aversion,
one gets heated; sloth-and-torpor [lethargy and mental dullness]
results in stagnation; through restlessness-and-worry one is tossed
about; and [paralysing] doubt obscures.

Contemplation of the five hindrances includes being aware of whether
they are present or absent and how they arise. Being mindful of the
hindrances also includes being aware of how to work with and let
these tendencies go if they have arisen and how to prevent them from
arising in the future.

Mindfulness is possibly the most effective tool to transform the
obstacles, or patterns that bind, into forces that liberate. As well as
mindfulness there are antidotes for each of the hindrances. In addition
we can each devise and tailor personalised strategies based on our own
habits and temperament.

Obsessive (sensual) desire

Some say that love (when it is based on lust) is blind. When our perceptions are coloured with the dye of sensual craving they become
distorted and we can easily mistake, misperceive and misunderstand
what we are experiencing. As discussed in Chapter 1, desire can be
helpful, especially when we need energy to follow our valued directions in life. However, desire becomes a hindrance when clinging
and grasping drives it. Traditionally this hindrance refers to desire of
the senses. In Buddhism the senses include the five senses as well as
heart-mind. Therefore we can desire everything that we smell, touch,
taste, see, hear and perceive, including ideas and concepts. Obsessively
wanting pleasant experiences and resisting inevitable change creates an obstacle to meditation and the path to health and wellbeing.
There is nothing wrong with enjoying life and everything that life has
to offer. If, however, we cling to the objects of our enjoyment when
they eventually change then we are destined to be unhappy. A revered
English-born Buddhist monk[4] once said that one way to be happy is
to want what we already have. If we constantly want what we don't
have then we will be unhappy. If we habitually look for happiness

outside our current experience we will be dissatisfied with what we already have.

Obsessive desire can be subtle or extreme. At a subtle level, this hindrance could come up as clinging to expectations in our meditation. We may, for example, have one meditation where we become very calm and relaxed and our body feels blissful and in the next meditation session we may expect the same thing to happen and be disappointed. Unfortunately this expectation is an example of an unhelpful desire because it pulls us out of current experience and leads us to dissatisfaction with the way things are. Planning to do something other than what we are doing, or being lost and enchanted with fantasies, regardless of what they may be, when it would be best to focus on current activity are subtle forms of obsessive desire. We can be deceived and blinded by the object of our wanting, rather than seeing clearly. Many desires are illusory. We believe that once we have what we desire we can finally be satisfied. However, satisfaction is rarely delivered.

Steadiness and stability of attention are antidotes for a mind filled with sensual desire that jumps from one possibility of pleasure to another. Other strategies include:

• Noting 'desire', 'wanting' or 'craving' as it arises in one's mind.
• Reflecting on the impermanent nature of all things.
• Cultivating generosity and gratitude for what we already have
• Simplifying one's life and being content with moderate levels of pleasure.
• Maintaining good friendships and having useful conversations.

Hostility and ill will

In Chapter 1, aversion was referred to as one of the root causes of *dukkha*. However, just as desire can be helpful, aversion can be a natural response that is necessary for survival and protection from harm. For example, one characteristic of aversion is avoidance of physical and emotional pain. Nonetheless, when our heart-minds are disturbed by ill will, they become contracted and cramped, darkening our vision and creating divisions within ourselves and the world around us. Hostility and ill will includes unconstructive and unfounded criticism, condemnation, and negative judgements towards others and self. Those who are depressed are often trapped by aversion and ill will in the form of self-hatred. Just like desire, ill will can deceive us by exaggerating, distorting and clouding our perceptions of life, ourselves and other people. It is as if we project our aversion out onto the world and it bounces back. Aversion, when it is an obstacle, works to isolate, contract and cut us off from the world and people around us. At a subtle level boredom can also be a form of aversion because we reject the reality of the present. Mulling over what we perceive as life's injustices is also aversion.

As aversion often manifests as anger, many of the strategies described in the previous chapter to work with unbalanced anger can also be used with this hindrance. Loving kindness, acceptance and tolerance are direct antidotes for this hindrance. Curious investigation of how this obstacle comes up within us, the factors associated with it, what maintains it and how it is released, are other ways it can be addressed.

Lethargy and mental dullness

The mind hazed with lethargy and dullness lacks the mental clarity required to clearly perceive the characteristics of existence and the relationships between experiences. This hindrance blocks the path to psychological health and wellbeing because we cannot see clearly enough to develop understanding. Mental dullness clouds awareness and may appear as sleepiness when in fact we do not need sleep. Our minds become stiff and inflexible, thick and foggy, as if the contents of the mind are impenetrable.

Sometimes mental dullness can be caused by an energetic or physical imbalance and we may need to open our eyes or move our bodies or somehow address the energetic blocks. At other times it can be a form of avoidance or resistance to difficult or painful experiences. As we cultivate our heart-minds the process may uncover painful memories and shutting down our awareness may be one way we habitually deal with these experiences. Even though avoidance may be a way to cope, it can also keep us bound to the *dukkha* of *samsara*.

Sometimes we may think that the hindrance of lethargy and mental dullness is present, when all we really need is to sleep. It is important to have enough regular sleep and to allow ourselves to rest and recuperate when needed. Sleep is necessary and has a restorative function. Many of us live our lives constantly sleep deprived and when we have an opportunity to stop, sleepiness envelops us. It is very important that we do not treat ourselves harshly and often the best solution to sleep deprivation is to kindly give yourself what you need and catch up with your sleep. This hindrance can also masquerade as calm and tranquillity when it is in fact the blissful oblivion of falling asleep. At these times our period of formal meditation practice may pass very quickly indeed!

How do we work with this hindrance? If you have had enough sleep and this obstacle to cultivating the heart-mind is truly present, then there are many strategies that can be used. One of my meditation teachers, Venerable Sayadaw U. Pandita, once said that a way to transform mental dullness is to have right aim (Pandita, 1992). I interpret this as focusing clearly on one thing at a time rather than letting one's attention be dispersed. Right aim may be practised by intentionally focusing on the minute details of an action or experience. On one retreat I focused with curiosity on the subtle sensations of my head falling forward as I was slumbering off into mental dullness and quickly my mind became very clear! In this way I used interest and investigation as a way to wake up. When this hindrance is related to energetic blocks it is useful to open your eyes, stand, walk or move in some way. If you are in a warm and stuffy room, go outdoors, or take off your coat or blanket and try looking at light.

Restlessness

Restlessness, agitation and worry cause the mind to jump about making it unable to focus. Some features of restlessness are arousal, agitation, worry, rumination, guilt and the feeling that we cannot trust, rest in and appreciate our current experience. At a physical level it may feel as if we just can't sit still. At an emotional and mental level our mind may be agitated flitting from one thing to the next, never staying focused long enough to see deeply. The fourth hindrance blocks the path because it disperses attention so that there is no depth in our concentration.

The hindrance of restlessness is similar to lethargy in that sometimes it may result from a physical or energetic imbalance. It is, however, very different from being in a haze, because restlessness can have a quality of sharp alertness. Unfortunately this alertness is not balanced with calm and doesn't have the strength to move beyond the superficial.

Sometimes meditators experience restlessness when they try too hard, or they take the meditation practice too seriously. This unbalanced effort easily turns to tension, and the mind cannot concentrate. A good antidote for this is to simply relax, 'chill out' and do something enjoyable. Restlessness can be transformed by engaging in enjoyable and interesting activities that focus attention. Enjoyable activities vary from individual to individual. For me, some enjoyable activities include going for a walk or a long ride on a bicycle in natural surroundings, sweeping a path, surfing, scuba diving, playing guitar or playing some basketball. Serenity meditation practices are also often recommended for restlessness. The mind can easily focus and become calm when it absorbs into meditation objects that have happy, pleasant or interesting themes.

Restlessness may be a common experience for those who suffer from depression or anxiety. As mentioned in Chapter 4, mental proliferation (*papanca*), which is common in depression and anxiety, can be a feature of the fourth hindrance. A good way to work with proliferating thoughts is to practise 'bare attention'. Remember, bare attention involves paying attention to the raw experience of the senses, free from the filters of conceptual thoughts. Bare attention will be discussed again later in this chapter.

Another factor often associated with restlessness is remorse and guilt about unwise and harmful actions that we have done in the past. One approach to working with these experiences is learning from the past and committing to act ethically in the future.

An analogy of restraining a wild bull with force is useful in considering how to manage restlessness. When constrained, a bull's agitation may escalate. But if it is freed and allowed to roam in a spacious paddock it may calm down. Giving a sense of spaciousness to restlessness helps to quell, calm and transform this hindrance into peacefulness. Some strategies to work with restlessness are as follows:

- Emphasising movement, such as physical exercise or walking, rather than forcing oneself to sit still for hours meditating.
- Bringing a sense of spaciousness to our meditation by, for example, directing attention to things outside ourselves such as sounds or expansive views.
- Utilising 'open awareness' (explained later in this chapter) where attention does not focus on selected and narrow fields of awareness.
- Seeing restlessness for what it is, not identifying with it, letting go of the need to control it and cultivating deep acceptance.

Paralysing doubt

The fifth hindrance, paralysing doubt, has been compared to mud because it obscures our reflection and is thick and difficult to move through. Paralysing doubt can also be described as debilitating uncertainty. It has been compared to a man at the fork of a road not knowing what direction to take; he becomes paralysed unable to take any path and remains stuck where he is. Doubt can be a sense of scepticism or uncertainty about something. In many circumstances doubt can be helpful. When we question the validity and usefulness of our actions doubt can lead to understanding and the ability to make informed decisions. In circumstances where doubt takes the form of unwarranted scepticism, however, it can be a hindrance to developing understanding and happiness.

As well as indecision, doubt can manifest as judgemental and narrow-minded cynicism. When the questioning mind becomes entangled with cynicism we can become stuck in intellectual analysis. When doubt arises in meditation we may become unwilling to practise. We may question the usefulness of what we are doing and think that it is a complete waste of time. We may find ourselves thinking something like, 'How could being aware of the movement of my feet as I walk [in walking meditation] help in any way with my anxious or depressed moods? This practice is ridiculous . . . the people who practise these meditations are deluding themselves', and so on. This type of mental activity restricts motivation and attention, and ultimately the ability to learn and cultivate understanding. When we are paralysed with doubt we are unwilling to take the risk of a new experience. Without experience there is no opportunity to learn from experience. When there is an unwillingness to practise there are no results from the practice.

The natural antidote to paralysing doubt is faith. Here faith can mean the trust or confidence that a particular path of action will lead to a helpful outcome. Trust is the acknowledgement of a possibility even though we have not yet experienced that possibility. Confidence, on the other hand, comes from experience. If we have tried something at least once and experienced a positive result we can develop confidence that doing something similar will bear similar results. Hopefulness is another way of understanding faith. In this context, hope does not mean wishing and craving for a particular outcome. Rather, it refers to a form of inspiration that is the opposite of hopelessness. Faith is cultivated in a circular, interdependent manner. When we have faith that freedom from stress is possible and meditation may be helpful, we are willing to make an effort to practise. When we are motivated and bring awareness (mindfulness) to an issue, it helps us to focus and see the issue clearly. With mindfulness and concentration, wisdom arises. Wisdom or understanding then helps to reinforce faith and the cycle continues (Figure 6.6).[5]

As described above, some of the antidotes to paralysing doubt include:

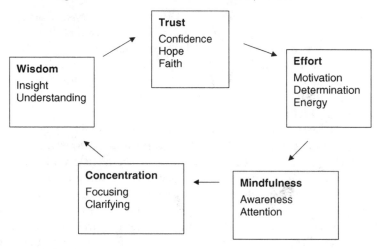

Figure 6.6 The five faculties

- Cultivating faith.
- Reflecting on what is helpful to short-circuit reactive cycles.
- Recognising doubt when it arises and choosing not to get caught up in the stories that doubt generates.
- Cultivating commitment and acting in accordance with commitment.
- Learning, understanding and discussing how *dukkha* develops and is managed.
- Developing helpful friendships and having useful conversations.

2. Contemplation of the 'self'

This contemplation focuses on the self. It is our 'self' that experiences *dukkha* as well as wellbeing and happiness. Therefore it is important that we understand what it is that we call the self and how we develop this understanding. From a Buddhist perspective the self is the changing elements of mind (heart-mind, mentality) and body (form). The Buddhist understanding is that there are five groups of experience, that together are called 'I', 'mine' and 'myself'. In Pali these five groups are called *khanda*. This is often translated as aggregates or clumps because each is made up of many different experiences clumped together. The first group relates to body and the other four relate to mind. Mind is considered to be that which knows and experiences. Body is considered as phenomena that cannot know or experience. Mind and body are interactive and interconnected. If we cut our hand and it hurts, the 'body' as solid matter is cut, but the 'mind' experiences the pain.

The five *khanda* are:

1. *Form*, which refers to solid tangible matter. We experience the most basic elements of body or form as experiences of hardness and softness, temperature, movement and a sense of cohesion.
2. *Feelings (vedana)* (as described in previous chapters), refers to the emotional tones, or flavours, of pleasantness, unpleasantness or neither. Feelings can arise dependent on the changing nature of physical phenomena or on the changing nature of mind.
3. *Perceptions*, which involve the mental functions of remembering, recognising, perceiving and naming objects. Perceptions may only last a moment. They are nonetheless distinct moments of recognising something. Recognising sound vibrations that hit the ear drum as the sound of a car, or a bird, or our son or daughter calling, are examples of perception.
4. *Mental formations*, which involve thought and the creative nature of thought. This group of experiences involves the construction of concepts, including those related to who and what we conceive ourselves to be.
5. *Consciousness*, which involves the sense of knowing and awareness at basic and refined levels. Sometimes consciousness is considered to be the same as heart-mind as it has been described in this book. Volumes have been written about consciousness and there are many different perspectives on what it is and what its different layers are. At its most basic level, however, consciousness occurs in every moment of waking life in reference to specific objects of sight, sound, smell, touch, taste and mind. In other words consciousness arises when there is a coming together of an object to be aware of and the perception of that object. Consciousness brings a sense of cohesion to the patchwork of experiences related to self.

These five groups of experience are interdependent and constantly changing. Confusion about the nature of these experiences is at the core of *dukkha*. Clinging to the five groups of experience that together are called 'I', 'mine' and 'myself' is a subtle form of *dukkha*. One way to remedy this confusion is to use mindfulness to develop an understanding about the self. The *Satipathana Sutta* instructs us to bring attention to these experiences or *khanda* in order to develop insight. According to the Buddhist monk, Analayo (2003), the Buddha spoke about the contemplation of the *khanda* as being a 'lion's roar' because of its powerful potential to awaken insight and psychological freedom.

We can contemplate the *khanda*, or the experiences that make up the self, at any time, whether we are formally meditating or not. Moreover, every aspect of our personal experience can be used to help cultivate insight into the nature of self. For example, noticing the physical experience of sitting on a chair at work (form), the unpleasant feelings of being in traffic (feelings), the recognition of a person's voice on the phone (perceptions), planning for a project (mental formations) or simply recognising that we are aware (consciousness) at moments throughout the day. There are also situations and formal meditation practices where contemplation of the *khanda* can become a focus. For example, if we were to sit alone in a dark cave in silence and pitch black darkness we would be confronted with the *khanda*. There would be nothing for us to be aware of except mind and body.

When we are mindful and able to notice and distinguish these various experiences we realise they are impermanent. Contemplating the *khanda* and seeing their impermanence changes our perspective of the 'self' as a fixed identity or possession or something that we can control. Sometimes it helps to question who or what is experiencing the immediate experience? Where, what or who is the essence of what I call I, mine and myself?

Who or what am I?

Curious investigation or enquiry has been described in numerous places throughout this book. Curious enquiry is an ally to mindfulness and a defining feature of insight meditation. When we investigate the nature of painful thoughts, emotions and physical sensations, for example, it can help us to be free from the reactions that lead to further suffering. Sometimes, investigation may involve some reasoning or discursive thought. In Buddhist meditation practices, however, investigation is a quality of mind which is much deeper and more intuitive than logical verbal thought processes.

Koans are powerful meditation practices in some Zen Buddhist traditions. As far as I understand, Koans are paradoxical questions, which can be used to cultivate the quality of curious investigation. 'What is the sound of one hand clapping' is an example of a Zen koan. Other popular koans include: 'what is life?', 'who am I?', 'what is it?', 'what is the truth?' or 'what's this?' The underlying theme of a koan seems to be an unanswerable question about whatever is being examined. The questioning is not meant to provide a rational answer but to awaken a sense of mystery and awe.

We can bring curious investigation to the five *khanda*. This can include: sounds, smells, tastes, sights, sensations, thoughts, emotions, feelings, reactive patterns and what it is that knows all these experiences. The following is an example of how we can practise contemplating the self.

Enquiry about the self

Begin your meditation practice by using whatever strategies are useful for you to establish mindfulness. This will vary from individual to individual but could include bringing attention to any of the primary objects of meditation described in this book such as: body scan, general relaxation, sound or breath.

When you feel that your body is relaxed and your mind is relatively calm and peaceful ask yourself what is strongest in your experience in this present moment. It could be sights, sounds, smells, tastes, physical sensations, breath, thoughts, a mood state, a hindrance, a factor of awakening or something else. Then ask yourself 'what is this?' or 'what is really going on here?' Remember that even though your mind may come up with smart and logical answers and stories about what is happening, the emphasis is on cultivating the quality of investigation and knowing the three characteristics of life (change, interdependence and uncertainty). This process may be exasperating and frustrating or very interesting and calming. Whatever the reaction or response that arises, let it also be the object of penetrative enquiry with the question 'what is happening here?' You may have thoughts, ideas, concepts, views, etc., about who is doing the enquiry. If so, let these self concepts also be the object of curious investigation. Remember to step back into the depths of awareness without dissociating or cutting yourself off and merely notice all the ideas with a sense of questioning curiosity.

Questions such as 'who or what is watching, witnessing, knowing, listening being conscious of all of these experiences?' may arise. If so, then let consciousness be the object of enquiry and contemplation. You could try this by feeling as if you are stepping back into a deeper perspective of awareness. You may also feel there is nothing you can do other than be present and aware. After a while it may feel as if the questioning becomes very refined and falls away to give rise to simply being present. Notice this experience and when it changes notice how it changes. Always allow mindfulness to be your refuge.

Remember that if you feel overwhelmed, lost or falling apart with this or similar meditation practices, you are free to apply grounding and anchoring strategies by shifting attention to something tangible such as: the breath or bodily sensations, movement, being active, becoming engaged in a concrete task (such as doing the housework) or finding someone to talk to.

Continue with the questions of enquiry until the allotted period of time for your practice is completed then spend a few moments reflecting on insights you may have gained by doing this practice.

When you are ready you are invited to participate fully with your daily activities with awareness and peace.

3. Contemplation of the six sense spheres

The instructions in the *sutta* for this sub-domain are to bring attention to the sense organ and the sense object. According to Buddhist psychology the six sense spheres are: sight, sound, smell, touch, taste and heart-mind.

In the time of the Buddha there was a seeker called Bahiya who, sensing that his death was imminent, wanted to receive the pith of the Buddha's teachings before it was too late. Seeing the Buddha on alms round, he went up to him and asked for the essence. The Buddha, being aware of Bahiya's determination to realise awakening before dying, gave possibly the shortest discourse recorded. An extract of the discourse as translated by Thanissaro Bhikkhu[6] follows:

> In the seen there is only the seen; in the heard, there is only the heard; in the sensed, there is only the sensed; in the cognized [mentally perceived], there is only the cognized. This Bahiya is how you should train yourself.

According to records, the seeker realised Nirvana when he heard this discourse. This short discourse describes a practice of bare attention.

As mentioned in Chapters 1 and 4, bare attention refers to the moments of awareness of something before we begin to identify and conceptualise. It is called 'bare' because the objects of attention are not covered and filtered by concepts and views. Settling the mind in its natural state, as described in Chapter 4, is an example of bare attention in which we bring attention to objects of heart-mind, such as thought.

The practice of bare attention is quite common in contemporary psychology to short-circuit reactive cycles. Bringing attention to raw sensory experience can slow down and stop the descending spirals of rumination, in depression or calm the escalation of worry in anxiety. Paying attention to the experience of sound or sight, for example, can short-circuit panic attacks.

Paying attention to sounds, as described in Chapter 1, is an example of contemplating the six sense spheres. We can note the impermanence of sounds as well as the tendency to cling to pleasant sounds or reject and condemn unpleasant sounds. In this way we develop an understanding of how craving and clinging manifest and how they can be released. The following meditation script is an example of one way to practise contemplating the six sense spheres.

Open awareness

Settle your body and mind and make yourself completely comfortable. Make the resolve to incline towards stillness and clarity, relaxing tension and being present for the period of this exercise. Allow the wide and broad experience of this moment to be the object of attention and bring attention to experience in a relaxed, open-minded and compassionate manner. Release any striving to achieve a goal and enjoy, with non-attachment, the simplicity of being. Be content with this simplicity.

You may like to leave your eyes slightly open but let their focus be diffuse, or, if you want you can close your eyes. Whatever you choose retain a sense of awake-awareness that seems to spread in all directions.

Don't force your mind to focus on any one particular experience but allow attention to settle onto whatever seems particularly predominant. Let awareness go where it wants to go. Be open to and aware of whatever is happening in this present moment as it changes moment to moment. Do not focus on anything in particular but let whatever is predominant come into your awareness without feeling that experiences should be other than how they are. Be attentive to sights as sights, sounds as sounds, smells as smells, tastes as tastes, touch and sensations as sensations and mind and objects of mind such as thoughts and moods just as they are.

Being present, let your aware mind be open and wide like the sky. Like the sky your mind is spacious enough to contain all experience – sights, sounds, smells, tastes, bodily sensations, thoughts and mind-states. Be attentive to and notice whatever happens in the immediate present. There may be sounds, there may be thoughts or there may be emotions. There may be various sensations or visual images. Whatever the experience, be present with the experiences as they arise and then notice how they pass away.

As sound arises, you can note 'hearing'.

As thought arises and passes, you can note 'thinking'.

As smell arises and changes, you can note 'smelling'.

Be mindful of sights as sights, smells as smells, sounds as sounds, sensations as sensations, thoughts as thoughts, feelings as feelings, states of heart-mind as states of heart-mind.

Noting and naming these experiences may help you maintain a perspective of spaciousness with them. Note whatever presents simply and objectively. There may be hearing hearing, or thinking thinking, remembering remembering, sitting sitting or the in and out of the breath. Note and be aware of whatever is central in the wide sphere of your awareness.

If noting is too cumbersome be content to merely notice these experiences. Just as the sky rejects or denies nothing, be willing to accept the experiences that arise in your mind with open-hearted compassion. Just as the sky cannot claim ownership, neither cling to nor hold on to anything. Be allowing and open to whatever arises and passes without preference. Take refuge in this present moment; willingly observe experience from the perspective of awareness. Settle back into the spacious and expansive nature of your awareness and watch the show.

Observe thoughts and states of the heart-mind like clouds across the sky. Sometimes they are delightful with beautiful shapes and colours. Sometimes they are clearly insubstantial, light, thin and almost translucent, moving and changing with the wind and passing by.

Sometimes thoughts and states of heart-mind are like thick, dark, heavy and menacing storm clouds that block the sky. Though turbulent and sometimes frightening, know that such storms in the mind must pass. Know also that such storms are deceivingly illusive and insubstantial. Know that they are not you and you need not identify with them. Know that the spaciousness of the aware mind is untouched by these emotional storms. Take refuge in the spaciousness of awareness. Being present and being aware in the moment has the power to calm all mental and emotional storms.

Be present with whatever arises in this wide sphere of awareness without focusing on anything in particular. Notice how it changes. Notice also how experience arises and passes because other conditions change. Notice how one experience leads to another. Attend to the continuous arising of momentary events and their relationships, this leading to that. Notice the causal patterns and their relationships.

Now, silently observe the play of experiences arising and interacting and passing.

(Silence for whatever period is suitable)

Now that you are coming to the end of this formal meditation period assess if open awareness gave you a sense of peacefulness and freedom. If it has, know that you can choose, with wisdom, suitable and appropriate moments in your busy daily life where open awareness may provide a sense of spaciousness and freedom.

If you have chosen to end this exercise, begin by mindfully moving your fingers and toes, then the rest of your body. Remember where you are and what you are doing. As you stand and go about your daily activities do so with presence, purpose and attention.

4. Contemplation of the seven factors of awakening

Just as there are five obstacles to meditation, there are seven factors that lead us to psychological health, wellbeing and awakening. These seven factors are:

1. Mindfulness/awareness.
2. Investigation/curiosity/enquiry.
3. Effort/energy/determination/motivation.
4. Rapture/joy/emotional wellbeing or lightness of heart.
5. Tranquillity/calm/serenity/relaxation.
6. Focused attention/concentration.
7. Equanimity/unshakable understanding/peacefulness.

The seven awakening factors have the opposite function to the five hindrances or obstacles and their cultivation is therapeutic. Two opposing football teams could be used as an analogy for the relationship between the seven factors of awakening and the five obstacles of meditation described earlier. The 'factors of awakening' team needs to outmanoeuvre, outskill and overcome the 'five obstacles' team. On the 'factors of awakening' team, mindfulness could be compared to the goal kicker. The goal kicker, however, does not work alone nor is she/he acting without significant training, practice and fitness. To overcome the 'five obstacles' team and score a goal requires skill, training, fitness and the whole 'awakening' team working together. Each team member (or factor) needs the other team players to complement their skills as well as support their mutual aims. With the 'awakening' team, concentration, for example, provides power and precision to the play. Effort provides the fitness and energy whilst joy the reward and positive inspiration to continue. Further to this, investigation provides the understanding of strategies that work, whilst equanimity and tranquillity, the graceful poise that is needed to achieve the goal.

Just as each member of a football team needs time, training and practice to refine their particular skills and learn to work with other team members, so too does each awakening factor benefit from cultivation. Awakening factors such as mindfulness, motivation, calm relaxation, joy, concentration, peacefulness, etc., are basic components of many contemporary psychotherapeutic approaches and some of these contemporary strategies have been discussed in this book. Strategies for how to cultivate each factor are also listed in popular as well as classic Buddhist texts such as the Abhidhamma (Bodhi, 2000a; Pandita, 1992). Please see Appendix B for examples.

Similar to the factors of the eight-fold path, the seven factors of awakening have refined and basic levels. Refined levels usually occur at advanced levels of meditation practice. Basic levels can occur in daily life. They are factors that lead to awakening about what is happening in our life, the world and our self. In the Abhidhamma (Bodhi, 2000a), the seven factors are described in terms of three aspects: their main characteristics, how they function and how they manifest or appear in the heart-mind.

1. *Mindfulness*:
   - The characteristic of mindfulness is non-superficiality. That is, it penetrates experience.
   - The function of mindfulness is non-disappearance or to keep the object in view.
   - The manifestation of mindfulness is confrontation, or a coming face-to-face with experience.
2. *Investigation*:
   - The characteristic of investigation is an intuitive knowledge about life including *Samsara* and the way to exit reactive cycles.
   - The function of investigation is to 'dispel darkness' or to clarify whatever is not clear.
   - The manifestation of investigation is clarity of understanding.
3. *Effort*:
   - The characteristic of effort is enduring patience with difficulty and hardship.
   - The function of effort is to support wholesome mental states.
   - The manifestation of effort is courage (to face up to experience) and boldness.
4. *Joy*:
   - The characteristic of joy is delight, satisfaction and happiness.
   - The function of joy is a light and buoyant energy.
   - The manifestation of joy is sensations of lightness.
5. *Tranquillity*:
   - The characteristic of tranquillity is a calm mind and a relaxed body.
   - The function of tranquillity is to calm agitation and restlessness.
   - The manifestation of tranquillity is a calm mind and a relaxed body, a non-agitation of body and heart-mind.
6. *Concentration*:
   - The characteristic of concentration is 'non-dispersal' or a mind that is not scattered.
   - The function of concentration is to collect the mind or gather in attention.
   - The manifestation of concentration is stillness and peace.
7. *Equanimity*:
   - The characteristic of equanimity is the balancing of opposing mental states.
   - The function of equanimity is to reduce where there is excess and fill in where there is deficiency or lack.
   - The manifestation of equanimity is ease and balance.

Like limbs on a tree, the seven factors grow and send out new branches and sprout new leaves. When *mindfulness* grows or is cultivated, it leads to curious *investigation* or *enquiry*. With meditative enquiry we may ask something like, 'what is happening here?' or 'what is it?' or 'what is really going on here?' or 'what is the truth of this experience?' Though some questions about life cannot be answered, enquiry can lead to understanding and provide insights. This understanding is liberating and can give rise to *motivation* and *courageous energy* to break binding habits. Being willing and enthusiastic also awakens us to emotional freedom and a realisation of the beautiful aspects of life. Realising freedom and beauty naturally leads to *joy* or a *lightness of heart*. This rapture can be felt in both our bodies and our hearts in a way that seems to bubble up and through our being. Joy gives rise to a sense of comfort both within ourselves and with the world around us. A sense of ease is the way that a *calm* and *tranquil* mind and a *relaxed* body are experienced. Tranquillity leads to the ability to collect the mind and *concentrate* attention appropriately. With a unified heart-mind we can absorb ourselves with what we focus on, and the sense of separation is dissolved. Feeling intrinsically connected both within ourselves and with the things around us naturally gives rise to a sense of ease and peacefulness or *equanimity*, which is unshaken by the changing, interdependent and uncertain nature of life.

The instructions in the *Satipathana Sutta* are simply to observe whether the factors are present or not, then to apply strategies directed at cultivating and maintaining them. In other words, notice when a factor is present and become familiar with it, pay attention to what caused it and understand how it can be cultivated. We can then act in a way that will reinforce and develop this helpful quality. The following script is an example.

Contemplating the hindrances of and factors to awakening

Ensure that you are at ease with your posture and your body is free from constriction and discomfort. Set the intention that for the period of this exercise you will first settle the body, inner speech and mind in a way that is relaxed, still and aware. Also set the intentions to bring curious attention to the patterns of mind that hinder psychological freedom as well as those patterns of mind that are factors of awakening.

Let awareness centre on a chosen object. It may be the experience of sitting or the rising and falling of your abdomen. It could be strong sensations in your body or sounds. Whatever you choose let that object be like an anchor or a place of reference you can bring your attention back to when you need. Allow your mind to quieten by being centred and enjoy the silence for a few moments.

Now open your awareness 360 degrees to illuminate all fields of experience – both body and heart-mind. Attend with curiosity to the continuous arising of momentary events and their patterns.

Engage with a sense of honest enquiry and ask yourself 'is awareness obscured by unwholesome patterns or is it engaged with qualities of mind that lead to happiness and freedom?'

Pay close attention and notice what happens. Examining the appearances of all six senses, apply discerning intelligence to distinguish those patterns that hinder the path to liberation from factors that support and enhance awakening of the heart-mind. Attend closely to both unhelpful patterns as well as those that are helpful on the path. Remain face-to-face with reality, attentive, engaged and vigilant, without slipping into distraction or excitation. Maintain an ongoing flow of awareness.

Do not limit your attention to the patterns that are classically described such as the five hindrances or the seven factors of awakening, but use these qualities of heart-mind as a reference point.

Is your heart obscured by obsessive desire? Are you in the grip of fantasies or cravings? If so what makes them stronger and what helps to release their grip? Notice how these patterns change and pay close attention to how the mind is hijacked and deceived.

Enquire and ask yourself if aversion is present. Is there ill will and hatred boiling the heart, or is aversion present in subtle forms such as boredom, mild irritation or simmering resentments? In an objective manner, investigate the factors that may be associated with aversion. Then, if you choose to abandon this hindrance, open your heart and bring kind awareness to the experience.

Ask yourself if your heart-mind is obscured with dullness, mental stiffness or lethargy. Bring sharp-minded clarity to your experience. Investigate, with energy, the factors related to this lethargy and dullness, and with mindfulness wake up to the experience.

Ask yourself is your heart-mind-body agitated with rest-lessness and worry? If so courageously explore what factors agitate it more and what factors calm and settle the mind. If you can, relax and focus, centre, settle and stabilise. Let your awareness be open and broad. Do not struggle and try to make it better. Simply focus, relax and calm your mind.

Ask yourself is paralysing doubt hindering presence? Is procrastination about commitment and uncertainty about the worth of the practice blocking attention? If so, remember your commitments and resolve and bring attention to this present moment, with confidence.

How do the hindrances arise? How are they present? What effect do they have on the body, mind and the way things are seen and understood? What factors reduce their strength and power over you? How can you release them?

Allow mindfulness to flourish and grow. Foster curious enquiry and notice if there is a sense of enthusiasm. What factors strengthen mindfulness, investigation and energy? How do they arise and once arisen what helps to maintain them? Having energy and enthusiasm you may notice a calming rapture arise. If so, enjoy this experience in a non-attached manner and let it nourish tranquillity. Support a calm, serene and peaceful heart while continuing to maintain awareness and enquiry. How do these qualities arise? How are they present? What effect do they have on the body, mind and other aspects of life? How can the wholesome factors arise and be nurtured and how can the unwholesome be released? Allow the heart-mind to become absorbed in the process. Clear and still, focused and calm. Finally, look within your heart-mind and ask yourself if your heart is peaceful. Is your heart unshaken by the changing, interdependent and uncertain nature of life? This peacefulness is also called equanimity. If equanimity is present note and be aware of its presence and know how this quality arose and can be maintained. Know that mindfulness, investigation, energy, joy, calm, concentration and equanimity all work together and lead to awakening.

5. Contemplation of the four noble truths

Contemplation of the four noble truths is the last contemplation described in the *Satipatthana Sutta*, and as such it is possibly the most refined and sophisticated. The four truths can be understood in two ways. The first way has been described throughout most of this book. That is, as two cause–effect relationships: *dukkha* and its causes and freedom from *dukkha* and the causes of this. Another way that the four truths can be understood is how the Buddha described them in his first discourse.

In the first three weeks following the Buddha's complete awakening, it is said that he stayed put and simply enjoyed the peacefulness of liberation. At first he thought that his realisations were too profound for others to understand and he was content to be solitary and keep his insights to himself. However, it is said, the Buddha's compassion compelled him to help other beings to also find peace. He sought out the five ascetics who were previously his friends and fellow seekers and spoke to them about the four noble truths and began 'turning the wheel of Dharma'. In this first discourse the Buddha spoke about the four noble truths as if they were sequential tasks or stages, the first leading on to the second and so on. In summary, the four noble truths as tasks could be understood as follows:

1. Embrace the full catastrophe of life, face up to this reality, get to know *dukkha*.
2. Realise the root causes of *dukkha* including unhelpful patterns and destructive habits, and let them go.
3. Realise freedom by releasing, abandoning or relinquishing the causes of *dukkha*.
4. Live a life of freedom. Follow and practise the path.

In relationship to the first truth, the task the Buddha suggested was to become familiar with *dukkha* and understand it. This requires the courage to kindly turn towards our suffering rather than habitually reject it. This is not easy and it is one of the reasons that awakening is so difficult. Nonetheless, when we are able to face up to the reality of *dukkha* and become intimately familiar with it, we are able to gain insight into its causes, the second truth. The task of the second truth is not only to realise the causes of *dukkha* but also to release our grip on what is keeping us bound in *samsara*, our reactive cycles. In accordance with dependent arising, when there is no cause of *dukkha*, then there is no *dukkha* which is freedom, the third truth. The task of the third truth, freedom from *dukkha*, is to awaken to it. Once we realise freedom from *dukkha* we need to live according to our realisations. When we have an insight into freedom it makes it very difficult to go back to the habits and patterns that caused our suffering in the first place. Therefore the task of the fourth truth is to follow a path that is free from destructive patterns of body, mind and speech and to live a life of freedom.

Approaching the four truths as if they are tasks emphasises the need to become familiar with suffering. In order that our investigations lead to understanding we need to approach suffering with open-minded and compassionate curiosity. Of course the Buddha did not suggest that we create suffering so that we can become familiar with it, but he did highlight a principle that many contemporary trauma therapists utilise. This principle is exemplified by the saying: 'what doesn't kill you makes you stronger'.[7] Please do not interpret this as indicating that I am trivialising or minimising the pain and suffering of trauma, because I am not. The principle does indicate, however, that difficult life situations, even horrific traumas, can be opportunities for the development of wisdom, and thus great freedom. Many trauma therapists, for example, will help their clients find some form of meaning or philosophical resolution to their ordeals. The work of putting the traumatic past to rest and finding purpose to move forward requires the cultivation of wisdom. The sequence of the four truths as it is outlined in the first discourse provides a framework for understanding suffering as a possible cause of wisdom. I often ask participants of groups that I conduct about the meaning of wisdom. I also then ask what causes wisdom. Almost everyone says that wisdom is based on life experience. They add that it is mostly the difficult experiences of life that give rise to wisdom. Wisdom is not easily come by and we could say that one cause for wisdom is suffering. It is most often in retrospect that we realise the opportunities that suffering can bring, because when we are experiencing it, it is often unbearable. Unless, of course, we have already developed some wisdom and an understanding of the four truths and this then enables us to see suffering in a different perspective.

This final sub-domain or area of the last application of mindfulness involves bringing attention to both the interactive and sequential nature of the four truths. We can be attentive to the four truths at different levels ranging from the basic and mundane, the painful and difficult and the most subtle and profound. We can see *dukkha*, its causes, freedom from it and ways to be free at both coarse and refined levels. The whole of the Buddha's teaching is directed at the realisation of the four truths at all levels. For example, irritation at getting a flat tyre can be an opportunity for us to realise the four truths. The cause of the *dukkha* of irritation is not the flat tyre but our clinging to the idea that we should not be blocked in going somewhere we want to go when we want to go there. If we pay attention to the cause–effect relationships we may also realise freedom from the *dukkha* of irritation. It is much more challenging when our experiences are intense or traumatic. Nonetheless, if the potential of psychological freedom can be realised it can be profoundly liberating. The guidance and instruction provided in this book is directed at helping us to be able to notice the principles of the four truths in our daily lives. During our everyday activities of work and social interaction as well as during those periods of quiet meditation, it is possible to tune in to and notice the relationships between causes and effects, evident as the four truths.

Contemplating life

Find a place, possibly outdoors, where you can listen to and observe life. It could be in a natural setting such as by a creek in the forest, on top of a mountain in the wilderness or by the sea. It could be at a busy market place, shopping mall, railway station or airport. Wherever you find yourself, sit, stand or stroll comfortably. Put aside worries and concerns and let your attention centre compassionately in the present moment and be aware. Watch, listen and notice, open-mindedly, with interest and curiosity, the interplay and arising and passing of the events that we call life. Release any condemnation and censorship and simply open to the five physical senses and whatever arises in your mind. Notice experience internally and externally, both within your own heart-mind and the world around you.

When you notice that you begin to judge the events of the world happening around you or the experiences within, observe your judgements regardless of whether they are positive or negative. Allow the events of life and your judgements to unfold in a completely natural and uncensored manner. If you start to judge your judging, notice that experience with compassion. Endeavour to not get caught up in thoughts that you have to work it all out. Let insights arise completely naturally. Be allowing and aware and simply observe, listen, feel, taste, smell and be conscious of the experience of life as it unfolds.

If you found this contemplation useful, remember you can bring this open perspective to your life and interactions with the world whenever you need. Thank you for your attention.

Notes

1 This common analogy used for karma is found in classic Buddhist texts such as the Dharmapada.
2 See, for example, Nidana Samyutta, in Bodhi (2000b, p. 552).
3 In Dharma talks he has given I have heard Stephen Batchelor, a prominent Buddhist scholar and meditation teacher, refer to dependent arising as 'life'.
4 That is, Ajahn Brahmavamso the highly respected abbot of Bodhinyana monastery, Australia in a discourse I heard him give when I was staying at his monastery in 2013.
5 In Buddhist psychology these five qualities are called the five faculties. When they mature and strengthen they are then called the five (spiritual) powers.
6 The Bahiya Sutta, U.d.1.10 according to Thanissaro Bhikkhu see: www. accesstoinsight.org/tipitaka/kn/ud/ud.1.10.than.html.
7 With acknowledgement, this is part of a title for a book about overcoming trauma written by Maxine Schnall (2009).

References

Analayo (2003). *Satipatthana: The Direct Path to Realization.* Birmingham: Windhorse.
Batchelor, S. (1997). *Buddhism without Beliefs: A Contemporary Guide to Awakening.* London: Bloomsbury.
Bodhi, B. (2000a). *A Comprehensive Manual of Abhidamma.* Onalaska, WA: BPS Pariyatti Editions.
Bodhi, B. (2000b). *The Connected Discourses of the Buddha: A Translation of the Samyutta Nikaya.* Somerville, MA: Wisdom Publications.
Forsyth, J. P. and Eifert, G. H. (2007). *The Mindfulness & Acceptance Workbook for Anxiety: A Guide to Breaking from Anxiety, Phobias and Worry Using Acceptance and Commitment Therapy.* Oakland, CA: New Harbinger Publications.
Fryba, M. (1989). *The Art of Happiness: Teachings of Buddhist Psychology.* Boston, MA: Shambala.
Huxter, M. J. (2007). Mindfulness as therapy from a Buddhist perspective. In D. A. Einstein (ed.), *Innovations and Advances in Cognitive Behaviour Therapy.* Bowen Hills, Qld: Australian Academic Press.
Marlatt, G. A. (2002). Buddhist philosophy in the treatment of addictive behavior. *Cognitive and Behavioural Practice 9*: 1 44–50.
Pandita, Sayadaw U. (1992). *In This Very Life: The Liberation Teaching of the Buddha.* Boston, MA: Wisdom Publications.
Schnall, M. (2009). *What Doesn't Kill You Makes You Stronger: Turning Bad Breaks into Blessings.* Boston, MA: Da Capo Press.
Segal, Z. V., Williams, J. M. G. and Teasdale, J. D. (2002). *Mindfulness-Based Cognitive Therapy for Depression.* New York: Guilford Press.
Wells, A. (1997). *Cognitive Therapy of Anxiety Disorders: A Practical Manual and Conceptual Guide.* Chichester: John Wiley.

7 Presence, ongoing practice and aspirations for the future

Chapter overview

Putting into practice all the ideas and strategies explored in this book is an ongoing journey. This final chapter will look at our journey so far and the meaning of progress. It will provide some ideas for ongoing practice and ways to prevent lapsing back into ways that may not have been helpful. It will also address the importance of having meaningful aspirations for the future whilst finding contentment where we are, here and now. We will conclude with aspirations for happiness in a guided loving kindness meditation.

The journey so far

The path of freedom always starts from where we are as there is nowhere else we can be. As we come to the end of this book we may start to wonder what we 'got' from reading it or wonder about our progress along the path. If we remember that Nirvana was described as the absence of *dukkha* in Chapter 1, then we may be more inclined to think about what we have released and abandoned rather than what we have gained from our journey together.

There are many ways to journey along a path of psychological health and wellbeing. Some people choose to develop mindfulness and related skills in intensive retreats and can spend years, if not their lifetime, perfecting these skills. The benefits of such practices are likely to be proportionate to the time and commitment that is given to them. To the extent that one can stay present, in an open-minded manner, to current experiences, to that extent, problematic mental tendencies such as worry and unhealthy rumination can be reduced.

One aim of this book has been to help us find contentment. According to some of my Islamic clients there is a saying in the Koran that says contentment is the greatest treasure. This book has outlined skills we can put into practice to work towards contentment and psychological health and wellbeing. Together we have explored and covered many different strategies with an emphasis on the four applications of mindfulness as they were explained by the Buddha in the *Satipatthana Sutta*. Paradoxically, mindfulness is a means to an end where the end is the means. In other words, the aim of remembering to be here now is to 'be' here now. Being present is intrinsically rewarding. For the most part the result of presence is being content to be present. Awakening to the realities of this present moment and being content is, in my view, freedom.

From my perspective psychological freedom is not limited and bound by a fixed end point or static state but is a dynamic way of relating to the changing events of life. When the four truths are understood as a sequence, as they were in the previous chapter, living and practising according to the principles of the eight-fold path is the result of awakening to freedom. Awakening to freedom can be as simple as deciding not to get upset when we have a flat tyre or as profound as the release from life-long destructive cyclic patterns. Regardless of whether we have profound awakening experiences or not, journeying on the path of freedom is an ongoing life endeavour.

If you still feel just as stuck in *dukkha* as you were before reading this book then please be kind to yourself. Remember harsh self-judgement usually increases the suffering we feel when what we really need is some self-kindness and compassion. Please do not feel discouraged if your judgement is that you are still far from even a moment of contentment, presence and peace. Beginner's mind, as it was explained in Chapter 1, is the type of attitude that we need to pick up the pieces of whatever our experience is and start again. The benefits of mindfulness and practising on the path can only be realised by each of us for ourselves.

Progress

Progress along this path is difficult to judge. If we monitor ourselves over short periods of time it may seem that there has been little progress or that we are sliding backwards. When we are getting over difficult times in our lives recovery takes time and so it may be better to assess progress in terms of change over months and years rather than days or weeks.

For some of you, this book may have provided helpful strategies or strengthened the skills you already have. Some of you may have noticed dramatic positive shifts in your lives. For others there may have been little change or things may even have become worse. If you feel the severity of your *dukkha* has increased, please try not to be overwhelmed by feelings of disheartenment. Significant change usually takes time. Being able to step back and see the bigger picture helps to get a more realistic perspective.

It is helpful to compare journeying on the path of psychological freedom to hiking up a steep mountain or going along a forest track in rugged terrain. If we were to climb a very steep mountain on a path that criss-crossed the slope, at times it may seem as if we were actually going back down the slope. If we step back, however, and view the path from a distance, we realise that, even though the path goes backwards and forwards and up and down, it eventually reaches the summit.[1] The path has ups and downs and some challenging obstacles but these obstacles are not impassable.

For many, the path of psychological health is also a spiritual path. In classic Buddhist teachings, as well other spiritual traditions, it is understood that meditation practices have stages of development indicating progress. Regardless of the tradition, these markers describe insights, knowledge and experiences that are intrinsic to the process of developing skills and awakening to destructive patterns and subsequently being free from them. In many cases the experiences are the same. However, across the traditions how they are interpreted varies and therefore how the experiences are integrated into a person's life also varies. Something that is consistent in all the traditions is a period of increased *dukkha* after a stage where a practitioner may feel they have made significant progress. In Christian traditions this has sometimes been called 'the dark night of the soul' and in some Buddhist Insight traditions it is called the stage of *dukkhanyana* (insight knowledge into *dukkha*). These experiences are so common that they are often thought of as a necessary component of a spiritual path.

The road to healing and recovery is never straight and even. It has many twists and turns as well as ups and downs. Be careful not to get caught up in obsessively comparing your progress with another's. Remember that everyone is different and that we all progress along the path at a pace that is appropriate for us.

Lapses are to be expected and are a realistic part of our progress along our healing pathways. A lapse is experienced like a slip or a backward step on the path of our progress. Lapses can provide us with the opportunity to learn how we can let go of unhelpful patterns or tendencies. A relapse, on the other hand, is when we fall back into old unhelpful patterns of thinking, emotions and behaviour.

The term relapse prevention is popular in mental health services and it refers to being proactive in our healing journey so that we avoid slipping back into old destructive patterns. If we feel that we are relapsing, it is important not to be overwhelmed by despair, but to remember what seems to be helpful for us. It is a matter of starting again. Starting again should not be considered a failure. Starting again is a reality of the path and a reflection of beginner's mind. With every new moment we can have a fresh beginner's mind and start again.

Relapse prevention is best managed by considering how we can integrate mindfulness and the path into our daily life, in an ongoing and consistent manner. To progress along our path and prevent a relapse we need to maintain a practice. We think nothing of putting in time and effort to clean and nourish our bodies. We wash and eat every day. The same attitude can be brought to mental and emotional health and wellbeing by developing routines and firm intentions to practise.

If you feel like you are losing your way and you are experiencing deterioration in your mental wellbeing, please do not hesitate to consult a mental health professional. Though not all mental health professionals may be familiar with mindfulness and meditation, they are trained to assess and care for individuals when they are going through a difficult time. Please do not underestimate the help they can provide.

Ongoing practice

If possible, choose a time once a day when you can commit to a formal exercise such as sitting quietly with awareness or mindful walking or moving postures (such as yoga). After particularly stressful days, be kind to yourself and devote special time to recovery and recuperation. If you can't find time to devote to formal practice, remember to be present with life as it unfolds. In other words, put an emphasis on being mindful with your everyday activities, no matter how mundane and boring they may seem.

Throughout the day, find a few moments to be mindful of simple events such as breathing in and releasing a breath of air, listening to the sound of a bird, watching a cloud change with the wind or smelling freshly brewed tea. Try listening to the sound of the phone for a precious moment before racing to answer it. Be mindful whilst you do physical activities and whilst you communicate with others. Choose some specific activities that you can use as 'touchstones' or reminders to be mindful. For example, washing up, washing your face, opening doors, brushing your teeth, combing your hair, having a cup of tea, eating a snack, checking the mail, putting the garbage out and so on.

Don't forget to notice things that you may not have noticed before. It can be helpful to access media that is meaningful for you and immerse yourself in it on a regular basis. Find time to listen to inspiring speakers or read inspiring fiction and non-fiction books. Watch meaningful movies or informative documentaries about life. YouTube clips can also be very helpful, but don't let your consumption of electronic media consume you.

Connecting with nature whenever we can and wherever we are seems to cleanse our mind and naturally inclines us to be present. Mixing with wise and kind friends is also an important aspect of the practice. Having inspiring figures in our lives is helpful. Joining a group of people who regularly meditate and having discussions with friends about pathways of psychological freedom are helpful activities. We can also cultivate presence by attending retreats devoted to awakening and healing. If you decide to attend a retreat, it is wise to ensure that suitably qualified teachers conduct it so that when challenges arise they can provide appropriate guidance. It is also important to develop a healthy sense of humour and to be kind to yourself.

Related story: Jasmine re-establishes her practice

Jasmine had a severe panic disorder and her GP referred her to an eight-week mindfulness course to learn skills to help her manage her panic attacks. After the course Jasmine felt confident that she could manage her panic reactions and whilst they had not completely disappeared they had improved significantly. To help keep up the practice Jasmine decided to maintain a daily meditation routine and attend a local meditation group once a week.

Things went well for Jasmine and after a few months she managed to get part-time employment and started a TAFE (Technical and Further Education) course. Life became hectic and soon she found that she didn't have time to do any formal meditation practice. Nonetheless, she felt confident that mindfulness in daily activities would be enough to help her manage her stress.

Despite being busy Jasmine continued to go well for months. Then, unfortunately, her youngest child became ill and needed ongoing care at home. Jasmine made her daughter's health a priority and as a result couldn't attend her TAFE course. Jasmine was concerned about her daughter and she started to worry excessively. Life became stressful. One night Jasmine woke from her sleep having panic symptoms. Then, a few days later when she was stuck in traffic she had another panic attack.

Jasmine started to fret because, after months of having no panic attacks, they were beginning to re-emerge in her life. Jasmine made an appointment with the psychologist who had conducted the mindfulness group and together they reviewed the situation. It was clear to Jasmine that the mindfulness skills she had previously learnt were valuable and needed to be maintained. Despite her best intentions she had not kept up the practice.

The psychologist pointed out that most people take it for granted that if they want to maintain oral hygiene they need to brush their teeth daily. Similarly to maintain mental health a daily practice is necessary. Jasmine realised she needed to renew her commitment to practise regularly. Re-establishing her practice was difficult and it required effort but Jasmine knew it would help prevent her falling back into her old patterns. She found her CDs from the course and used them to guide her meditation practice until she re-established her meditation routine.

The stressful situation eventually settled and the panic attacks were no longer a problem. Jasmine felt good that she had started to meditate again. She felt her daily meditation practice was like eating a healthy meal every day. Meditation provided her with emotional and spiritual nutrition; for her it was the fuel needed to walk on the path of wellbeing.

Aspirations for freedom and happiness

Aspirations are wishes and visions for the future arising as intentions in the here and now. Aspirations can be wholesome and part of the eight-fold path, or unwholesome and lead to entanglement in reactive cycles. As discussed in Chapter 4, pessimism or thinking negatively about ourself, the world and the future can serve to shape miserable or anxious lives. Optimism, on the other hand, even when the odds are not in our favour, provides the opportunity to see possibilities for action and alternatives to dire situations. Creative visualisations or other forms of imagination enhance a person's ability to speak, act and think in ways to enable their wholesome visions of the future to become a reality. Sports people for example, often creatively imagine performing their sport skilfully and musicians often practise a piece of music in their minds.

A growing understanding of the brain and how it works helps us understand what is happening when we use creative visualisations. Current understanding is that the brain is made of millions of cells called neurons and that over time these neurons make connections or pathways when we learn or practise skills. In neuropsychology there is a saying that goes: 'that which fires together wires together' (e.g. Siegel, 2009) meaning that we can create neuronal pathways and change our brains. The terms neuroplasticity and neurogenesis refer to how neuronal pathways can be developed and strengthened with experience and practice.

The act of creative imagination works in a way that reinforces the neuronal pathways required for peak performance. In the previous chapters we have explored how the habits of mind can reinforce destructive mental, emotional and behavioural patterns. It is often difficult to see a future beyond the suffering portrait we paint of ourselves. However, the same imaginative processes that can be used to enhance peak performance in sports people and musicians can also be used to create a happier future.

Being able to let go of the habitual images we may have of ourselves and creatively imagine a happy and liberated self, may actually change the neuronal pathways that correlate with this reality.

The direction and vision we have for our future is an important part of the path of wellbeing and happiness. A young boy's vision of becoming a guitar-playing rock star will motivate him to put in the hours and hours of practice required to develop his musical skills. His aspirations can help him to make the choices necessary to shape that dream into a reality. Wholesome aspirations can be a way for us to endure and overcome hardships and therefore lead a happy life.

This book has primarily focused on mindfulness meditation practices as a means for us to overcome *dukkha* in our life, but there are other Buddhist practices that also support us on the path of wellbeing. Loving kindness meditation or *metta bhavana* (Pali) is a serenity meditation practice and one of the four *Brahma Viharas* (Pali). *Brahma Viharas* translates as divine abodes or places of wellbeing. The other abodes are: compassion, appreciative joy and equanimity or peacefulness. The four divine abodes are both meditation practices and ways we can be in the world.

Loving kindness or *metta* includes qualities of warm friendliness and universal good will. It is the ability to see the good in ourselves and in others. It is evoked by tuning in to happiness and the beautiful aspects of life, and aspiring to happiness into the future. Loving kindness meditations are based on aspirations for happiness for ourselves and for others. These meditations help to create happiness in the here and now and in the future. There are many ways to practise loving kindness meditation and words and visualisation are often part of the process. The words 'may I' or 'may you' are often used. Obviously we are not asking for permission but using these words to set a helpful desire in motion. I invite you to practise the following as just one example. This loving kindness meditation is also my way of thanking you for reading this book and wishing you all the best for the future.

Loving kindness: caring for oneself, caring for all beings

Ensure that you are at ease with your posture and your body is free from constriction and discomfort. Set the intention that for the next 20–30 minutes you will first settle your mind by remembering to be present here now, and then will cultivate aspirations of good will and happiness for yourself and for others.

Bring your attention to the present moment and anchor yourself in this moment by turning attention to what is experienced in the here and now. Settle into being at peace with the present moment experience.

(Silence 2–3 minutes)

Bring to mind themes of happiness. Perhaps you can remember a time when you have felt happy or if not, how such happiness could feel. If you can bring to mind a happy event this can help you connect with the feeling of happiness. Contemplate a happy event as if it is happening right now. Imagine you can see the scene, hear the sounds, smell the smells and generally feel the ambience. As you bring to mind the happy recollection your heart may respond by opening to this happiness. Let this feeling in your heart bloom and grow, and put the word 'happiness' to this flourishing feeling.

It may feel like light buoyancy in your heart. Be curious about how this feeling is experienced, and nurture it by bringing attention to it. Note and name the experience as 'happiness'.

Silence

Bring attention to this experience and let the thoughts about the happy event grow. Do not try to force it but let the feeling of happiness grow so that it fills your chest and radiates to every cell of your body and every part of your being and life.

Let it grow by bringing gentle and delicate attention to the area around your chest.

Say to yourself:

May I be happy.

May I truly be happy.

Completely let go of resistance and struggle and let happy feelings grow and flourish, and soften and melt with these feelings. Feel nurtured and healed by the aspirations of happiness in whatever way that seems appropriate to you. Tune in to the words and make them relevant for you.

May I be happy.

May I truly be happy.

Now bring to mind thoughts of peacefulness. Peacefulness includes being completely free from the burden of ill will and resentment. A heart liberated from bitterness and hatred is a heart at peace. Perhaps you can cultivate this feeling by thinking about someone who is peaceful or remembering a time when you were peaceful. Bring this time or person to mind and let peace be your heart's response.

Let peacefulness fill your heart and spread to every part of your being. When your attention wanders do not struggle but merely bring attention back to the feeling of peacefulness and let it grow.

May I be peaceful.

May I be peaceful.

Reflect on what it may mean to be healthy in body and mind. Perhaps you can tune in to a feeling of vitality and ease here now as we meditate, or you can bring to mind how such feelings could be. A healthy mind may be one that is free from remorse and regret, uplifted and at peace. A healthy body may feel relaxed and energised, vital and pain free. Whatever a healthy body and mind may mean to you, reflect and contemplate the idea of freedom from troubles of mind and body. Tune in to how this feels and be open to resonate with these the feelings of health.

May I be healthy in body and mind.

May I be healthy in body and mind.

Now, with a mind filled with self-love, project your thoughts into the days, weeks or months ahead. See yourself going about your daily activities and meeting the challenges and joys that life brings. If, as you project into the future, you see a heart constricted with fear or gloom, bring kind understanding to these projections. Realise projections of the future are not necessary the reality of the future. Remember that mindfulness, actions directed by wisdom, compassion, joy and warm kindness have the power to transform suffering. Remember that wise actions of body, mind and speech can protect your happiness. Here now, in this present moment cultivate the aspiration to take mindfulness, wisdom, compassion, joy and warm kindness with you as protectors as you move through life. Perhaps you can see yourself moving through life meeting the challenges of life with wisdom, peace and joy, calmly and with ease.

May I be able to protect my own happiness.

May I be able to protect my own happiness.

Reflect on what it means to love oneself by opening your heart to yourself. Realise that all other beings are also in your heart and that by bringing warm kindness and compassion to yourself you also bring warm kindness to other beings.

Say and connect with the words:

May I be happy.

May I be peaceful.

May I be safe, free from harm.

May I be healthy, free from troubles of mind and body.

May I be able to protect my own happiness.

Let the energy and aspirations of loving kindness shine out beyond the confines of what we usually call ourselves into your surroundings and out into the world around you. Let this loving kindness energy touch the hearts of other beings. Let it touch people in the streets, people as they work, beings in the skies and in the oceans. Beings in other lands and beings who are very different to us.

Whatever beings there are:

May their hearts be filled with happiness.

May their hearts be peaceful.

May they know true joy.

Let this soft and gentle kindness spread around our precious planet and universe.

May the hearts of all beings be filled with loving kindness.

May all beings, be at peace.

May all beings be truly happy.

May all beings be free from conflict and hardship.

May all beings abide in joyous harmony.

May all beings be happy.

Now come back to being aware of yourself your own heart and where you are in this room. Realise that you can access this quality when you need. Realise you can radiate loving kindness in daily activities in contact with the world around you or during periods of formal meditation practice. You can practise simple acts of kindness in many different ways.

Reflection

Now that we have come to the end of this chapter and this book it is time for us to reflect on the journey we have made together and what we have discovered and learned. In summary, we have briefly considered the practice of mindfulness as it is applied in the context of a path that leads to psychological health and wellbeing, freedom from *dukkha* and genuine happiness. Mindfulness is, of course, just one aspect of the path and without the other factors it is meaningless and not effective. The other aspects of the path include: wise discernment and ethical and healthy lifestyles. Other essential components of our journeying on this path are inclining towards warm friendliness, compassion, the joy of appreciation and peace for our self and others.

May you truly be happy, peaceful and free, now and into the future. May you fare well in your ongoing journey.

Note

1 This analogy originally came from the first major text on ACT, Hayes et al. (1999).

References

Hayes, S. C., Strosahl, K. D. and Wilson, K. G. (1999). *Acceptance and Commitment Therapy*. New York: Guilford Press.
Siegel, D. J. (2009). *Mindsight: Change Your Brain and Your Life*. Carlton North, Victoria: Scribe Publications.

Appendix A

Response/reaction record

Our responses or reactions to situations have consequences that affect our thoughts, emotions and physical feelings. Sometimes they impact on the people and the world around us. Complete the record below as a way of considering response options for each situation.

Trigger/ situation	Response/ reactions	Consequences: How did your response affect yourself and/or others around you?	Was it in line with or in opposition to your goals and values?	If it was in line, how can you increase these types of responses?	If it was in opposition, what are some alternative responses?

Appendix B

Strategies for cultivating the seven factors of awakening

Strategies to cultivate mindfulness

- Applying effort to practise basic and broad mindfulness practices such as mindfulness in daily activities.
- Association with mindful people.
- Inclining the mind to the development of mindfulness.

Strategies to cultivate the quality of investigation

- To ask questions about life and meditation practice.
- Tidiness and cleanliness with oneself and the immediate environment.
- Avoiding unwise people.
- Associations with the wise.
- Reflecting on the teachings of wise ones.
- Commitment to the cultivation of investigation.

Strategies to cultivate effort

- Bringing wise attention to experience.
- Reflection on how miserable it is to be stuck in reactive cycles due to the lack of courageous energy.
- Reflections on the benefits of cultivating effort.
- Appreciation and gratitude for acts of generosity and support on the path of freedom.
- Reflection on the positive qualities of wise ones such as the Buddha.
- Reflection on the benefits of practising.
- Avoiding those individuals who may be lazy.
- Association with those who display courageous energy.

Strategies to cultivate joy

- Thinking about the advantages of being free from emotional distress.
- Remembering personal actions that have been in accordance with our ethical values.
- Recalling our acts of generosity.
- Reflecting on the nature of peacefulness.
- Avoiding the company of aggressive, angry and insensitive people.
- Cultivating friendship with people who are warm, loving and refined.
- Reflecting on, hearing or reading about how anguish is reduced or abandoned.
- Inclining the mind towards, or committing oneself to, the development of joy.
- Relaxing.

Strategies to cultivate tranquillity

- Living in a suitable environment with an appropriate diet and agreeable weather.
- Having a comfortable posture.
- Making effort that is balanced, without strain and struggle.
- Avoiding the company of cruel, bad tempered and insensitive people.
- Cultivating friendship with calm and gentle people.
- Inclining the mind towards, or committing oneself to, the development of tranquillity.

Strategies to cultivate concentration/unification

- Bringing order, simplicity and cleanliness to our environment.
- Applying continuous mindfulness to what we are doing.
- Remembering how to uplift the mind when it is pulled down by depressive states.
- Remembering how to calm the mind when it is over-excited.
- Remembering how to bring lightness to one's heart when it is overwhelmed with pain.
- Associating with calm and collected people and avoiding those who seem agitated and scattered.
- Reflecting on the types of peacefulness that are possible with deep states of concentration.

- Inclining the mind towards, or committing oneself to, the development of concentration.

Strategies to cultivate equanimity

- Practising mindfulness or wise attention based on the intention to cultivate equanimity.
- Endeavouring to not get too attached to anyone.
- Having a balanced attitude to material things such as property.
- Avoiding people who tend to be very possessive and lack equanimity.
- Association with people who seem to be emotionally balanced and peaceful and not too attached to material possessions or people.

Appendix C

Stress reactions cycle breakdown exercise

Consider a stressful situation and break down the chain reaction that led to the stressful situation. Try to be aware, as best you can, of every component in the reactive cycle.

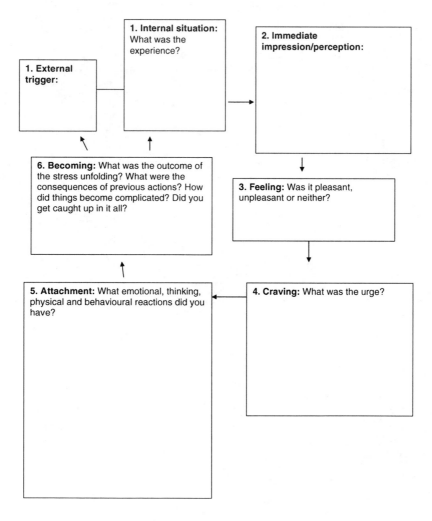

1. External trigger:

1. Internal situation: What was the experience?

2. Immediate impression/perception:

6. Becoming: What was the outcome of the stress unfolding? What were the consequences of previous actions? How did things become complicated? Did you get caught up in it all?

3. Feeling: Was it pleasant, unpleasant or neither?

5. Attachment: What emotional, thinking, physical and behavioural reactions did you have?

4. Craving: What was the urge?

Alternative response possibilities to stress reaction cycles

Consider the reactive stress cycle on the previous page and then think and write down exit possibilities or alternative responses to automatic reactions.

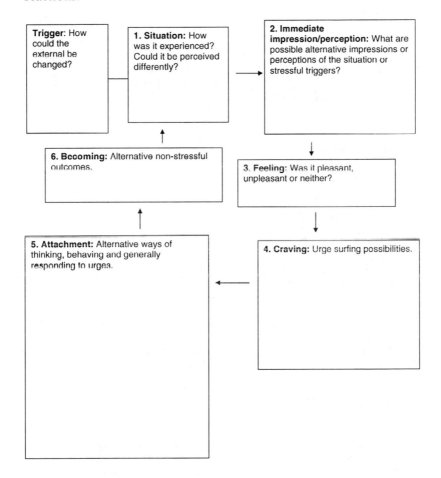

Trigger: How could the external be changed?

1. Situation: How was it experienced? Could it be perceived differently?

2. Immediate impression/perception: What are possible alternative impressions or perceptions of the situation or stressful triggers?

6. Becoming: Alternative non-stressful outcomes.

3. Feeling: Was it pleasant, unpleasant or neither?

5. Attachment: Alternative ways of thinking, behaving and generally responding to urges.

4. Craving: Urge surfing possibilities.

Index